D1824340

THE FISHERMAN'S BASKET

by

Noel C. Gibson

Published by:

FREEDOM IN CHRIST MINISTRIES

THE FISHERMAN'S BASKET CONTENTS

- Sketching the gospel for all ages
- Making and using visual aids and object lessons
- Adults' and childrens' open air evangelism—
  Biblical and practical know-how for Western and
  developing nations
- Heading people to Christ, and problems often
  faced
- The community religious survey
- Door-knock evangelism
- Literature evangelism
- The evangelistic home meeting
- Industrial evangelism
- Prison evangelism
- Hospital evangelism
- Camping ground or trailer park evangelism
- Teenage evangelism
- Secondary school evangelism
- Indoor childrens' evangelism
- Equipment for outdoor evangelism and film
  showings
- The theology of evangelism
- Principles of communication
- Using a personal testimony in evangelism
- Guides to forming a personal counselling plan
- Preaching basics
- . . . and lots of resources

First printed 1984

ISBN 0 9591100 0 3

Printed by
MISSION PUBLICATIONS OF AUSTRALIA
19 Cascade Street Lawson NSW 2783

A dedication   Dedicated to my two life-partners, one invisible, one visible, without either of whom I would not be the person I am and this book would not have been possible.

An explanation   The initials OAC represent Open Air Campaigners, an interchurch mission society which commenced in Australia just before the end of the 19th century. The ministry is now established in 11 countries, with training and outreach programs in many more countries.

While the major ministry of OAC International is open-air evangelism, many other forms of evangelistic outreach are used to reach people of all ages, in fellowship with local churches. A regular training ministry is also conducted with churches, Bible colleges, theological colleges and other mission societies.

In recognition of the time the author spent in the preparation of these materials during his ministry with OAC, the publishers will have pleasure in making a donation toward the ongoing evangelism of OAC Ministries Australia for each copy sold of *The Fisherman's Basket.*

An acknowledgment   Unless otherwise stated, Scripture references have been taken from the New International Version, published by Hodder and Stoughton.

A tribute   Special thanks are due to Mr Stewart Dinnen, M.A., M.B.E., F.R.G.S., of WEC International for his warm encouragement, advice and objective evaluations which greatly assisted in shaping the book's format and presentation.

To another friend, Mr Graham Chaseling, special thanks for some very 'effishient' support sketches.

The publishers   Freedom In Christ Ministries Trust C/- 8/58 Wrights Road Drummoyne NSW 2047 Australia. The Trust is dedicated to facilitate, encourage or promote the preaching, teaching and ministry of the gospel of Jesus Christ internationally.

PREFACE

No writer on a subject as extensive as evangelism could ever claim adequacy or originality. What follows is but a compilation of the teaching and example of others, or what the Holy Spirit has revealed in the writer's 26 years' ministry with Open Air Campaigners. Prominence has been given to open-air evangelism as it is a largely forgotten method which is still being proved effective and because little is available in writing on the subject. Where possible, credit has been given to people whose ideas and sketches have been used. To each one, and to those who have not been identified, we say thankyou.

Because evangelism means many things to many people, Section 4 of the Lausanne Covenant has been taken as the definition of the stand taken throughout the book:

'To evangelise is to spread the good news that Jesus Christ died for our sins and was raised from the dead according to the Scriptures, and that as reigning Lord He now offered the forgiveness of sins and the liberating gift of the Spirit to all who repent and believe. Our Christian *presence* in this world is indispensable to evangelism and so is that kind of dialogue whose purpose is to listen sensitively in order to understand. But evangelism itself is the *proclamation* of the historical Biblical Christ as Saviour and Lord, with a view to *persuading* people to come to Him personally and so be reconciled to God. In issuing the Gospel invitation we have no liberty to conceal the cost of discipleship. Jesus still calls all who would follow Him to deny themselves, take up their cross, and identify themselves with His new community. The results of evangelism include obedience to Christ, incorporation into His church and responsible service in the world.'*[Author's italics]*.

Three words have been italicised because of their significance to the format of writing:

Presence   or that quality of the resurrection life of Jesus Christ which should be seen in every preacher of the gospel to validate his message.

Proclamation or the variety of ways and means of communicating the relevance of the historical biblical Christ as the only Saviour and Lord of all cultures.

Persuasion or the aim of all evangelistic preaching: to persuade men, women, teenagers and boys and girls to be reconciled to God on the basis of the blood shed at Calvary, to enter into a faith relationship with Jesus Christ and to submit to his lordship in true discipleship.

Whether this book blesses or bores you may depend upon your experience and the degree of your commitment to the ministry of evangelism. It carries no guarantee of instant success, but to everyone willing to pay the price of discipline, practice, and application a new dimension of effectiveness in winning souls to Christ will be reached. May it be fuel to the fire of the Holy Spirit, swelling the size of the harvest in the day when workers in God's harvest field will give an account of their stewardship.

Noel C. Gibson

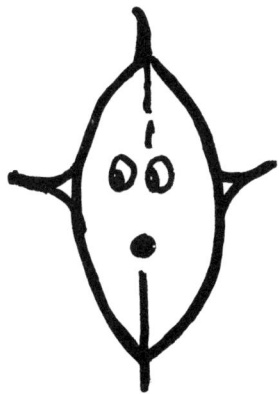

FOREWORD

Throughout the centuries open-air preaching has been used by the Holy Spirit as one of the most popular and effective means of making known the gospel. Moses preached in the open air, and so did the prophets of old. Our Lord also used this method, and the early church dutifully followed His example. It is interesting and instructive to note, moreover, that the three most revolutionary movements in the history of the church—the Crusades, the Evangelical Revival under Whitefield and Wesley, and the work of the Salvation Army—all advanced by open-air testimony. Trends and techniques have changed through the years but the need for open-air evangelism has remained the same. Indeed, there are multitudes of people who can never be reached in any other way. As someone has put it: 'We must go outside if we are to win the outsider'.

Some of my happiest days have been spent in open-air campaigning. Before and during World War II I led teams in open-air evangelism in the towns and villages of Wales. While I was pastor of Duke Street Baptist Church in Richmond England, I preached in the open air every Sunday from May to September—from a plinth of the statue on the banks of the river Thames. This, of course, was a church-supported effort which not only helped to draw a crowd but supplied the supporting testimonies, music, talent and counsellor personnel. The same was true in New York City when I was minister at Calvary Baptist Church for fourteen years. During this period the workforce was trained by the Open Air Campaigners. I will never forget those mighty soul-winning times at Columbus Circle, Central Park!

There are three main reasons why I am sold on open-air evangelism. First, it is the *least expensive* way to reach people with the gospel. I am disturbed by the enormous financial outlays that are incurred in modern evangelism. By way of contrast, all that a pastor or an evangelist, needs is a well-equipped van and PA system, or even less. The second reason is that open-air evangelism is the *most extensive* way to reach people with the gospel. By this means preachers can impact the smallest groups (without apology or embarrassment), or the largest crowds, such as Billy Graham has addressed in places like Korea and elsewhere. It is also important to bear in mind that this form of outreach takes the preacher, or team of speakers, *anywhere*, provided local laws are observed and people are present. In New York we witnessed on Wall Street, on university campuses, in the ghettos, in the parks and at housing projects. The third reason is that open-air evangelism is the *best expressive* way to reach people with the gospel. No-one who employs this method of evangelism can afford to be pedantic or parsonic. The preacher may attempt this with a captive audience; but not in the open air. There, he must draw a crowd, then *hold* the crowd. Under the anointing of the Holy Spirit he must exude serenity. Without being arrogant or assertive he must show that he is in command and knows what he is doing. He must effuse sincerity. The outsider (though unregenerate) is very sensitive to vibes. Reality turns him on; pomposity turns him off. Once again, he must ensure simplicity. Theological jargon, evangelical cliches, or even biblical words, are a no-no, unless the terms are explained *simply*. In his book on *Preaching*, G. Campbell Morgan says that the delivery of a sermon demands 'truth, clarity and passion'. All three are needed in the open air, especially clarity.

Anyone reading this Foreword will gather by this time that I am *for* open-air evangelism! This is why I must heartily commend Noel Gibson's excellent book on the subject. As an experienced evangelist he rightly emphasises the preacher's presence (the spiritual quality of life); the preacher's proclamation (the what and how of preaching); and the preacher's persuasion (the aim of all gospel preaching). But to this main thrust he adds a wealth of helps and hints on open-air work in all its varied aspects.

As this book goes forth on its mission it is my prayer that pastors, evangelists and Christian workers who read it will 'launch out into the deep' of open-air evangelism. It has been a neglected area of Christian endeavour, and we need to redress this failure on the part of the church. In my judgment no-one can remedy this situation like the Open Air Campaigners; so we must seek their expertise and encouragement. Then with the truth in our hearts and the tool in our hands we must make sure that *The Fisherman's Basket* is full when we meet our Master face to face.

Stephen F. Olford
President, Encounter Ministries
Wheaton Illinois USA

Throughout the book, measurements are given using the imperial standard. Below is a conversion to metric for the convenience of those using that standard.

	IMPERIAL		METRIC
1″	one inch	=	25 mm
2″	two inches	=	50 mm
3″	three inches	=	75 mm
4″	four inches	=	100 mm
5″	five inches	=	125 mm
6″	six inches	=	150 mm
1′	one foot	=	300 mm
2′	two feet	=	600 mm
3′	three feet	=	900 mm

THE FISHERMAN'S BASKET contains helpful advice for all types of gospel fishermen; its contents designed to be used as needed.

HERE ARE THE CONTENTS OF THE BASKET

AUTHOR'S INTRODUCTION

WHATEVER HAS FISHING GOT TO DO WITH EVANGELISM?

On one of those delightfully cool tropical evenings so typical of the highlands of Papua New Guinea, the writer sat chatting to an old-time missionary pioneer from the Solomon Islands. It was past his usual bedtime but his memory was sharp, and judging by the smile that flickered across his weather-worn face he enjoyed re-living his early days of attempting to make the gospel understood in the local culture. After he went to bed I sat for a while thinking about what he had said, particularly one story which threw a light on bringing people to Jesus Christ. It concerned a novel method of fishing used on Santa Ana Island.

It seemed that the local custom was for fishermen to replace the traditional hook and line with a decoy fish and a piece of fishing line knotted firmly through its upper jaw. It was kept 'parked' inside a floating log anchored offshore in between fishing trips. The practice was for a fisherman to collect his decoy on the way out to the reef, tying the end of the line to the canoe's outrigger arm so that the fish would follow under its own power, like a dog being taken for a walk on a leash. After anchoring close to a promising-looking gap in the reef the fisherman would transfer the end of the fish line to a long pole to be held in one hand and pick up a long-handled net with the other hand.

The method of fishing is very simple, but highly effective. By manipulating the pole, the fisherman guides the captive fish over the gap and into the shadows under the rock ledge where it can be seen by the reef fish, then pulls it quickly back toward the surface of the water. The fisherman knows from experience that the presence of a strange fish will quickly raise an alarm and that a reef fish will immediately dart after it with a 'get out of here trespasser' look set on its jaw. Unfortunately for the brave defender swimming toward the light, it cannot see the inverted net that has been slipped between itself and the decoy. The rest is easy. A quick

1

flick of the wrist, a jerk of the net, and one very startled reef fish drops into the canoe at the fisherman's feet. The process can be repeated time and again until enough have been caught. The decoy is then returned to its log, fed, and left for future use. My friend told me that he had known of up to twelve reef fish measuring up to two feet in length having been caught by this method during one fishing trip.

The room where I was sitting was well lit, but another light was beginning to fill my mind as I thought about that story. It seemed to me that God is a Master Fisherman wanting to reclaim for himself people hiding like fish in the shadows of guilt and fear under a rock ledge called 'sin'. To do this he sent his Son down into our environment to startle us out of the complacency of sin so that we might follow him out of darkness into the light of a new spiritual relationship with himself. It follows then that evangelism is the means of bringing Jesus Christ to the attention of sinners in their own environment, and that the net is the ministry of the Spirit of God reclaiming men, women, and children to a new spiritual state—the Kingdom of God.

This shed a new light on a ministry to which the writer had been called many years before, and as to why the Lord Jesus said to partners in two family fishing businesses at the Lake of Galilee, 'Follow me, and I will make you fishers of men' (Matthew 4:19,21). Jesus obviously did not mean us to think of spiritual fishing as either a pastime or a commercial spiritual exercise. It was the prophet Habakkuk who made the first rather spine-chilling comparison between people and fish being hunted by the cruel Chaldeans with hook and net:

'You have made men like fish in the sea,
    like sea creatures that have no ruler.
The wicked foe pulls all of them up with hooks,
    he catches them in his net,
he gathers them up in his drag-net; and so he rejoices and is glad.
    Therefore he sacrifices to his net and burns incense to his drag-net,
for by his net he lives in luxury and enjoys the choicest food.
    Is he to keep on emptying his net, destroying nations without mercy?'
                                                              —Habakkuk 1:14–17.

Habakkuk's words have much more than historical significance. There is another and more wicked enemy in the soul-fishing business, and the first two he ever landed with his hook and net were Adam and Eve. Since then no-one has been able to avoid his lures or escape his net.

It is therefore not surprising that the Saviour of sinners chose a fishing illustration to emphasise soul-winning, and again, it centred on one of the fishing brothers. He had just completed speaking to the crowd from Peter's boat, and despite Peter's scepticism had rewarded him with a magnificent catch of fish. It was too much for the hardy fisherman. Overcome with guilt and unworthiness he just sank to his knees among the fish and asked that Jesus would leave him—his conscience was smarting. It was at that moment that his Master spoke those immortal words:'Don't be afraid [Simon]; from now on you will catch [Gr. zogreo, to capture alive] men' (Luke 5:10).

Soulwinning therefore is the harvesting of people out of Satan's captivity to the glory of their God and Saviour Jesus Christ.

The Apostle Paul wasn't on board Peter's fishing boat that morning, but he did get some private tuition from the same Master Fisherman later on in Arabia, and he also learned the lesson. In turn he passed it on to Timothy in one Greek sentence found in 2 Timothy 2:24–26:

> 'And the Lord's servant must not quarrel; instead, he must be kind to everyone, able to teach, not resentful. Those who oppose him he must gently instruct, in the hope that God will grant them repentance leading them to a knowledge of the truth, and that they will come to their senses *and escape from the trap of the devil, who has taken them captive [Gr. zogreo] to do his will.'*

The word *zogreo* is used only twice in the New Testament. Jesus used it in connection with the harvesting of souls, and Paul used it to show who has captured the souls of men.

There are four interesting fishing hints in this passage.

(1) *Escape from the Devil's human fish-trap is only possible through the power of the truth of the gospel.*
No other message is truth. Only submission to it, which involves repentance, will bring a captive back to his proper senses so that the will to escape may be activated.

(2) *Good fishermen don't scare the fish away.*
'. . . he must gently instruct.' The facts of the gospel should be given as good news. The subjects of *hell* and *judgment* should not be used as openers. Truth is never offensive though, regrettably, the package in which it is sometimes delivered may be offensive.

(3) *In spiritual fishing the fish needs to co-operate. There is an order to be followed:*

- **Repentance comes first.** When the light of truth shines in, the will needs to respond positively, forsaking its habits practised in spiritual darkness.

- **The revelation of truth follows.** Jesus Christ himself is the light to which a person is turned when his eyes have been opened by the Spirit of God. But knowing what he says is not enough.

- **There must also be an acceptance of the authority of that truth over the sinner,** and a submission to it. So a response must be an intelligent one on the basis that without Jesus Christ no release from the grip and penalty of sin is possible.

- **Escape from the devil's clutches calls for a deliberate choice by the action of the will.** When faith is placed in Jesus Christ as Saviour he alone releases the captive into a new environment. This is called the new birth or being born again (John 3:3,5; Titus 3:5).

- **The result brings both the blessings of relationship and the responsibilities of discipleship.** The *will* spoken of in verse 26 is not the

3

devil's will, but God's. The Amplified Bible puts it this way: 'And that they may come to their senses (and) escape out of the snare of the devil, having been held captive by him, (henceforth) to do His (God's) will'.

(4) *Paul even describes the character of the person he considers would make the ideal fisherman.*He must be kind to everyone, not a resentful person, an able teacher, and gentle towards those who are troublesome students.

OPERATION RECOVERY

Before Jesus Christ returned to his Father he revealed his master plan for a world-wide program of capturing people alive. We know it as the Great Commission (Matthew 28:18-20). He also made it clear that there were great conditions to be fulfilled first (Acts 1:4,5,8). Luke tells us that the whole act came together and that Peter became the spokesman for those filled with the Spirit of God (Acts chapter 2).

It is interesting that Peter became the spokesman, and one cannot but wonder whether he had a memory flashback: 'put out into deep water, and let down the nets for a catch' (Luke 5:4). In any case, he did, and the nets held 3000 souls.

The disciples had fulfilled the word of the Lord to the letter. Their obedience holds some keys for us. But first of all, an overview.

THE THREE PHASES OF THE MASTER STRATEGY FOR EVANGELISM

1. THE GREAT COMMISSION (Matthew 28:18-20)	2. THE GREAT CONDITIONS (Acts 1:4,5,8)
(1) Divine pre-eminence in evangelism *'All authority in heaven and on earth has been given to me . . .'*	(1) The preachers' preparation *'Do not leave Jerusalem, but wait for the gift my Father promised . . .'*
(2) Divine purpose for evangelism *'. . . go and make disciples of all nations . . .'*	(2) The preachers' promise *'But you will receive power when the Holy Spirit comes on you . . .'*
(3) Divine presence with evangelism *'. . . And surely I will be with you . . .'*	(3) The preachers' priority *'. . . and you will be my witnesses . . .'*
(4) Divine priorities of evangelism • GO: Outreach evangelism • BAPTISE: Obedience in action • TEACH: Christ-centred teaching	(4) The preachers' pattern • To WAIT: preparation of heart • To RECEIVE POWER: the fullness and control of the Holy Spirit • To ALL NATIONS: the ends of the earth.

THE DIVINE OBJECTIVE-MAKE DISCIPLES OF ALL NATIONS

JERUSALEM . . . .
Chs.2-4

JUDEA . . . .
Chs.2-4

SAMARIA . . . .
Ch.8

THE ENDS OF THE EARTH . .
Ch.9 to today

3. THE GREAT CONFIRMATION (Acts chapter 2)

• They *waited* for God's timing (v.2).
• They *received* God's power (vv.3,4).
• They *witnessed* as instructed (vv.5-11).
• They *went and preached* the gospel (v.22).
• They *baptised* obedient ones (v.41).
• They *taught* the people what Jesus had taught them (v.40).

The more they carried out the divine plan, the more people became disciples of Jesus Christ.

And now for a little more detail.

THE GREAT COMMISSION

Divine Pre-eminence in evangelism

The great commission opens with a superlative statement on the sovereignty of Jesus Christ over the cosmos. 'All authority in heaven and on earth has been given to me" (Matthew 28:18). His supreme authority is a divine endorsement of the preacher and his gospel, and God will vindicate them both provided they remain faithful to his revelation. He did so in the ministry of Jesus Christ. '... even though you do not believe me, believe the miracles, that you may learn and understand that the Father is in me, and I in the Father' (John 10:38). He did so in the ministry of the early church. 'Then the disciples went out and preached everywhere, and the Lord worked with them and confirmed his word by the signs that accompanied it' (Mark 16:20). If you have been called to preach the gospel, recognise and wisely use the power of your authority and expect God to confirm it with signs following.

Divine purpose for evangelism

The aim of the Great Commission is found in its verb: 'make disciples'. The three commands—'go', 'baptise', 'teach'—are progressive priorities toward the goal of making disciples, never ends in themselves. The disciples obviously understood:

- **to go** meant two important things. Firstly, it was their responsibility to take the gospel to people wherever they could be found, rather than merely to open an office for enquirers. Secondly, there was no misunderstanding concerning the gospel message itself. Jesus had told them: 'Go into all the world and preach the **good news** to all creation' (Mark 16:15), and that '... **repentance and forgiveness of sins'** would be preached in his name (Luke 24:47). There were no cheap 'Come to Jesus and be happy' sermons in the first century.

- **to baptise** meant performing a public act in which a believer was identified with the death, burial and resurrection of Jesus Christ by being immersed in water. It signified a break with the system of Levitical sacrifices and bondage to the Law (Hebrews 6:1-6). Baptism in the book of Acts was normally the first act of obedience after faith in Jesus Christ followed by the filling of the Spirit. Some who had received the power of the Holy Spirit first were baptised immediately afterwards. This obedience-blessing sequel is found in Acts 2:41; 8:12,36; 9:18; 10:48; 16:15,33; 18:8; 19:5.

- **to teach** meant instructing new believers to obey the teachings of Jesus and the revelations of the Holy Spirit to bring them to spiritual maturity. Of course the early church had no departments of Christian education, but they knew the principles and put them into operation. 'They devoted themselves to the apostles' teaching and to the fellowship, to the breaking of bread and to prayer' (Acts 2:42).

5

Disciples are the end result of this process of evangelism in which time is not always the most important factor. Some missionaries and evangelists have wept many tears, spent years in dedicated preaching, and even died for the gospel's sake, without seeing a single soul saved. But where God is at work there must be results to his glory. What an eye-opener heaven will be for some preachers who were discouraged by an apparent lack of results.

Divine Presence with evangelism

'And surely I will be with you always.' What electrifying words! This should launch every preacher into the quality of expectant faith which will produce results. No wonder the proverb says: '. . . the righteous are as bold as a [young] lion' (Proverbs 28:1).

THE GREAT CONDITIONS

These tell us a little more about how this holy boldness comes about. Three instructions need careful attention. The first is:

'wait'

The 10 days the disciples spent together in the upper room healed wounds, restored unity after the confusion caused by the betrayal of their leader, and prepared them for the promised return of Jesus Christ in the invisible form of his Holy Spirit. The fire spoken of in Luke 12:49 swept down from heaven when '. . . a sound like the blowing of a violent wind came from heaven and filled the whole house where they were sitting. They saw what seemed to be tongues of fire that separated and came to rest on each of them. All of them were filled with the Holy Spirit and began to speak in other tongues as the Spirit enabled them' (Acts 2:2-4).

The presence of the Spirit of God in the Body of the Church has not changed the instruction to wait. There must always be deep personal preparation of heart and soul before asking God for his power in evangelism. If we as preachers do not wait for God to reveal what spiritual house-cleaning we need to do he will certainly wait until we do. The early disciples waited in joyful anticipation, knowing that God could be neither early nor late in keeping his promises. The Holy Spirit delights to fill clean hearts who submit to the Lordship of Jesus Christ (John 7:37-39). But do we need to tarry as the early Church did? No. The Holy Spirit is not a divine favour to be begged but a promise to be joyfully received, when conditions are fulfilled.

'receive power'

The Twelve were given both authority (Gr. exousia) and power (Gr. dunamis) to fulfil their ministry (Luke 9:1). The authority was from Jesus himself (Matthew 28:18), the power from the Holy Spirit (Acts 1:8). Gospel preachers need both. Just as an incoming president of the United States of America has authority to nominate people to assist him in office but without power to perform until he has been sworn in, so after Jesus Christ had been received into glory he was able to use his authority to give power of performance to those whom he had chosen to continue his early ministry. It is vital that every person who desires to be involved in evangelism understands this, so that he will not be limited by inferiorities or human limitations but produce the results God expects, using delegated authority and power (Corinthians 2:3-5). '... This salvation, which was first announced by the Lord, was confirmed to us by those that heard him. God also testified to it by signs, wonders and various miracles, and gifts of the Holy Spirit distributed according to his will' (Hebrews 2:3,4). 'Philip [the only named evangelist in the New Testament] went down to a city in Samaria and proclaimed the Christ there. When the crowds heard Philip and saw the miraculous signs he did, they all paid close attention to what he said. With shrieks, evil spirits came out of many, and many paralytics and cripples were healed. So there was great joy in that city' (Acts 8:5-8). 'by the power of signs and miracles through the power of the Spirit ... I [Paul] have fully proclaimed the gospel of Christ' (Romans 15:19).

'witness to me'

When preaching fails to uplift and to glorify Jesus Christ it ceases to be the gospel. It is possible to preach his words and teachings, follow his example in the relief of suffering and misery and uphold the justice he showed, but all this amounts only to religious rhetoric if Jesus Christ is preached only as some historic patron saint. The New Testament shows him to be alive in the power of an endless life, and this sin-sick world needs preachers who will present Jesus as the living and reigning Christ who exercises limitless authority over the affairs of daily living and the kingdom of darkness. Witness faithfully to Jesus Christ in the way you live and what you preach, and people will see and feel his anointing on you and your ministry. They will not be able to resist the Jesus you know and show.

THE GREAT CONFIRMATION

Pentecost was the crucible in which the ingredients of man's obedience and submission and God's power were fused together. As a result people became disciples of Jesus Christ. The event was historical, but the process is continual. The Great I AM never changes. To him, time is not significant. But people are significant because blood was shed for them. Because '... He is patient ... not wanting anyone to perish, but everyone to come to repentance' (2 Peter 3:9), and because he '... wants all men to be saved and to come to the knowledge of the truth' (1 Timothy 2:4), he is still saying: 'Come, follow me ... and I will make YOU fishers of men' (Matthew 4:19) [my capitals]. May God impress the sign of the fish— the symbol of the early Church —on your soul as he sends you out to labour in his harvest field, even at the eleventh hour.

Like its real-life counterpart, the *Fisherman's Basket* has compartments containing supplies for a variety of fishing needs. It may be read progressively or selectively. Aids and methods follow in Part 1. Readers who prefer to commence with theological, doctrinal and practical preparation for a personal or public ministry of evangelism would benefit by commencing at Part 5, before returning to Part 1. Make good preparations, and have an exciting time fishing.

Noel C. Gibson

Part 1—INDEX

OF FISHING IN GENERAL—
BAITS AND LURES IN PARTICULAR

Chapter 1

MAKING THE BAIT ATTRACTIVE

Listeners have a right to expect a quality dividend for investing their time in a speaker. And speakers should aim to see they get it. The repeated yawn, looking at the watch—or matt-glazed eyes often are sure signs that the listeners consider they are being short-changed.

Most of us began to learn by associating pictures with words and still find this principle effective. This is why we are selective in buying articles to assemble, choosing those which have diagrams which make them so much easier to get working. And ladies always choose dress patterns with instructions they can most easily follow.

Preachers who use visual variety will also help their hearers understand and remember their messages. Few churches provide teaching aids such as a permanently mounted chalk or white board, or an overhead projector, and few preachers think of holding up pictures or words to help their listeners understand or remember. No wonder some congregations stagger home full of words and terms which mean little to them, and still feel starved of the spiritual food they needed so badly.

One simple communication aid which could help change that is THE SKETCHBOARD. Its advantages are many:

- It can be carried anywhere indoors or outdoors, and stored so easily when not in use.
- It can be made adjustable to suit the height of any speaker.
- Any writing medium can be used, such as chalks, paints, crayons, spirit pens and charcoal.
- It can be lit at night, and an ultraviolet lamp (black light) can add a spectacular effect.
- It is inexpensive to make.

There are three vital factors about sketchboard preaching. **Firstly,** no special artistic ability is needed to be effective. **Secondly,** practice will help *anyone* become proficient. **Thirdly,** a variety of board designs and materials can be used.

1. No special artistic ability is needed

If ever a statement will be hotly disputed this is surely the one. The use of a sketchboard seems to produce an instant brand of audience inferiority, and someone is bound to say: 'I could never do that', or: 'It's all right for you, you're an artist, and I'm not'. Both statements are wrong because no previous experience is needed and no art is involved. Of course there is greater scope for an artist, but anyone who can draw a reasonably straight line qualifies.

To show how simple it is, the following sketches have been prepared in two stages. The first is the basic outline which can be prepared before speaking. The second is the completed sketch. The middle column shows how message and the sketch develop together. Try them first with a ball-point pen on a sheet of paper or some felt-tip pens on a large sheet of white or brown paper before using a sketchboard. Keep practising and you will gain confidence, and the chances are that others will think you are just great!

Before commencing to preach prepare your paper like this:

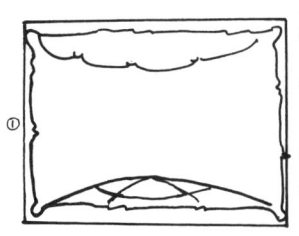

Develop your preaching and sketching in stages:

1. Fill in 'God' and 'Man'.
2. Draw horizontal line of cross in red. Sin separated from God.
3. Speak of God's love in Jesus to break the sin barrier. Draw red vertical line completing the cross.
4. Three famous words. Write in 'Faith', explain meaning.
5. 'Hope': write in. Speak of Hebrews 6:19, make anchor.
6. 'Love', complete heart, apply.

This is how your final sketch should look:

1. Fill in man with his burden of guilt. Speak of **sin**, the cause.
2. Fill in consequences: 'Lost', 'No hope', 'Judgment' in order, and elaborate; then 'Hell'.
3. Outline the cross and speak of the substitution of Jesus Christ—'Saved'.
4. Explain 'Life', and challenge.

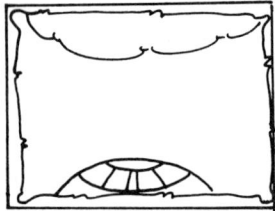

1. Fill in 'A holy God'. Speak of creation, God's intention for man, the fall.
2. Draw in 'sin'. Speak of God's attitude to sin (**must judge**)—did so with Adam.
3. Noah—righteous—built an ark. God judged the world.
4. Fill in ark. All lost except eight.
5. Fill in cross. Lost without Christ.

1. Fill in 'Death'—everything in life points away from Jesus and ends here.
2. Fill in 'Frustration'—everyone has that too.
3. Fill in 'Hell'—Satan's destiny—for man without the Cross.
4. Fill in 'Life' etc. Speak on what Jesus offers. Challenge.

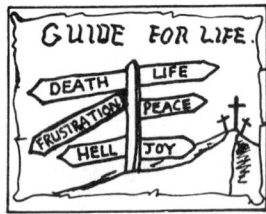

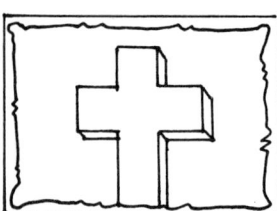

1. Speak of God's personal and unique revelation in His Son Jesus Christ.
2. Jesus reveals the holy nature of God as the Light of the world.
3. Jesus reveals the love of God in his death for us.
4. Jesus gives the life of God through resurrection.
5. Jesus brings total liberty to all who trust him.

Fill in the words in turn. Each letter speaks of a different aspect of PEACE. There is a choice with the final letter 'E'. There can be no true peace without Jesus, so ensure he features prominently.

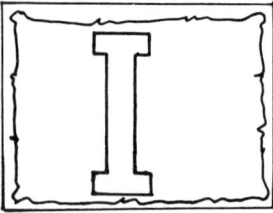

This simple talk revolves round the great spiritual sickness: 'I' disease. It has been said that the letter 'I' is just a minus sign standing up and making an idol of itself. It is the no. 1 sin—and the centre of it. Christ alone can cancel it out through his cross.

Now that you have the idea of moving from the basic outline to the completed sketch as you preach, here are four completed sketches for you to work out your basic outline and message.

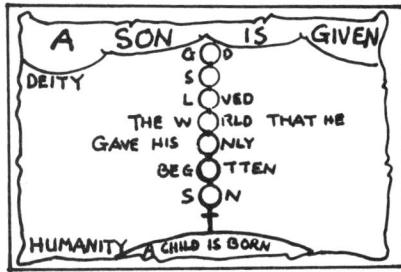

Some alternative types of lettering will also add variation to your sketches.

Large letters underlined in an alternative colour.

SALVATION _– RED_

Colour patch printing

 — yellow background

Mystery writing This ⌣⌣⊃ᴊᴧᴦᴧ⁻ becomes JUDGMENT.

Letter outlines HE DIED FOR ME

Shadow lettering JESUS CHRIST

By now you must be bursting with ideas of your own. Why not jot them down in a little notebook. If you want a fancy title for it, call it your 'Homiletical Seed Nursery'. In other words, you are bedding seed thoughts in the soil of your mind where the Holy Spirit can water and warm them in time, causing sermons to grow.

A member of Youth With a Mission (YWAM), training in Sydney Australia, decided he would try his hand at a sketchboard sermon. He put his ideas on paper and gave them to the writer. The idea was terrific. All it needed was a little reshaping.

The sketch as submitted   **The sketch as suggested**

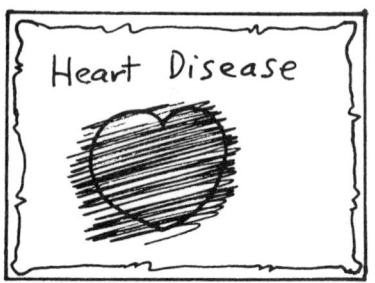
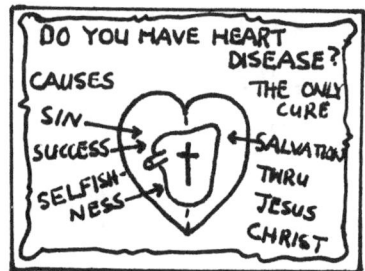

The subject is of topical interest to all, as heart disease is a major cause of death.

There are many good comparisons between the causes of both physical and spiritual problems, but only Jesus can give a new heart which will not be rejected by the body.

Give interest to your sketch. Let it clearly emphasise the points of your message, and aim for the climax to centre in response to Jesus Christ. If it is an outdoor message make sure the words can be read clearly. The board remains a silent witness after the sermon ends. After you have given a sketch talk make what changes you feel would improve it and write them down in a special book. The Spirit of God may rewarm it in your soul's microwave oven for re-use.

2. Practice will help anyone become proficient.

- Two lines should surround each sketch. One straight line in yellow and a wiggly line in black make a nice combination. This frames the whole sketch, making it appear tidier.

- Do as much preparation as possible before speaking, without giving your message away. Once your service or open-air program commences, there will be no time for preparations before you preach your sketch message. A spare sheet of paper may be used to cover the preparations.

- Avoid gaps between speaking and sketching as much as possible. By moving to one side of the board and using your outstretched arm you should be able to let your audience see most of what you have completed while you develop the next point. When your back is turned to your audience speak more loudly, and directly into the board so that your voice will still be clearly heard and the continuity of what you are saying will not be lost.

- Fill in words *after* you have finished speaking about each point, particularly if it is your last point. Aim to hold their interest right to the end so that no-one will turn off—or walk away without hearing your climax if you are outdoors.

- Even though you may have finished sketching, continue to hold the paint brush or chalk in your hand as it will help to hold interest.

- Newspapers full of headlines are never eye-catching, and sketchboards filled with words and pictures don't give a clear message. The use of colours and well-spaced words is much more effective. The size of letters should be adjusted to suit the distance your audience is from the board.
- Sheets of ordinary newspaper are ideal for practice. The more newspaper you use the more proficient you will become.

3. A variety of board designs can be used

Every person who uses a sketchboard for preaching seems to prefer to design his own, so there are no end of designs. For reasons of space only two can be shown here; others are in the resource section.

This is the budget model. It costs little, can be made quickly, but is awkward to store.

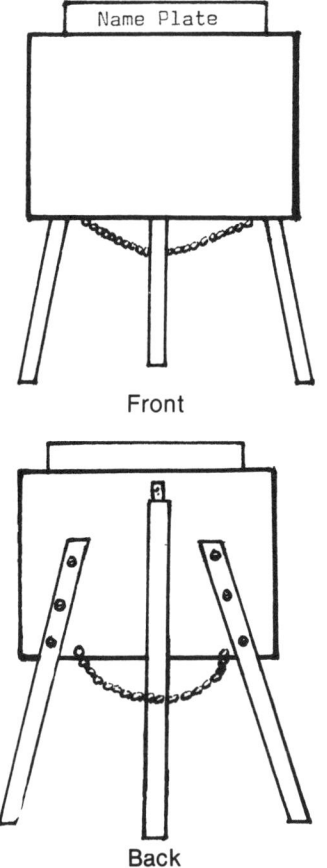

Front

Back

The board itself is made of 5-ply wood or particle board. Marine bonded plywood is ideal. The legs are lengths of wood 2 in x 1 in screwed in the back of the board. The back stay is attached to the board by a hinge. A length of light chain will hold the back stay in position.

This is the popular model used by OAC in college seminars in the United States and Canada. It lends itself to mass production, is effective but bulky.

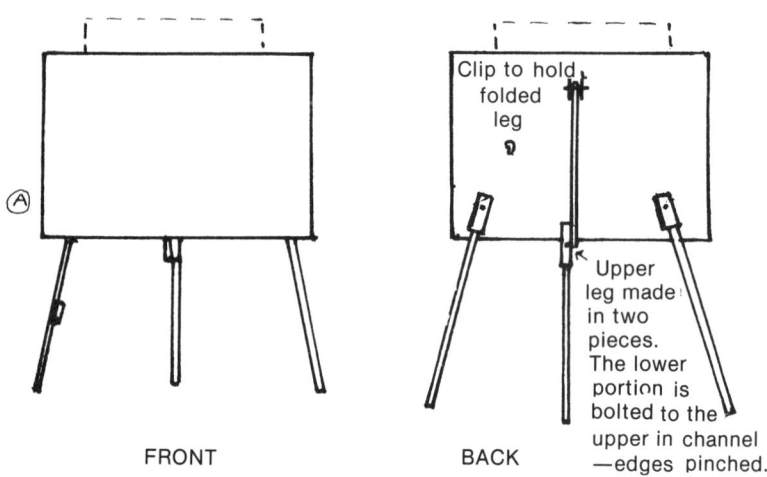

FRONT   BACK

The plywood board is the same size as the other models. The main difference is that the legs are made either from used metal piping called conduit, (the type used to protect electric wiring) or of aluminium. Each should be ½ in diameter. The legs are attached to pieces of aluminium channel which are securely fastened to the board by a ¾ in machine screw to a smashed 'T' nut on the front of the board. The legs are free to swing up and be folded away as shown in the following diagram. The ends of the channel are pinched slightly to grip the pipe legs when open. When the lower legs are closed they are gripped by a piece of pinched channel (marked 'A'). The back leg folds in half and is held by a clip (marked 'B'). Some of the specialised fittings are shown below.

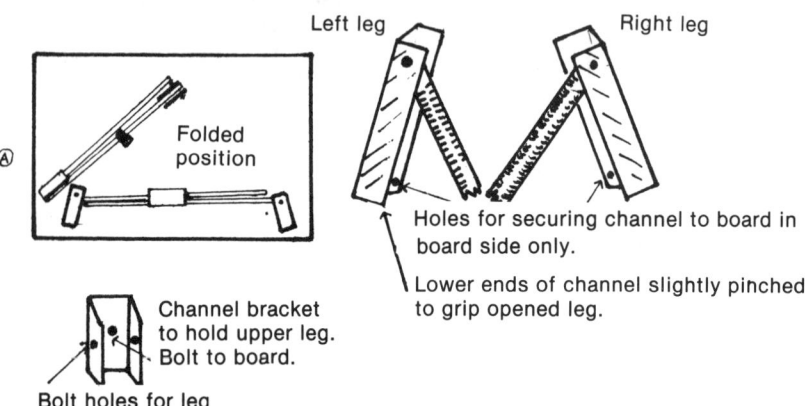

16

All boards should have rubber feet fitted to the legs to grip on all surfaces. Where boards are used outside church buildings or by inter-church missions it is advisable for an identifying nameplate to be used. This will save confusion with cults, and encourage passers-by to pay attention. One advisable piece of extra equipment is a rubber bungie with hooks at each end. This will enable your board to be fastened to a fence, tree or pole to keep it from blowing over in the wind. Flying boards can become very expensive when they do damage, or injure some unfortunate listener.

Other useful boards include the roll-up slat board, enamelled magnetic metal board, and aluminium frame board over which canvas can be stretched. For further details check the resource section.

A variety of materials can be used . . .
for sketching or visual displays

Newsprint. The ends of rolls of newsprint are generally given freely by printing works to churches and charitable institutions. To cut the correct-sized paper for a board, roll off a long sheet on a floor with a smooth clean surface. Measure the width of your board, add six inches to give a three-inch overlap each end, then mark and fold that piece of paper over, and crease. Continue this process until about 12 strips have been measured off. Take a sharp knife or pair of scissors and cut both folded ends, and your paper is ready. Attach the paper to the board with large paperclips or drawing-pins (thumbtacks).

Suitable sketching aids

- **Powder paints** obtained in bulk from art suppliers. These are made up with water as required, but may smell offensive if not used quickly. No-smell pigment paints are now available from some paint manufacturers. Suggested colours are red, yellow, blue, green, black.
- **Showcard colours**. These are colourful but expensive and brushes must be washed thoroughly after use.
- **Fluorescent paints** in powder and liquid form. The colours are bright for daytime use as well as under black-light at night.
- **Plastic house paints** provide a great variety of colours for artists.
- **Wide-tipped spirit pens** are useful. Those fed by capillary action are preferable to the liquid gravity-fed type which cause delays in re-inking the tip.
- **Chalks** are ideal for quick, colourful work. Lecture squares three inches by one inch by one inch are preferable to the round demonstration chalks which sometimes tear newsprint because of their silicone content.

Fine cotton material, or heavier types of artistic paper. These materials are ideal for more permanent use with acrylic paints. Cotton material and acrylic markings are washable.

Green chalkboard paint will prepare any smooth surface for use with stick chalks available in every country in the world where there are schools.

Clear plastic stretched over a piece of white material provides a good surface for felt-tipped pens. Experiment first with colours, as some have a

17

chemical reaction with the plastic, leaving marks which cannot be removed with water or thinners.

Felt for flannelgraph use. This is not ideal outdoors in windy weather.

Plasticographe—the plastic alternative to flannelgraph, with reversible overlays—hold well in the open air, though from some angles there may be a reflection problem.

Thin sheets of tin covering a board will hold magnetic based materials.

For general needs

A container for paints and/or chalk. Tool boxes, fishing boxes, or hand-made wooden boxes are ideal. Paints should be kept in small glass jars or plastic wide-mouthed containers with air-tight lids to prevent evaporation or loss through spillage. Containers of powders or pigment and a small bottle of water will provide instant supplies when needed. Make sure there is room for brushes and absorbent clean-up materials.

Brushes. A soft ½ inch bristle brush with a non-rust copper ferrule is ideal for sketchboard work. Brushes need to hold a reasonable amount of paint and be capable of making both thin and wide lines as needed.

Paper clips. Some people use drawing-pins (thumbtacks) for holding the paper to the board so that sheets can be torn off with ease. Others prefer wide spread bulldog clips (stocked by stationers) to keep the paper surface taut and to minimise wind interference outdoors. Three are recommended for each side of the board.

Indoor sketchboard users who wish to keep their friends and influence others to love them will place a sheet of paper on the floor under a sketchboard to prevent the expense of cleaning spilled paint from the carpet.

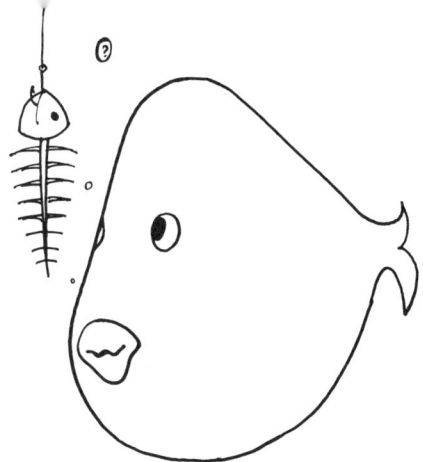

Chapter 2

KEEPING THE BAIT ALIVE

'As dead flies give perfume a bad smell—so do dead sermons give the gospel a bad name.'

The first half of that quotation comes from the wisdom of King Solomon (Ecclesiastes 10:1). The second is an observation on much of what goes for present-day preaching.

The gospel is the good news of God, and it needs to quicken the spiritually dead rather than engrave their epitaphs. In other words, sketch-board users need vitality to keep the listeners from being sketch-bored. There are three aids to keeping them alive and attractive.

FIRSTLY: a quick method of printing.

SECONDLY: introduce a personality here and there.

THIRDLY: use a variety of approaches.

A quick method of printing.

Many years ago an OAC evangelist attended the Royal Sydney Show, one of the great international fairground attractions. What attracted him more than the entertainment, ring events, animals, produce, exhibits and certainly more than sideshow alley was a poster artist high up on a platform doing a most unusual advertising act. The late Rev. J. A. Duffecy, first International President of Open Air Campaigners, who was only one of thousands who stood and watched that day, but he later recalled his impressions: *'A poster artist was working on an oversized board with paint and chalk. He would make a couple of big 'ladders' on the white paper with a big paint brush, then add large circles and slabs of colour with chalk. Ex-*

19

pectation in the crowd increased as he moved up and down his board. Suddenly with a few quick strokes, a square of the 'ladder' would become a letter. Working backwards and forwards letters which appeared from nowhere didn't seem to make sense until the blobs of colour suddenly became people, and the letters in the 'ladders' became words. All of a sudden it was there, a complete advertising slogan. The crowd were delighted'.

Years later Jim Duffecy revisited the Royal Sydney Show and met the artist. He was delighted to hear that his quick method of printing had been used to make the gospel more easily understood. His ladder or lightning lettering is now in use worldwide as preachers, evangelists and missionaries learn it from those who first saw the method and copied it.

Another friend of OAC, Keith Thompson, who also saw the poster artist, recalled it in this sketch.

The method is so simple yet looks great. It not only attracts crowds out-doors as the sketchboard is being prepared, but people seem glued to the pavement as they see words appear from nowhere. Let's try it together. Too hard? Not at all! It is in fact very easy to learn.

Ladder lettering is as easy as writing your own name.

Just pick up a ballpoint pen, a pencil, paint brush or anything that comes to hand and let me prove it. First of all draw two parallel lines like this:

That's great. Now draw the 27 rungs of the ladder, one to start with, then one for each letter of the alphabet:

You're well on the way to being as good as that poster artist already. Now pretend you have the paintbrush in your hand and fill in the letters just as he did and you will soon have the alphabet completed.

If you are not sure of the difference between an **M** and a **W** just note where the two uprights of each letter point. The letter **M** stands on its legs, so they go at the bottom of the square. With the letter **W** they are up in the air, so put them at the top. Remember that and the battle's won. With the letter **Q** just blob out most of its seat—it won't mind; it's used to it. Next time you come to the letter **I** just make its box real narrow and that saves time. Now practise the alphabet. If you have some water colours or showcard colours handy, use a half inch brush on some old-newspapers until you can do them with your eyes closed. Well nearly.

Now let's try to put some letters together to get a gospel message across.

Hint directory as to how to be good at ladder lettering.

- **To get the right-sized ladder:**
  Draw an upright on your paper the height you want the letters to be.
  Now draw in one rung for each letter in your word.
  A three lettered word like *GOD* would be:
  Finally draw in the top and bottom lines and you have the ladder.
  You are now ready to fill in the letters so that your word can be seen.

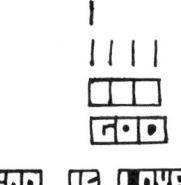

- **To put several ladder words together:**
  This can be done in two ways. First, with the words separated by one or two spaces.
  Secondly, they can all be in the same ladder, with the square between each word painted over. Don't forget to allow for the extra space to separate the words when filling in uprights for the letters.

- **What about a touch of colour?**
  Ladder letters are normally done with a black brush on white newsprint, but that can be varied by using other colours. Red, for example, is a good colour to use with the word 'salvation' or 'Jesus Christ'. A good contrast can be made by painting the whole area covered by the word in a background colour, then outlining the ladder squares with black. Yellow is a good contrast to black, but any light colour will be effective. Spelling out the letters of the word you have in mind, put an upright in place for every one, not forgetting of course the spaces between the words. Then paint over all the squares with the background colour.
  Let's demonstrate this with the text 'CHRIST DIED FOR OUR SINS'—step by step:

First: the uprights in the background colour.

Second: apply the colour so that it looks like a block of colour. (The uprights can be faintly seen).

Third: go over the colour block with the outline colour you have chosen and paint the uprights in again.

Finally: fill in the letters and it should be like this. As an alternative, outline the words with black on a white background, then with a coloured brush with most of the colour squeezed out streak the colour over the words from left to right.

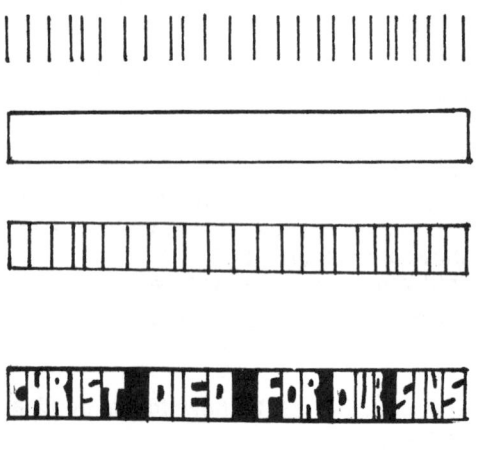

- **The most important hint of all: Practice.** When you have done that do some more practice, and when you are tired of that finish off with some practice.

- **Ladder lettering can be pushed into some very interesting shapes.**

- **And what if you make a mistake?**
Well, nobody is perfect. The best way to avoid mistakes is to pencil the shape of your letters in your ladder squares before you preach. The pencil marks will hardly be seen and you will feel more confident. With more experience you will be able to continue talking and fill in the words without pausing. Even then if you do make a mistake, all is not lost. Just tear off a small piece of paper from the lapover at the back of the board. Paint over the whole square in which you have made the mistake and while the paint is still wet, press on the small piece of newsprint. It will stick. Then re-outline the square and fill it out as you originally intended. Even in outdoor conditions your stick-on-letter will remain in place for the rest of the program.

Introduce a personality here and there.

Meet Mr Jet man (because he's generally drawn black) or his brother.

Mr Stick man (because he's always on a diet).

He will do anything for you ...   So will his wife and children.

WALK   RUN   PRAY   LAUGH

23

If you feel like varying their shape, why don't you? Many others have.

They are most co-operative; they will do anything you tell them to.

JUMPING   THOUGHTFUL   CRYING   ARGUING   HUMBLE   SLEEPING

PRAYING   KILLING   READING   RACING   FRIGHTENED

PLAYING   SWIMMING   DIVING   TUMBLING

EXERCISING   GYMNASTICS

CARRYING

SOLDIERS MARCHING

Use a variety of approaches.

The formula to reach this goal is:

General sketching
+ Ladder lettering
+ Jet figures
+ Different styles

= *VARIETY*

The following pages will illustrate this and double as a sketch library.

②

Lazarus and the rich man in Luke 16.

1. Describe the life of the rich man (contentment without God) and Lazarus.
2. Both brought to one level through death.
3. Positions reversed.
4. No chance of change because the gulf is only bridged in Christ during life.

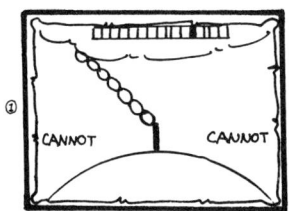

①

1. Jesus confused Nicodemus in order to change him. Without new birth we too *CANNOT SEE and CANNOT ENTER.*
2. Nicodemus said 'How?'. Jesus gives picture of New Birth to illustrate *EVERLASTING LIFE* (fill in each letter 'O')
3. Fill God's links to the Cross, our responses: succession of letters 'H'. John 3:16.

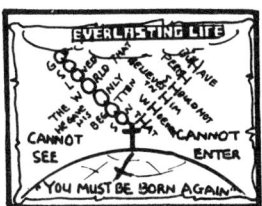

①

1. In Luke 5 Jesus is speaking to a crowd indoors.
2. Draw in four men carrying helpless friend.
3. No room, but they were determined. Draw third scene.
4. Jesus saw their faith—man's need—forgave sins eternally—healed body.
5. Fill in balance.

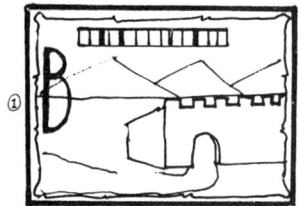

Mark 10:49
1. Write title: *'Believing is seeing'*.
2. Tell of Bartimaeus, and draw city.
3. Write in words as the story progresses.
4. Called for Jesus. Called by Jesus. Believed—saw—followed.

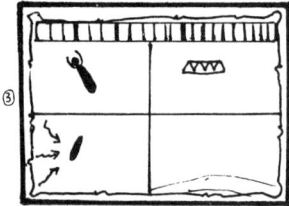

1. Cocoon of chrysalis designed to exert pressure to enable butterfly to fly.
2. Science says: pressure makes diamonds from coal.
3. All interested in profit. Can our pressures be turned into profit?
4. Yes, one has taken our pressures—*'... became sin for us'*.

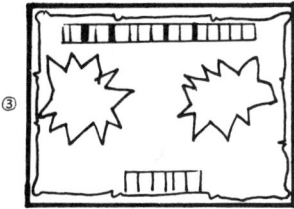

1. What if everyone did their own thing? A real mess.
2. Some advocate using technology, science and the media to 'control', really to manipulate, society.
3. There is only one way out. Jesus said, 'I am the way'. Up is better than out.

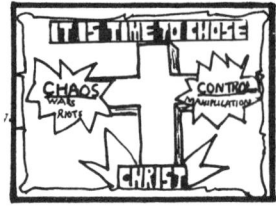

The wording of the text is done as you develop the message.
1. *The Lord*—who he is: God, and yet fully man.
2. His present reality: write in *is*.
3. Write in *Shepherd* first. Speak of job, laying down life etc.
4. Write in *my* and apply personally.
5. *I shall not want*. The result of having him as a personal Saviour.

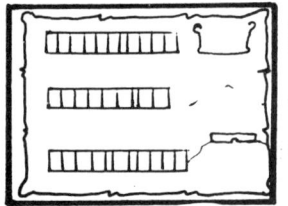

John the Baptist said three important things about Jesus.
1. SOVEREIGNTY. He was before him. Priority of existence and position.
2. SALVATION. *Behold the Lamb of God who takes away the sins of the world.*
3. SUFFICIENCY. The baptism with the Holy Ghost. Totally able. The way, truth, life.

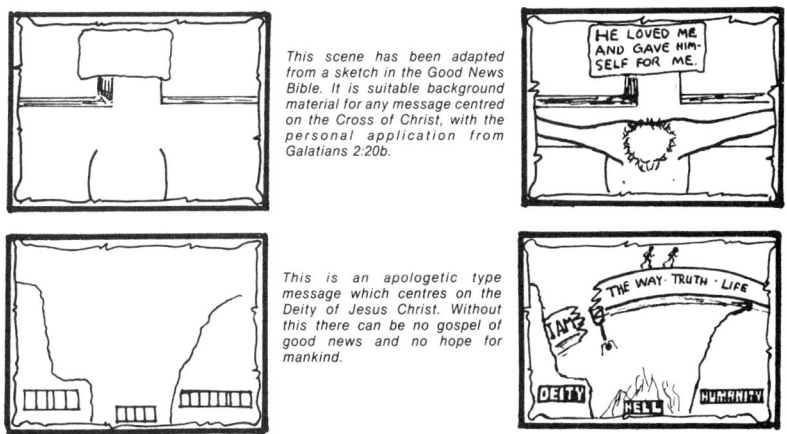

This scene has been adapted from a sketch in the Good News Bible. It is suitable background material for any message centred on the Cross of Christ, with the personal application from Galatians 2:20b.

HE LOVED ME AND GAVE HIM-SELF FOR ME.

This is an apologetic type message which centres on the Deity of Jesus Christ. Without this there can be no gospel of good news and no hope for mankind.

THE WAY · TRUTH · LIFE
I AM
DEITY   HELL   HUMANITY

Further examples and varieties of sketchboard messages may be found in the resource section in Part 7.

The multi-cultural sketchboard.

Here are some examples of the adaptable nature of sketch board messages.

Mandarin Chinese

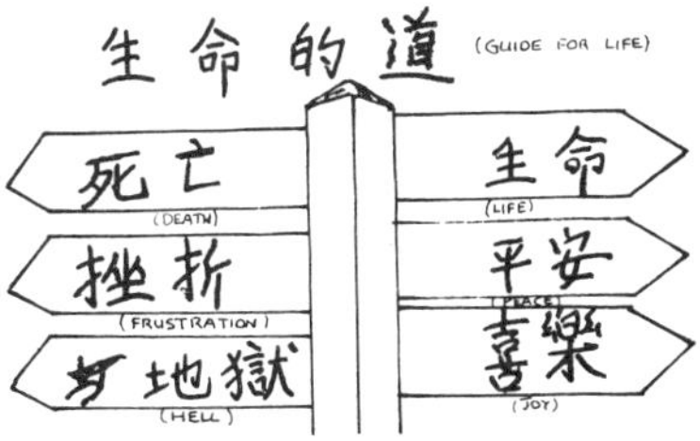

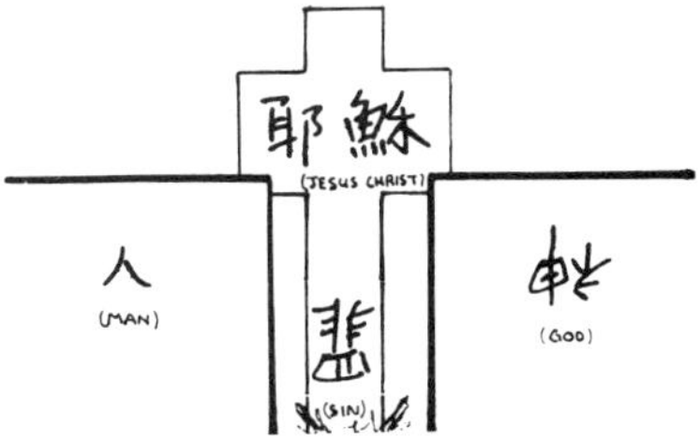

生 命 的 道 (GUIDE FOR LIFE)

死亡 (DEATH)   生命 (LIFE)

挫折 (FRUSTRATION)   平安 (PEACE)

地獄 (HELL)   喜樂 (JOY)

耶穌 (JESUS CHRIST)

人 (MAN)   罪 (SIN)   神 (GOD)

Portuguese   **Los Hechos Olvidados del Calvario**

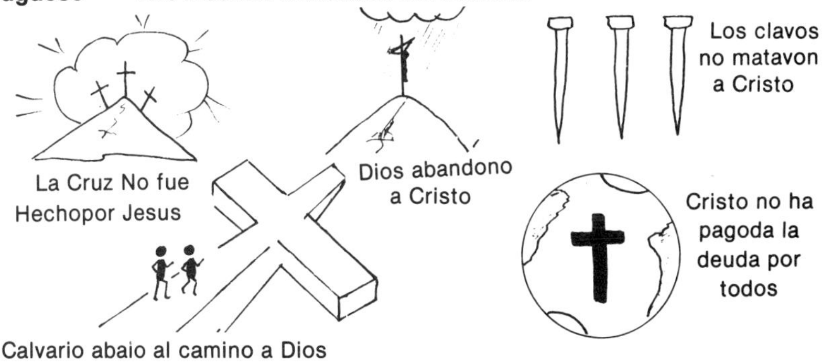

Los clavos no matavon a Cristo

La Cruz No fue Hechopor Jesus

Dios abandono a Cristo

Cristo no ha pagoda la deuda por todos

Calvario abaio al camino a Dios

27

Japanese   **New Guinea Pidgin**

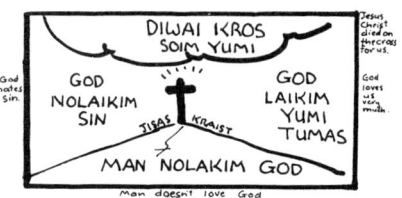

Acknowledgements: Chinese—D. Plummer, Portuguese—P. O'Gorman, Japanese—K. Kobayashi, Pidgin—G. Vines.

Chapter 3

SPECIAL BAITS FOR SPECIAL APPETITES

While the eternal gospel is unchanging, the manner in which it is presented needs constant review. It is in fact spiritual food which needs to arouse appetites some people are not aware they have.

A change of package will sometimes do this, such as a humorous sketch, or simple drawings which light up Bible words and terms people find difficult to understand. Cartoons which overemphasise the obvious also make truth inescapable.

Now before you throw your hands in the air and feel defeated before you have tried something a little different, you **still don't have to be an artist**. If you can copy, you'll do just great. The writer is no artist but can copy, and the more the practice the more the copy improves. Even at its very best no one could call it art! So you never know how much you can do and how well, until you try. Right?

Just in case there just happens to be one reader without enough confidence to try, why not look around for someone with a gift of sketching who can do it for you? Some of the guys in OAC have even married them when they have found them, and they both have had a great ministry, with Dad doing the preaching and Mum doing the sketching. Please don't take that as marrige guidance! There is sure to be someone in your circle of friends who would be delighted to use their gifts and abilities to make your preaching more effective, especially if they can't preach like you!

Some Papua New Guineans do not like stick or jet figures. They call them 'faceless people'. They have a point. At the best the outline represents a person, and the message should point out that that person could be the viewer. In some parts of Africa the nationals cannot understand perspective. They see jet figures as either pigmies, or giants with their heads in the clouds. One very good way to overcome this problem is to use cartoon faces which have more personal appeal. A whole story may be told around one large figure, or a series of faces or figures in sequence.

Mr Keith Thompson, a Sydney chalk artist of considerable ability whose writings are known internationally, has made character drawings his speciality. His latest book is *Sketch and Tell—Everyone can do it,* published by Anzea Books of Scripture Union in Australia is a must for all sketch artists. It is rich in resources for both adults and children's sketching. The following is reproduced by permission of the author from *Sketching and Telling* on Bible character drawing. The first series concerns the 7 steps in forming a male figure with chalks. They are the head—the body with a choice of shape—the hand shape—the beard—fact details and complete figure.

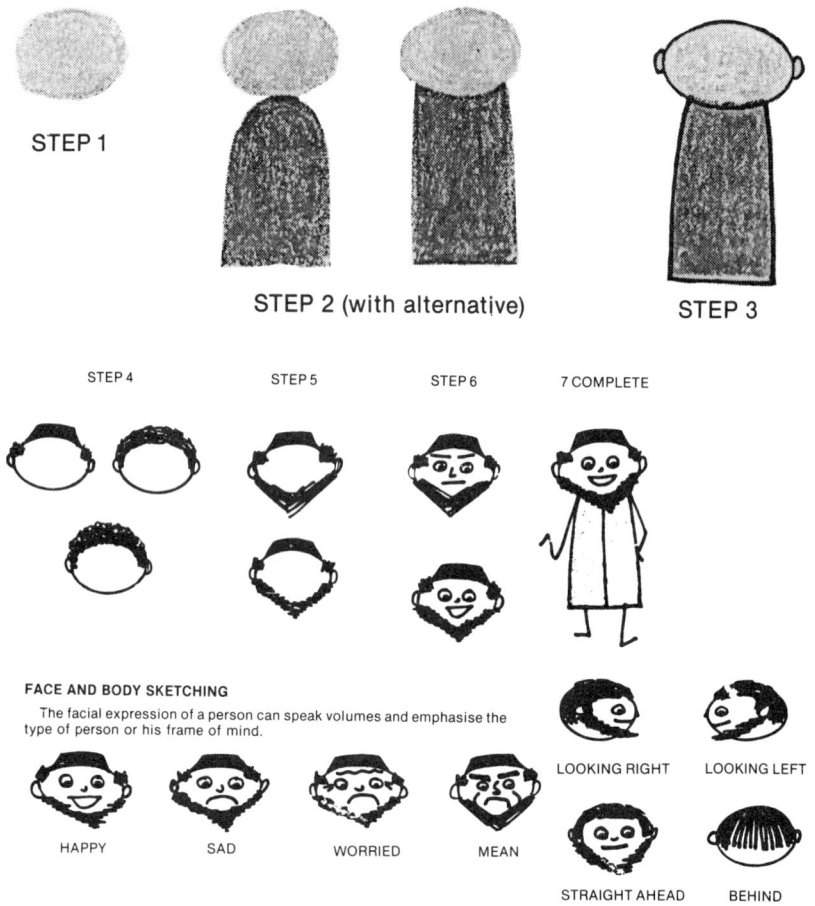

STEP 1

STEP 2 (with alternative)

STEP 3

STEP 4   STEP 5   STEP 6   7 COMPLETE

FACE AND BODY SKETCHING

The facial expression of a person can speak volumes and emphasise the type of person or his frame of mind.

HAPPY   SAD   WORRIED   MEAN

LOOKING RIGHT   LOOKING LEFT

STRAIGHT AHEAD   BEHIND

Different positions of the same person.

Notice that all background shapes to the faces and bodies are basically the same (shorter for sitting positions or angled for various other). Only the detail has been altered. Arms and legs are just simple strokes.

BIBLE WOMEN

Bible women can be drawn simply in several different ways. Here are some of them.

The sash across the body is a quick and easy way of showing a difference to the woman's body.

SITTING   BEGGING

RUNNING   KNEELING

CHILDREN

THE GOOD SAMARITAN

PREACHING

THE SOWER

YOUNG DAVID   JONATHAN

FISHING

Mr Robert Coyle of Youth Dimension Melbourne Australia has developed his own intriguing comic style figures which he uses most effectively with child, teenager and adult audiences. By special permission, over the page are some of the figures, faces and ideas he uses.

Serious and humorous cartoons will both attract and hold attention, particularly outdoors. In earlier generations a Mr Arthur Pace was well known for his series. Many writings for young people have illustrations which make excellent cartoons. The following examples have all been used in OAC outdoor programs to good effect by Mr Tony Martin.

Further materials on sketching are in the resource section in Part 7. These include sketches for children's stories, faces, animals trees and perspective.

Suggested reading on sketching

Why not try sketching? by Howard Miles—Mission Publications of Aust.
Sketch and tell, everyone can do it. by Keith Thompson —Anzea Publishers.

Sketchboard Sermons (Volumes 1 and 2) by James Duffecy —Open Air Campaigners International.
The little Jets Bible by Wade C. Smith—W. A. Wilde.
The little Jets Youth Talks by Wade C. Smith—W. A. Wilde.
Winning the Children to Christ by W. A. Guilford—Christian Press.
A Guide to Child Evangelism by Alan Bailey—Open Air Campaigners Aust.

Contribution Acknowledgements (by numbers)

J. A. Duffecy	1
P. Green	2
F. Kornis	3
G. Vines	4
E. Lowe	5
R. Coyle	6
S. Sexton	7
D. Franstone	8
P. Edwards	9
K. Thompson	1 0
W. A. Guildord	1 1
A. J. Martin	1 2

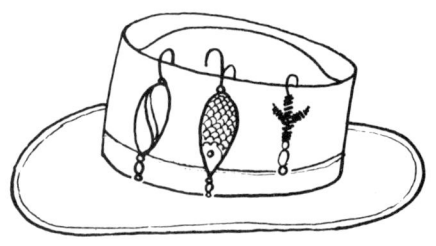

Chapter 4

THE VALUE OF THE REUSABLE LURE

Worms are usually messy and bait smelly, but lures are clean. Some fish are also diet-conscious, so dead bait doesn't excite them. But dangle something which looks alive, and jaws snap. The rest is a reel story.

Paints can be messy and equipment heavy, but lightweight visual aids are ready for use 24 hours a day. Like an accordion, they can be stretched out to fill the available time or squeezed into a minute or two.

When the Lord Jesus ran his school of evangelism he didn't have any prepared visuals.

His students saw communication principles in action by what he said and did. Simple stories and illustrations caused his hearers to 'see' what he meant, and when he wrote on the ground with his finger (John 8:6) he opened a new concept of visual aids. What he wrote in the dust must have been powerful. It quickly scattered the lawyers who were pushing personal hypocrisy to the point where a woman's life was at stake. A visual aid can pack a punch—without a word being said.

The term 'visual aid', like an umbrella, can cover many members of a family. Flashcards and flipcharts are in the family, so are picture rolls, posters, films, slides and overhead projector transparencies.

If you happen to be handy with a pair of scissors and felt-tipped pens, there are some visual aids you can make from lightweight card. Their lifespan may be considerably extended by the use of clear plastic art spray. If you want to create genuine hand-me-down heirlooms, cover them with clear adhesive plastic.

This visual, based on John 14:6, using both sides of three cards was made from leftover materials:

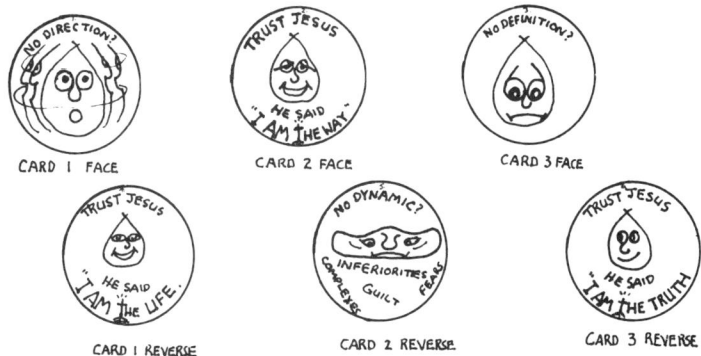

CARD 1 FACE   CARD 2 FACE   CARD 3 FACE

CARD 1 REVERSE   CARD 2 REVERSE   CARD 3 REVERSE

A small identifying number should be placed on each side to prevent confusion. When the face of card one has been shown, place it behind the other two, similarly with card two. When the face of card three has been explained, turn it round and place it in front of the other two cards, which should be reversed together. When number four (the reverse of card one) is used, it is put at the back of the other two, followed by the fifth (the reverse of card two), leaving the sixth face, which is the reverse of Card three to be shown last.

The next visual requires five cards in the shape of a circle with a handle, being fastened together at the base of the handle by a heavy paper fastener. Each card is allowed to fall after use, exposing the face of the next card. The theme is the cause of unhappiness in the unbeliever and joy in the believer. The negative side should be shown first. The visual may be used for teaching, to illustrate a gospel message, or as a final challenge.

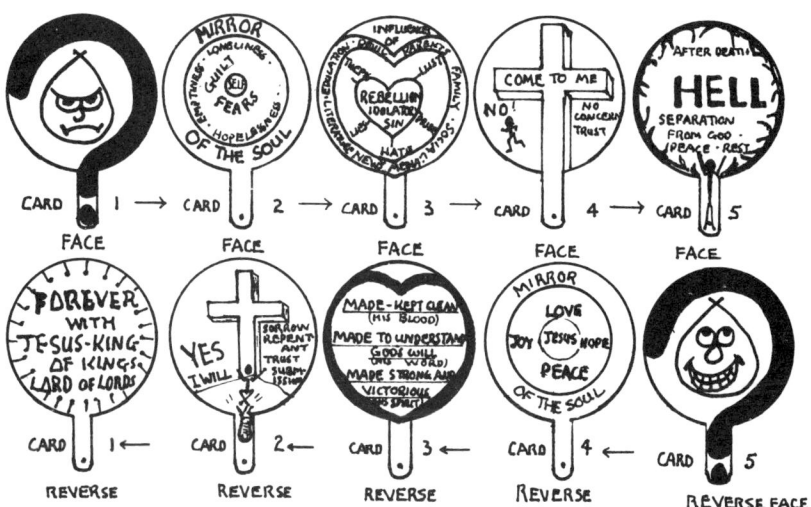

CARD 1 → CARD 2 → CARD 3 → CARD 4 → CARD 5
FACE   FACE   FACE   FACE   FACE

CARD 1 ← CARD 2 ← CARD 3 ← CARD 4 ← CARD 5
REVERSE   REVERSE   REVERSE   REVERSE   REVERSE FACE

The following visual is a communication bargain—two for the price of one. It is shown like this with the words appearing in the slots as projecting circle is turned.

Side one is a message on the type of person who needs to be saved.

Side two shows the attitudes people on their way to hell frequently show toward the gospel and Jesus Christ.

The words which appear on side 1.

UNSURE OF WHAT COMES
AFTER DEATH

DISAPPOINTED IN
CHURCH OR RELIGION

NOT ENJOYING THE
FULNESS OF GOD'S LOVE

BURDENED WITH
GUILT OR FEAR

INTENT ON EARNING
GOD'S FAVOUR

DEEPLY DISAPPOINTED
WITH LIFE

UNABLE TO GET FREE
FROM SIN'S GRIP

LOOKING FOR
INNER PEACE

The words which appear on side 2.

DON'T ANNOY ME
YOU SPOIL MY FUN

WHAT'S THE HURRY
THERE'S PLENTY OF TIME

WHY SHOULD I BELIEVE?
GOD'S NEVER HELPED ME

ME A CHRISTIAN?
MY FRIENDS WOULD LAUGH!

PROVE GOD TO ME—
THEN I'LL BELIEVE

I'M OK. I'VE GOT
MY OWN RELIGION

GOD'S NOT GOING
TO RUN MY LIFE

GET OUT PREACHER
I DON'T NEED GOD

So much for the preview, now for the workbench.

Step One   Cut the two covers from the light card and complete artwork. Cut out slots for words.

Step Two   (a) Cut a circle with a diameter one inch less than the width of the cover.
Use a pencil to divide each circle into eight segments.
(b) Then mark the size of the word slot in exactly the same place on each of the segment lines (c).

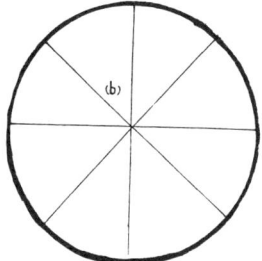 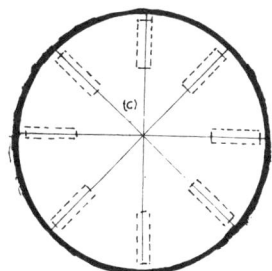

Step Three   Print the headings in large letters on both sides.

Step Four   Place one cover face down on a table, then the circle with matching words so that the edge of the circle projects half an inch beyond the edge of the visual, for turning purposes. Cover with the appropriate side, and align. The visible words should fit the slot exactly. Secure with a brass fastener through the centre hole, and tape around the edges.

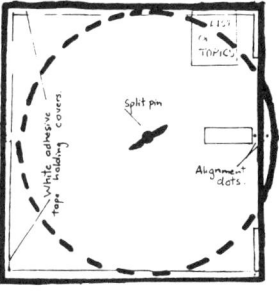

Finally   Place two alignment dots on each side of the cover and turning circle so that you will not need to check the side facing away from you when preaching.

A list of topics clipped to the side facing the user will show the words facing the audience without turning the visual around.

Those you adapt from existing materials

The scope is limitless for the imaginative person. Gospel illustrations will jump at you from sketches on tracts, illustrations from books, comic strip characters and a host of other little ideas from magazines, advertisements, newspapers, in fact any reading matter. The following simple four diagram foldout is a counselling book adaptation which illustrates the way of salvation. In diagram one the shaded area of holiness round GOD and MAN should be coloured yellow. In the following three diagrams it should be red, a symbol of sinfulness. The two crosses should also be in red.

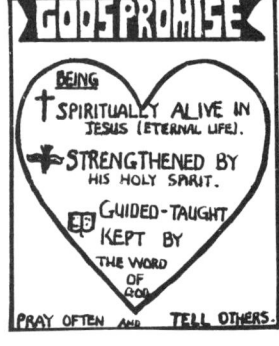

Do each section on a separate card, then fasten them together by white or clear adhesive tape as shown in the small diagram. Section four folds across behind number three, then the two together fold behind number one. Number three is then folded back behind those two, and you are ready to commence with the first card. The second card swings across, then the third with number four behind it is allowed to drop down. When ready, the final card is allowed to swing across. Note, there is no adhesive tape between cards two and four.

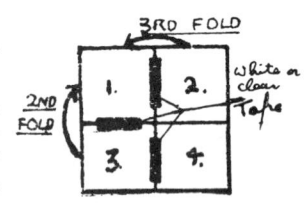

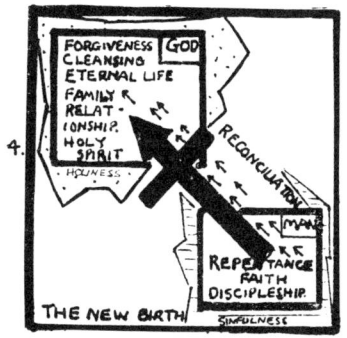

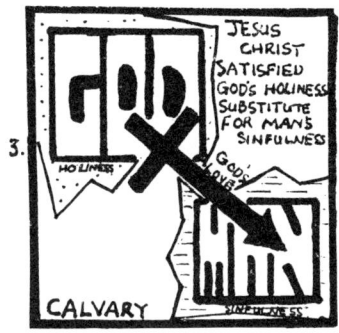

One picture can be more effective than a thousand words

.... especially when people are having a hard time listening. The Bible likens sin to the colour red, the same as blood—its means of atonement. (Isaiah 1:18.)

Because certain shades of red disappear under translucent red cellophane, a delightfully simple visual aid can demonstrate how the blood of Christ removes the stain of sin. It may be necessary to try a variety of shades of red to find the one which disappears. A red indelible pencil has been found ideal. Basic materials include white card for nine heart shapes to your selected size, and a sheet of cellophane in the colours red, blue, green and yellow.

To make up:

- Draw the outline of a large heart on a piece of cardboard, then cut out. Using this piece as a template, cut eight heart shapes.
- Cut out the inside portion of each of the eight hearts, leaving heart shapes 1–1½ inch wide.
- Glue a different cellophane colour to 4 separate heart cut-outs, trim, and allow to dry. Then paste the four remaining heart frames to cover the glued cellophane. (See fig. 1)
- Write the wording of your preference from either figure two, three or four on the first heart shape in your selected colour of red.

Presentation

Speak of how impossible it is to remove the stain and guilt of our wrong-doings, no matter how hard we try.

41

Those who believe they can buy their way out of anything, and expect to bribe God, are shown to be mistaken by covering the red marked heart with the yellow cellophane heart. The wording remains clearly visible. Quote Psalm 49:6-9, particularly the Living Bible paraphrase.

Next speak of the intensely practical do-gooder who aims to earn forgiveness. Cover the sin with the green heart. The words will still be clearly seen. Those people are like the Pharisee in Luke 18:9-14.

Then use the blue heart representing the religious person who thinks that his church record will be so good that God will be obliged to wipe out his debt. His name is Mr Pious. But the words under the blue cellophane remain. (Ephesians 2:8,9; Titus 3:5).

Finally, the red heart represents the person who realises he cannot do one thing for his own salvation and who throws himself upon God's mercy, and trusts in Jesus for what he did for him on Calvary's Cross. This time the words cannot be seen. As long as the red heart remains in place there is no record to condemn. The effect of this illustration will long be remembered.

. . . and one picture can also introduce five important words.

The picture is:

The words are:

P for Pardon—Isaiah 55:7
E for Eternal—John 3:16
A for Abundant—John 10:10
C for Costly—Romans 4:25, 5:1
E for Enjoyable—Ephesians 2:14

Finally, try being as wise as a serpent

The last thing one would expect to find in an attractive-wrapped gift package would be a gospel message, but some people will listen only when they are caught by surprise. This visual aid, wrapped in gift paper and tied with ribbon, can be used to make people curious, and when it opens into the shape of the Cross shows the heart of the gospel.

Take a sheet of white card and mark on it the lines shown in figure 1, making sure each square is of equal size. A sheet 24 inches by 18 inches will divide into six-inch squares. Glue a sheet of colourful gift-wraping paper to the reverse side, then cut away the shaded areas with a sharp knife and reinforce the edges with adhesive tape. Use large press-on letters, or a felt-tipped pen to write the letters shown in figure 2.

Finally, by folding the cross into the shape of a box with the letters on the inside an attractive-looking gift is ready to be tied with ribbon. When not in use unfold and keep in a large manilla folder to preserve the edges.

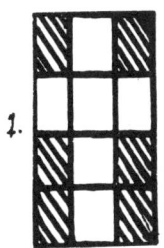

1.

2.

3.

Chapter 5

BAIT THAT EXCITES THE CURIOSITY OF THE FISH

All living things seem to have one thing in common—curiosity. Birds will flock, animals will gather, and people will almost trample over one another to see something unusual. When the gospel is wrapped in an unfamiliar and faintly mysterious package it is possible to use this irresistible urge to get people to stop and listen.

The Lord Jesus never had trouble gaining attention. Unkown and mystical in the beginning of his ministry, what he said and did aroused curiosity and people quickly developed a love-hate relationship with him. He used object lessons to emphasise important truths (the denarius, the children on his knee, the little boy's lunch), and explain truths (miracles to show forgiveness of sin, or the power of faith). As Saviour, Healer and Deliverer, Jesus was never a showman.

Modern object lessons can be effective in evangelism, but any implied association with magic or spiritual powers should be avoided at all costs. Openness without an explanation as to how the effect will be obtained will keep the user from being accused of deceit. Those who use object lessons sold in 'magic' shops need to be sensitive and keep a clear conscience before God so that his Spirit is not grieved.

The following object lessons are simple to make and use:

- **Some almost explain themselves**
  Many books are available with simple talks using objects such as a clock, a compass, a fountain pen, worn out money bags, lamps of all descriptions, keys, magnets, torches and the like.

  However, there is one effective lesson which does not appear to have

caught the attention of writers. It concerns a cheap imitation ring in a little transparent plastic box, which costs less than one dollar. The story (with appropriate demonstration) centres on an imaginary suitor who arrives at his young lady's house complete with a very fine sheath of flowers and a magnificent ring. He proposes and is accepted. The young lady takes the ring out of the box and tosses it idly aside while gushing effusively over the little plastic container. She admires the size, just right for her handbag. She likes the colour of the felt pad on which the ring had rested, because it matches her dress; but above all she likes the little click the container makes when it snaps shut. (A repeat demonstration on your little box emphasises this point). Finally the young man can't stand any more. He pockets the discarded ring and heads for the door. He leaves his ex-fiancee with the flowers, the empty container and his best wishes for her future happiness. A ridiculous story? Maybe, but don't laugh yet. Many people are so taken up with the bodies in which they live, mere containers designed to contain God's treasure, that they ignore or brush aside the greatest love gift of all, Jesus Christ. By creation and redemption he has the right to occupy the central place of every life.

Some need to be demonstrated

- **The downward pull of temptation and the strength of Jesus Christ gives to resist**

  Only two materials are required: a smooth block of wood approximately 3¼ in by 1½ in and a piece of light cord 4 feet in length. Prepare the object lesson as follows:

1. Using a wood-drill larger than the diameter of your cord, drill a hole from the centre of each end of the block of wood toward the mid-point, at a slight angle so that the two holes form an apex.
2. Thread the cord through from one end to the other. It may be helpful to push a piece of wire through first and use it to pull the cord through. Tie a small piece of wood to one end of the cord to prevent it from being pulled right through by mistake.

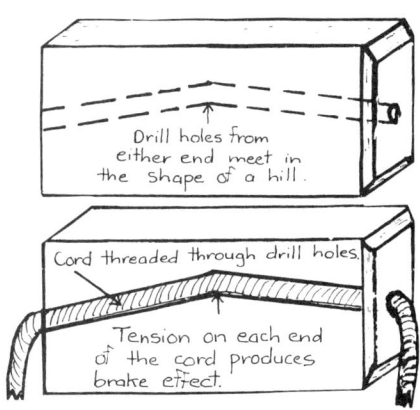

Drill holes from either end meet in the shape of a hill.

Cord threaded through drill holes.

Tension on each end of the cord produces brake effect.

The gospel application

Lift one end of the cord so that the other end touches the floor, then place your foot on it. Lift the block of wood with your free hand, then let it fall to demonstrate the unseen force of gravity which pulls any object downwards. Speak of the inflexibility of this law, and then compare it to the unseen force of spiritual gravity known as sin, which no one can resist.

The block should be dropped a few times while naming some obvious temptations to sin. Then introduce your audience to the person and work of Jesus Christ and speak of the deliverance he is able to give because he has broken the power of sin. As you speak, lift the hand holding the top of the cord so that it becomes taut, but not obviously. In fact, the cord could look taut (without pressure) all the time you are speaking.

To show the power of Christ to cleanse from sin and to deliver from its grip, remove your hand from the block of wood and it will remain in position. It may be moved up or down the cord when it is taut, and it will always stay where you leave it. Slacken the cord very slightly and the block will begin to slip slowly. This can then be likened to a Christian falling into sin. When he calls on the Lord for help he receives immediate strength to resist temptation. The block is then stabilised by tightening the cord. Restoration can be illustrated by lifting the block to where it was before it began to slide, and it will remain there. This effective illustration is simple to make. A commercial article is available in which the user can lock the cord in position so that it cannot be freed by anyone not aware of the locking device.

For added teaching a small magnet may be glued into a hole drilled in one of the surfaces of the block. A cardboard heart can then be cut from light card, painted black, and a small piece of tin or tinfoil glued to the reverse side. This will visually represent the effect of sin in the life. Another heart should be cut (this time white) and similarly backed to show the effect of forgiveness. A small red cross mounted behind it increases the teaching value. When the white heart backed with the cross is placed over the black heart the effects of sin can no longer be seen. Three simple diagrams illustrate this.

The cord is held in a vertical position

The black heart held by the magnet.

The white heart and cross over the black heart.

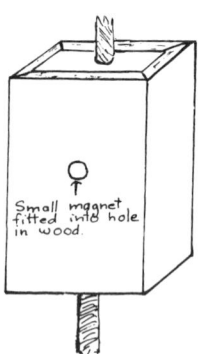

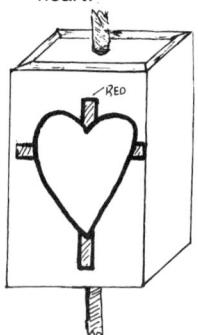

- **Jesus alone can make possible the impossible**

A piece of wood slotted near one end is offered to anyone standing around with a request that it should be balanced on the end of one finger. It is of course impossible, once again because of the force of gravity. However, when a man's belt is folded in two and the fold placed in the slot so that the two ends hang down in their natural position below the block of wood, the centre of balance is changed, and the piece of wood easily balances on the end of a finger.

It has been found that leather belts are more effective than the plastic variety because of their firmness. Plastic tends to go limp when hot. The overall size of the wood may vary, but the proportion and position of the slot should remain constant.

Position of slot.

Overall view.

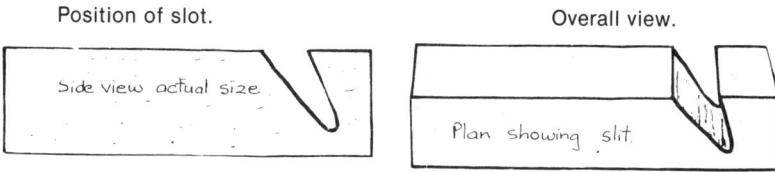

Side view actual size.

Plan showing slit.

Use of illustration

When anyone is unable to resist temptation they 'fall' into sin. Before using the belt, push some paper money into the slot and try the balancing act again, or use a sheet of paper with some good new year resolutions. Neither will be successful, of course.

From experience it has been found advisable to have a suitable belt ready for use as some offered by listeners may be too light. Practice will show how the belt should be placed in the slot. The weight of the buckle will determine this. The belt changes the centre of gravity in the wood, and a law of physics operates, just as an aeroplane uses the law of aerodynamics to counter the law of gravity. The comparison of the law of life in Jesus Christ over the law of sin and death completes the message.

The demonstration in action

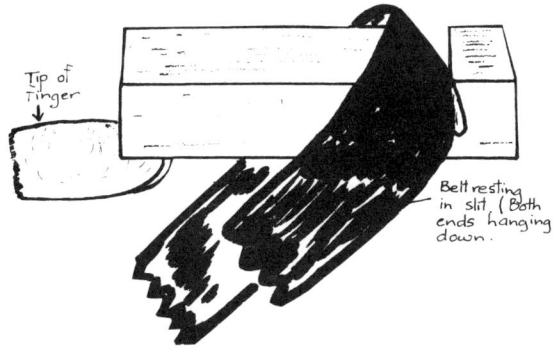

Tip of finger

Belt resting in slit. (Both ends hanging down.

- **Sin separates man from God. Only Jesus Christ can remove sin.**
  Requirements:
  - Three wooden blocks approximately 2½ in square with a ½ in diameter hole through the centre of each block.

47

- Two white nylon cords around ¹⁄₈ in diameter, and 4½ ft in length.
- A red scarf or cloth.
- A small spool of white cotton from which about 3 yds. should be wound on to a small piece of stick about 1½ in long.

Preparation:

- After thoroughly coating the wooden blocks with a suitable undercoat, paint the first block with dark blue enamel, the second with light blue enamel, and the third with red enamel.
- Paint the following words on the blocks after they have dried:
  * on the dark blue block paint 'GOD' in block letters in *white* enamel.
  * on the light blue block paint 'MAN' in block letters in *white* enamel.
  * on the red block paint 'SIN' in block letters in *black* enamel.

To prevent the enamel from chipping it is advisable to wrap each block in a piece of paper or cloth or carry them in separate plastic bags. All object lessons and visual aids should be treated carefully for long life, good appearance and best stewardship. They should not be handled by others, or their methods of operation explained.

By now you have:
* Three painted and lettered blocks.

* Two lengths of nylon cord about ¹⁄₈ in by 4½ ft.

* One small stick of wood with 3 yards of white cotton wound on it.

The final preparation is to find the midpoint of the two nylon cords and tie a simple reef knot round them both, then fold the doubled cords back with both ends together. (Steps 1, 2.)

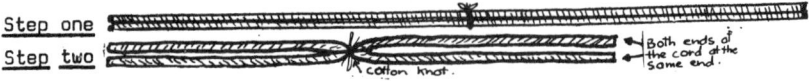

Presentation

1. Show the dark blue block and speak about the nature of God. The dark

blue colour reminds us that God the Creator lives beyond the reach of men in a place the Bible calls Heaven. The white lettering reminds us that God is perfect in all he does. There is no pollution of sin in Heaven.

2. Holding the dark blue block, pick up the light blue one with the word 'MAN' in white letters. Explain about God creating man with his inner nature like him spiritually, morally, emotionally and intellectually. Bring the two blocks together to show that God and man enjoyed a close friendship together in the Garden of Eden when there was no disobedience to spoil their relationship.

3. At this point ask for the assistance of two members of your audience to hold one block each. Then pick up the red block with the black letters 'SIN', and explain that God says our sin can be covered only by the whiteness of God's holiness (Isaiah 1:18). The black lettering speaks of the defilement caused by sin. Just as our hands get dirty when handling dirty things, so we become spiritually dirty when wrong thoughts and habits master us.

4. While the two volunteers hold the blue blocks, pick up the two ends of your prepared cords, left in some place where your audience can't see them, such as in a handbag. You can pick up the cords with the cotton tie hidden in the palm of your hand. This can appear quite natural by reaching into a bag and pulling them out. The audience can't see the knotted portion in your hand.

An alternative method can be used openly with practice. The tied cords can be picked up with the free hand while holding the red 'SIN' block in the other hand, focusing attention on it by lifting it up and speaking about the blockage sin brings into the life. People will not notice that the fingers of your other hand are feeling for the cotton reef knot in the middle of the two cords. Without even looking, it is possible to slip the right thumb and first finger between the cords and flick them apart so that the cotton join is safely in the middle of your palm.

Either way, still keeping the cotton knot in the palm of one hand, pick up the two ends of one doubled cord in the same hand and thread them through the hole in the middle of the 'SIN' block with the cotton knot still hidden from the audience by the back of your hand. Draw the two ends of the cord through the block until the knot disappears inside the block. Stop pulling when you estimate the knot is close to the centre of the block. The reason for checking the knot going into the block is to be sure that the two doubled cords are knotted together by the cotton thread. If the cords are only crossed over, and threaded through the block, you will never break nylon cords by a direct pull, in a lifetime. If you see you have made a mistake, continue to talk about the problem of sin, pull the cords out again, and go through the separation process again with your free hand and restart the threading process.

Most users of this object lesson make this mistake at some time, so before you ever use it publicly you must practise—then do some more practice.

49

5. When the cord threading process with the red block is complete, take either one of the two ends of the rope protruding out of each end of the block and tie the first part of a granny's knot on top of the block so that the effect will look like the illustration to the right. (See illustration.)

6. Finally, thread the ends of the two cords from one side of the red block through the dark blue block, and the others through the light blue block on the other side. If desired, the two volunteers from the audience can do the threading for you. When the three blocks are threaded together the separating nature of sin becomes very obvious. In fact, by grasping the two ends of the ropes in each hand and moving them vertically it will be seen to be impossible to bring 'GOD' and 'MAN' together because of 'SIN' between them. At this point the ends of the ropes should be handed to the helpers, who are asked to hold them apart but not pull on them.

7. The red cloth is then shown as representing the blood of Jesus Christ, who alone removes the sin barrier between God and man. Throw the cloth over the three blocks so that they cannot be seen. Speak of repentance, trusting Jesus for cleansing, forgiveness, salvation etc. and ask the helpers to pull the rope ends firmly. By holding your hands underneath the red block, you will catch it when it falls as the cotton tie is broken. Remove the red block inside the red cloth as a reminder that as 'SIN' cannot be seen when covered by the red cloth, so our sins will never be seen again when Jesus takes them away.

8. Put the red cloth and the covered block down, take the ends of the ropes held by the helpers, and show that now 'GOD' and 'MAN' are free to have the close friendship together again because the 'SIN' barrier is gone.

Please note:

The broken cotton will not be seen when the middle block is removed, being covered by the red cloth. After use, retie the cords with the cotton knot so that they are ready for the next occasion. This will mean that you will always be prepared, and could be saved embarrassment if people are around.

● **A novel use for safety pins**

Two pins make an ideal object lesson for showing the power of Jesus Christ to overcome sin. (Romans 8:13,26). This should be practised a number of times before attempting to use it publicly.

1. Have the points of each pin facing to the left.

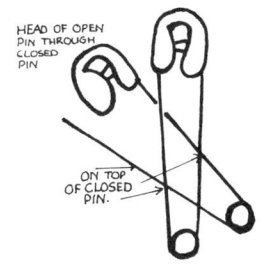

2. Close the left-hand pin, and hold it in the left hand. Put the head of the right-hand pin through the closed pin held in the left hand, and close.

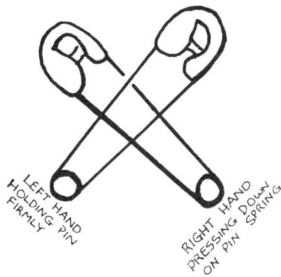

3. Grasping the right-hand pin at the bottom of the spring, turn it at right angles to the pin in the left hand and form a cross. Press down on the base of the pin in the right hand so that there is pressure on both pins.

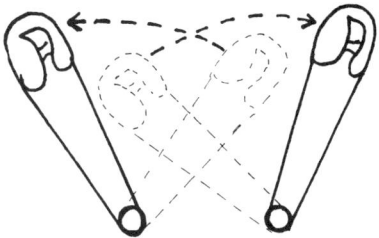

4. Move both hands outwards with a quick jerk, and the pins will separate, still shut. Only the cross of Jesus Christ separates sin from a sinner.

● **A new use for hacksaw blades.**

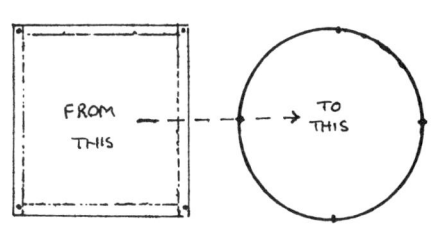

Lay the blades out in the form of a square. Then rivet or bolt the ends together in the same shape. The holes are already in place so that nothing has to be drilled. Make sure the rivets, or small nuts and bolts are not so rigid that no movement is possible. Now pick up the square with your two hands toward each other. By a quick flick of the wrists, the square is made into a circle. This illustrates what Jesus will do for us in making our lives like his. The circle is a perfect shape and is often used to represent God.

Paper cut outs are ideal for both preaching and teaching the gospel.

● The Cross of Jesus Christ.

Step 1.

Take a piece of writing paper or a single page of a tabloid newspaper, and fold it in the following manner:

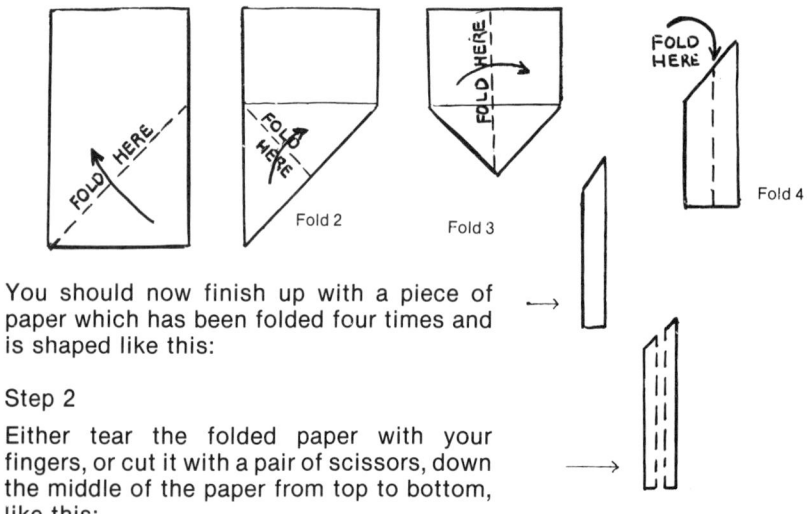

You should now finish up with a piece of paper which has been folded four times and is shaped like this:

Step 2

Either tear the folded paper with your fingers, or cut it with a pair of scissors, down the middle of the paper from top to bottom, like this:

Step 3

Unfold the pieces of paper. The left-hand piece, which is slightly longer than the other, will unfold into the shape of a cross. What remains will unfold into 8 separate pieces. The word 'HELL' may be made by carefully putting each of the 8 pieces in order. Except for the two letters 'L' which are obvious, the other letters have to be made up from pieces. A little practice will enable you to piece them together quickly. The letters will not be the same size, but the word will be easily recognised. It will look something like the illustration above.

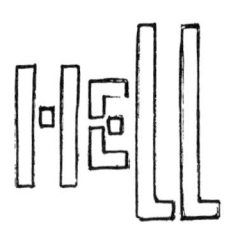

From this point, the 9 pieces of paper may be arranged into a number of positions for both teaching the gospel and illustrating the Christian life.

Step 4. (The gospel)

The scene of the Cross may be represented by placing the pieces in the following order:

52

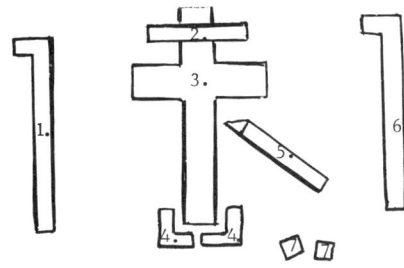

The scene

1. The unrepentant thief who turned his face from Jesus.
2. The superscription written over the cross.
3. The cross of Christ.
4. The hole dug for the cross.
5. The Roman soldier's spear which pierced Jesus' side.
6. The repentant thief who asked to be remembered.
7. The dice used by the soldiers to gamble for the clothes of Jesus.

When the story of the Cross has been told, the issues may be summed up in two words. The first is 'HELL', and the other is 'LIFE'. Both words cannot be made at the one time, as the same pieces of paper are required to make each word. When the word 'LIFE' is made, only 8 pieces of paper are used and one remains. This can be shown to be the letter 'I' and can be placed on top of the letter 'I' showing that a personal decision must be made to receive 'LIFE' in Jesus Christ. The two words appear like this:

Step 5.

There are several arrangements which apply to the Christian life. The first is that the new nature in Jesus Christ may be likened to His temple within us. 'Do you not know that you are the TEMPLE of God, and that the Spirit of God dwells in you?' (1 Corinthians 3:16 NASB) [author's capitals]. Two pieces of furniture in the various temples particularly represented the Lord Jesus—the altar of sacrifice and the seven-branched candlestick. In our lives there must always be an identification with the sacrifice of Jesus (Romans 12:1), and the reminder to walk constantly in his light (John 8:12).

The hidden light

Then there is the challenge to witness publicly. 'You are the light of the world. A city set on a hill cannot be hidden. Nor do men light a lamp, and put it under the peck-measure, but on the lampstand; and it gives light to all that are in the house. Let your light shine before men ...' (Matthew 5:14-16 NASB).

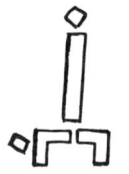

The light for all to see

• A simple visualised message

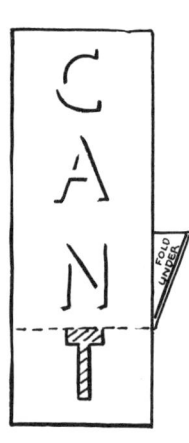

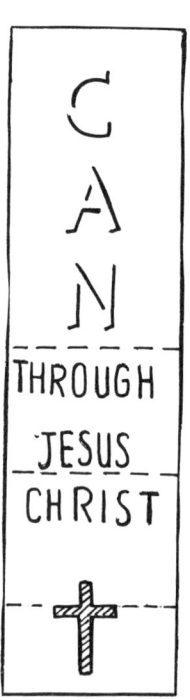

One of the most frequenty-used words in the English language is the word 'can't'. It is learned early in life and from then on either justifies us or excuses us from doing certain things. The big exception is that Satan deludes us into thinking that we can get right with God on our own terms, and he helps us work hard at it. But Jesus made it very clear that to get right with God he had to provide the link, and this is the one thing we just cannot do ourselves. '. . . for without me, ye can do nothing' (John 15:5 KJV). These two pieces of paper, or light cardboard, spell the message out very clearly. The one to the right is a scaled-down diagram of the complete strip, which you can make to the size most suited to the group of people you will be wanting to reach.

To use

Commence with the strip of paper, or card folded as shown in the left hand illustration, and talk about the word 'can't' and its frustrations. Then introduce the person of Jesus Christ; speak of all the things he was able to do because of his Deity. Finally speak of his greatest conquest of all— at Calvary's cross—and the victory he obtained on our behalf over sin and its grip and consequences. At this point the card may be folded and the last letter 'T' is then seen to be a cross; and the link between the cross and the change from 'can't' to 'can' is only through Jesus Christ. There is a natural progression from the simple gospel message which may be drawn from John 15:5 to the Christian's total dependence upon him for success in all exierences of life, as seen in Philippians 4:13 (NIV): 'I can do everything through him who gives me strength'.

Note: Be sure that when the word 'can't' is being shown the fold underneath is pressed tightly together with your fingers so that people cannot see the fold indicated by crease marks—enabling the cross to appear to be the letter 'T'.

• Paper rings and the gospel

For a message with three variations, three strips of paper are needed, approximately 4 ft in length and two to three inches wide. A roll of adding-machine paper is ideal. You will also need a pair of scissors and three pieces of adhesive tape the width of the strips of paper. Now to the messages.

1 Sin separates

Join two ends of one strip of paper with a piece of tape, then proceed to cut the ring through the middle so that two separate rings are made while you speak of the judgment of God which separates believers from unbelievers for eternity.

2 When sin is dealt with through Jesus Christ the believer is linked with God.

Take the second strip of paper, and while you share the gospel join the ends as in No. 1, except this time, without making it obvious, turn one end over a complete turn before securing. Proceed to cut through the middle of the circle. The result is quite unexpected. Two rings are linked together.

3 The limitless prospects of the Christian life.

Join the last strip of paper, this time unobtrusively, making two turns while speaking of the unity of God's family, the greater love, greater opportunities of fulfilment and the satisfaction which Christ brings to every area of life. Cut, and to the surprise of all there will be one large circle.

The object lesson's code of ethics.

If object lessons were to carry a code of ethics similar to a manufacturer's *Instructions for use, it would read something like this:*

BE POSITIVE
- Choose your object lesson for its ability to illustrate your teaching.
- Aim for those with an obvious application.
- Be interesting and concise to hold attention.
- Be honest at all times and avoid misrepresentation.
- Honour Jesus Christ in everything.

WHERE POSSIBLE AVOID:
- losing the value of your illustration by being too complicated.
- drawing attention to yourself by playing the 'smart alec' routine.
- any suggestion of powers of magic, because of demonic associations and scriptural warnings. Be sensitive to the Holy Spirit in this whole area. Many souls have been won to Christ through the ministry of so called 'Christian Magic', but some Christians have also been spiritually offended.
- passing on the know-how about the things you do. It spoils the effect for future use, and is unethical to those who may include those items in professional routines.
- centring your message and illustration on yourself. Don't cast a personal shadow over the truths you are teaching.
- using any object lesson which may offend the leadership of any church in which you may be a guest. If in doubt—check it out.
- allowing any object lesson to displace the dependence you need on prayer and preparation, and your dependence on the guidance of the Holy Spirit. Familiarity that leads to self-reliance breeds spiritual infertility.

Further reading.

A volume of small-book reading is available on visual aids and object lessons. A very small selection is:
Objects that talk and teach by Louis T. Talbot (Published by the author (probably out of print).

Bible object lessons for boys and girls by Betty Stubbs (the Standard Publishing Foundation.)

Illustrated gospel object lessons by W. T. McLean (Zondervan Publish House.)

Visual surprise sermonettes by Arnold C. Westphal (Zondervan Publish House.)

Part 2 -INDEX

Chapter 1

OPEN AIR EVANGELISM

THE OLDEST METHOD OF EVANGELISM
IN CURRENT USE

Fishing grounds can now be made to order by dumping several thousand used car tyres on the sea bed. Reef fish do the rest. In about two years they are ready for music lessons—the knife and fork symphony.

Open air evangelism is fishing where the fish are, not building a reef. People are usually divided in their opinion of open air evangelism. Those who do it, are sold on it. Those who don't, are mostly against it because of what they have seen, or because of what they imagine it to be.

It is true that lone gospel preachers do sometimes stand on street corners half choked with exhaust fumes, and barely able to be heard above the din of passing people and traffic. And some small groups do bravely sing and preach the gospel while being jostled, laughed at or heckled by those whose trade is cheap insults and hackneyed questions.

But fortunately, there are also open air preachers who build solid bridges of person-to-person relationships, and create such interest that people want to stand and listen. They preach the gospel meaningfully using modern methods of communication, and people outwardly respond to Jesus Christ in a challenge to repentance, faith and discipleship. Maybe an occasional scoffer or a good natured 'drunk' comments, but people listen well and are responsive.

Using Biblical basics and up-to-date approaches open air evangelism is still an evangelistic method which glorifies God and produces results in the 20th Century. Sometimes big results.

The following outdoor activities are often used for gospel preaching but fall short of the regularly used method of open air evangelism under consideration:

- The public rally preceded by a march of Christian witness.
- The open air forum for secular and religious speakers.
- The public stadium evangelistic rally.
- The church service outdoors.
- Seasonal celebrations, religious pageants or memorial services.
- The campfire service.
- The outdoor lead-up to an indoor service.

'**Open Air evangelism** as an established method of outreach uses modern and effective means of communication to present the gospel to people wherever they are found outdoors, based on the commands of Jesus Christ and the example of the early church. Its aim is so to present the claims of the living reigning Christ, that people of all ages will repent, trust Jesus Christ as Saviour, and become his committed disciples'. The principle is old but not outdated, the presentation must never be old, but continually updated. There are good reasons for this.

1. **Jesus did it and told us to follow his example; so there is no time limit.**
   The gospels clearly show that Jesus Christ fulfilled every detail of his Father's will in all he said and did. No-one and no thing stopped him. It was therefore no accident that he reached many more people outdoors than in the synagogues. The Gospels reveal that on 147 occasions Jesus preached outdoors as against 65 indoors. In 13 situations the location is indefinite.

He obviously went looking for people wherever they could be found, such as market places, the seashore, villages, public roads, and in the vicinity of the temple. He said he had come to find and save people, so open air evangelism was a logical first choice. The early church had no doubts about following his example, particularly as the more traditional places of worship began to be closed to them when they preached the resurrection of Christ. Preaching indoors soon became largely restricted to private homes.

'But', it may be argued, 'what about the enormous exansion of the printed and electronic media. Everyone who wants to can read, hear or see the gospel today in some form. Doesn't that make open air evangelism redundant?' Frankly, no! Availability is one thing, but receiving the gospel message in some form and understanding it is another matter. It is true that more Bibles are being printed, more good Christian literature is available, more Christian radio stations are on air and more Christian television programs screened than ever before. Yet in so many countries church attendances are dropping, while crime, vice, gambling, drug and alcohol consumption, pornography and occultism are rapidly increasing. Open air evangelism is able to reach those who will never see a TV screen, hear a Christian radio broadcast or ever be able to read.

2. Open air evangelism is a very personal method of reaching people with the Gospel.

An impersonal gospel newspaper advertisement may be passed over without any sense of embarrassment, and no one feels bad about ignoring church notice boards. Gospel literature offered in the street is easily refused or the distributor avoided. A radio voice or a screen image can be silenced without the speaker being aware he has been given 'the chop'. But somehow, eyeball to eyeball contact with a warm, communicating open-air preacher, seems to be another matter. Curiosity usually attracts interest initially and when the gospel is shared with sincerity, conviction and joyfulness by people in love with Jesus Christ, interest is often held, and prejudice and resistance melt away. Bystanders who identify with people giving personal testimonies, will wait to talk with them afterwards. And believe it or not, people are still drawn by old fashioned authoritative preaching, good music and singing, feeling no personal embarrassment when listening amongst a crowd. Even if people do not stay long, experienced evangelists will make sure that sufficient will have been said to challenge them concerning their relationship to Jesus Christ.

In the parable of the great banquet in Luke 14, the servant delivered his master's invitations to each invited guest in person, but when the time came, not one turned up. The spurned host was rightfully angry and sent his servant into the city streets and lanes to invite anyone he could find to the banquet. The beggars, the crippled and the blind came pouring in but there were still many vacant seats. The servant was sent out again to beat the bushes along the lanes and back country roads for anyone he could find. It was only by his urgent insistence that more came. The parable was surely prophetic. Open air evangelists are still going out to streets and country lanes urgently pressing people to respond to the gospel so that God's house may be filled.

3. Just add a preacher to people and the result is open air evangelism.

Just think of it. No pre-arranged seating, ushers, flowers, organs, hymnbooks, special dress, or starting time. If it is hot, people can listen in the shade. If it is cold they will be already rugged up for it, and perhaps-surprisingly, excellent open air evangelism can be held when snow is on the ground. If it is raining suitable shelter is usually not far away. Many OAC staff men have preached to audiences under umbrellas. For sheer versatility open air evangelism has no equal.

4. Outdoor evangelism will reach people who would never enter an evangelistic church.

Churches are regarded by some as outdated and irrelavent, dress-up affairs, exclusive clubs, or full of intolerant goody-goodies. The long-haired and bare-feet generation feel they would be out of place. Druggies, gamblers, prostitutes, socialites, and drunkards are too busy doing their thing to be interested. Atheists, sceptics, intellectuals, workaholics, jet-setters and Sunday sport fanatics limit their patronage to weddings and funerals. Jews don't make a habit of attending evangelical churches, neither do satanists, followers of Eastern religions, cultists, members of strict religious orders or anti-evangelicals. But all these people can be reached in many cities with the gospel outdoors without feeling threatened or disloyal to their beliefs. They feel secure in being anonymous in a group of strangers knowing they can walk away at any time they choose. As it was in the 1st Century, so it is in the 20th Century, London, New York, Rome, Toronto or Sydney.

5. **So much evangelism is to the few who hear it most and need it least; so little evangelism to the many who need it most but hear it least.**
It is a sobering fact that apart from Christmas and Easter a small percentage of people in the Western World attend church regularly. Churches have empty seats while hotels, social clubs, night clubs, casinos and all types of entertainment are full seven days and nights per week. The increase of civil marriage celebrants with secular alternatives to church ceremonies, helps to widen the gap. Of course open air evangelism cannot bridge that gap, but if people won't come to church, the church must go to the people. This is no option, but an obligation in the light of eternity.

6. **When the church has been insensitive to the voice of the Holy Spirit, God had used open air evangelism to bring revival to a nation.**
History shows that the 18th Century spiritual revival made a major contribution in shaping the destinies of both Great Britain and the United States of America. The names of George Whitfield and John Wesley are honoured for the parts they played in taking the great Reformation doctrines outdoors to the people. Denied the used of churches, vilified by the clergy, and sometimes attacked by ruffians, these men and others like them freed the gospel from its four-walled prisons. Bishop J. C. Ryle believed George Whitfield to have been the greatest English preacher who ever lived. He was capable of speaking without amplifiction to crowds of up to sixty thousand people at one time and ceaselessly rode all over England preaching massive sermons. His influence in America was no less extensive and effective. Wesley and his 'methodist' followers are said to have kept the bloody French Revolution from crossing the Channel to England. Had that not occurred, British history books may well have told a far different story. Revival is God's alternative to revolution, and open air evangelism brings the gospel to those who need it.

7. **Open air evangelism is probably the least expensive method of reaching people for Christ.**
Crusades are expensive if auditoriums and equipment have to be hired. Media evangelism is costly, particularly TV. Even literature evangelism has to be financed. But when a pastor and congregation take the gospel to a local park, beach, or shopping centre, no outlay is needed. Equipment and follow-up materials will be on hand.

8. **The Church gets a new image when its members take to the streets.**
Non-Christians do not understand that the church is a body of believers. The practice of writing the name of a denomination on church property confirms the misunderstanding that the building is the church. The only way to dispel misunderstanding and prejudices is to literally turn the church inside out. When vibrant, Spirit-filled believers are seen in open air programs, the church gets a new image. When those who live in a loveless world are exposed to loving, caring people, inevitably some respond to Christ. Church buildings or a noticeboard welcome don't radiate personal warmth, but when people in love with Jesus share that love where it is needed most, exciting things happen.

Much has been written about the spectacular growth of some denominations in South America, and no small credit is due to open air evangelism. The ministry of OAC itself has also resulted in churches being established through outdoor evangelism in Mexico, Ghana, the Philippines and Italy. Some of those churches have in turn sent missionaries to other countries.

9. **Open air evangelism attracts people looking for spiritual reality.**
'Cold canvas' personal work outdoors calls for a special type of dedication. Some time ago members of a YWAM outreach team working in Sydney, Australia, stayed until the early hours of each morning speaking to patrons of the night life of the King's Cross district about Jesus Christ. Night after night they walked the streets sharing Jesus on a one-to-one basis with all who would listen, but it was hard work. Before the end of their assignment they had learned some basics of open air evangelism, so they tried operating as a team. As they sang, testified and shared the gospel, people wanting lower-level entertainment drifted away, and the interested stayed. After a brief program they began personal conversation with those who remained and contacted many more people responsive to gospel dialogue than before.

10. **Open air evangelism offers greater scope for the use of spiritual gifts and abilities than any other form of evangelism.**
If that appears to be an over-statement, be assured it is not! Outdoor evangelism is open to both sexes without age limitation. It provides excellent experience for preachers, personal workers, musicians and singers. Artists gain confidence, and even those who claim little or no talent find there is personal fulfilment in making some contribution to the overall gospel program. It is here that principles of spiritual warfare are learned in practice, and pray-ers develop a new vitality. Love grows into a new dimension, and Christians experience the joy of working together for the glory of Jesus Christ.

11. **More people can be reached personally and more quickly in the open air than anywhere else.**
The last 20 years have seen increasing numbers taking to the streets for demonstrations. During national crises, governments often pro-

hibit more than two people assembling together outdoors for fear of activists. From the speech of Brutus at the funeral of Caesar to the overthrow of the Shah of Iran, the moods of crowds in the streets have changed history. But since Pentecost God also has truimphed outdoors. Over 1 000 000 people listened to Billy Graham outdoors in Seoul, Korea and he had been promised 5 000 000 next visit. In times of Holy Ghost revival, the gospel could be preached to more people at one time outdoors, than would ever be reached by local churches in a lifetime. It is interesting to note that in Revelation 11 the final testimony of God's two witnesses will end in the open air where their rejected bodies will lie while the world rejoices. The spotlight will remain on them for three days, then the power of God will stagger the watching world as they are brought back to life, and return to heaven. Make no doubt about it, major action will always be outdoors, where the people will be.

12. Open air evangelism is an ideal training ground.

Many church young people feel restless if restricted to a routine of teaching and social activities. What they need is an evangelistic outlet. There are young men longing to preach but they don't know where to begin. Talented young people with musical, singing and creative abilities need an outlet. Many would love to learn how to share their testimonies with friends without embarrassment, and others are keen to learn how to meaningfully communicate the gospel. Open air evangelism with children, teenagers or adults is certainly an excellent answer. There is scope for everyone. The minister of a large New Zealand church had a few problem young men who didn't seem to fit in with the rest. Then he hit on an idea, and asked OAC to take them over for a period of training and practical work. After two years these young men were so changed in outlook, co-operation and preaching ability that the minister became a strong supporter of open air evangelism. Any pastor who is prepared to lead his young people in this ministy, or make them available to others to do so, will find that his church will doubly benefit. Souls will be saved, and the young people will become deeply committed to Jesus Christ.

13. Open air evangelism causes spiritual renewal.

One thing is sure, backsliders and half-hearted Christians won't be volunteers. There is a price to pay in holy living if there is a chance that family members, friends, neighbours, school or work friends, business associates, or even creditors may happen to be in the crowd.

A teenager whose missionary parents were on field service, decided to give up active Christian living and drift with the world. One Sunday afternoon before he could act on his decision, he was brought to an OAC team prayer meeting and gospel outreach. He was never the same again. He entered Bible College, then began a full-time open air evangelistic ministry. Finally, married and with his young family, he went overseas as a missionary to a developing African nation. The change began when young people poured out their hearts for the lost whom they were expecting to reach in the afternoon open air program. Partnership in evangelism generated spiritual warmth.

14. The population drift is toward the cities where open air evangelism flourishes.

During the 1980 Consultation on Evangelism in Pattaya, Thailand, some interesting statistics came to light. In 1976, 131 cities throughout the world had a population of more than 1 million people. In 1979 this had grown to 175, an increase of 44, at a worldwide urban growth rate of 7.2% per annum. Nearly 45% of the world's 4.3 billion plus now live in cities, and that figure is rapidly rising.

One hundred years ago, the writer's paternal grandfather lived some 10 miles outside the city of Belfast, Northern Ireland. His Sunday practice was to walk into the city and preach the gospel in the open air, stopping at cross roads to preach to groups of people resting or passing. He repeated the process on the homeward journey. Now times have changed. Modern cities now provide masses of people, and preachers who want fresh audiences have only to walk one block, not 20 miles.

In Madras, India, one church commences open air evangelism in suburban streets each Sunday at 4.30 a.m. Members move from one district to another, sometimes with opposition, but invariably when they conclude just after 6.00 a.m. a large crowd has joined them, many having been made spiritually and physically whole.

15. Where climate and culture favour an outdoor life style, why herd people indoors to hear the gospel?

The world's greatest areas of population density are in Asia where the climate favours outdoor living. Many of these people do not have Western style houses, so life is freer and easier, without slavery to a clock. Many have not seen a church, know nothing about Christ, and are beyond the reach of the electronic and printed media, but are open to the gospel taken to them.

Operation Mobilisation have been pouring their resources into the Indian sub-continent for many years. Their teams criss-cross the country in trucks selling literature and doing open-air evangelism, often at considerable personal risk from religious fanatics. One of the most stirring experiences the writer remembers is when one of their leaders knelt and with tears asked for prayer that he would be given greater courage to preach Christ in the street where his family lived, on the concourses of railway stations and in public transport. He wept because of the great need, and the lack of workers to share Jesus. No! Open air evangelism is not dead. It never can be while Jesus is alive!

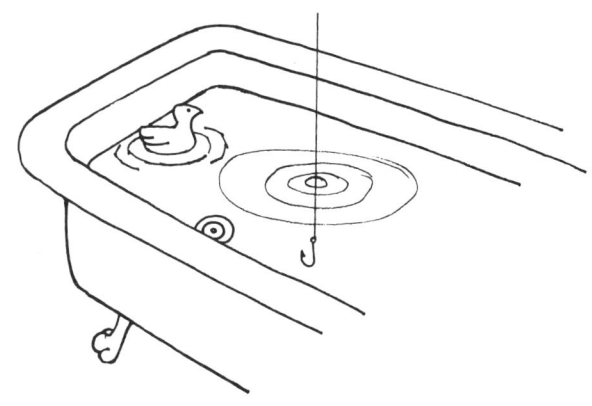

Chapter 2

YOU DON'T CATCH FISH IN A BATH TUB

... that is unless you have put them there for that purpose. Of course some fish shops and restaurants do just that. You select the one you would like, there is a swish of a net, a few thuds and you either carry your meal home with you, or sit down and relax while it is cooked.

But open air evangelism is not about captive fish but those who swim freely in the seas, rivers, streams, lakes and ponds. Just where can the best shoals be found so that structured or unstructured outdoor evangelism may be used to 'capture' people for Christ?

1. Where people live

That would probably be about the last place to think of having open air evangelism! But why not attract them out of their homes to hear the gospel? There was a time when the bands and songsters of the Salvation Army used to be driven around suburbs on the backs of large trucks on Sunday mornings stopping to sing, play, and preach the gospel while Corps members went from house to house offering literature, and receiving donations. The residents often showed their appreciation by lining their fences or listening from their doorways.

In an English town members of a local church and OAC have combined on summer Sunday afternoons to conduct gospel programs in a street of semi-detached two-storey houses. The writer walked down the street during one outreach and saw people listening behind front window curtains in almost every house. That day a little lady in her 80s was invited to give a brief testimony. At first she was reluctant, but finally agreed. When she got going she became so excited sharing her Lord that the compere was unable to recover the microphone for about 10 minutes! Some may shudder at the thought of such witnessing, but the only alternative to reach these people with the gospel would be to knock on their doors, and that may appeal even less!

Ethnic groups provide excellent opportunities for outdoor evangelism in some of the high density, high rise housing settlements of large cities. There are children by day and families by night. Where there is strong racial feeling, care needs to be taken not to inflame tensions, and night programs should be held in well-lit areas. Wherever possible, the presence of some of the older residents should be encouraged to prevent problems. The gospel can solve racial bitterness, and open air evangelism is a very genuine method of showing the Christian love to all races.

Two OAC staff members were driving through a town in the mid-west of the United States when a fire truck passed at speed. They followed knowing that a shiny fire truck is a great magnet to boys and girls, and found about fifty children gathered outside a house where fortunately the blaze had been confined to the contents of an oven. After receiving permission from the owner of a neighbouring house, the evangelists began a children's gospel program on his kerbside lawn. When the fire truck left, none of the children went, they were enjoying the gospel program too much.

During a visit to Taiwan, the writer went with his missionary host to two street film presentations at night. The first was at the end of a dead-end street in which the houses were surrounded by high walls and gates. The screen and projector were set up and in no time the whole available area was filled with people of all ages. Personal workers had a busy and fulfilling night. On another occasion the screen was put on the pavement outside a residential section of a business district, and within minutes neighbours had brought chairs and canvas seats and were waiting for the film. On both occasions a pastor closed with a gospel talk and challenge.

2. Where people work

No city or town of any size is without industry, and on fine days workers in small or large groups will sit outside in the sun or shade during tea and luncheon breaks. If they can be reached without having to walk onto private property which may be regarded as trespassing, and the approach is both friendly and interesting they generally respond well. Even those who are sitting on company property can sometimes be reached by the discreet use of amplification if they are close to the road.

The effectiveness of open air industrial evangelism should not be judged by numbers reached. One evangelist driving through an industrial area saw three men sitting on a concrete path outside a small factory. He parked, walked back, sat down with the men and shared Christ. Two soon made lame excuses and went inside leaving an audience of one. After listening very attentively to the gospel this man said, 'Last year I had a serious motor accident and suffered brain damage. I have just recently come back to work. After listening to you, I now know why God allowed me to stay alive. It was so that I could hear what you have told me today.'

There are thrilling opportunities with dock workers and employees working in railway workshops, timbermills, abattoirs, canning works and roadside gangs. Builders on industrial and housing projects, bridge construction gangs and public utility employees all provide potential audiences. Construction and maintenance workers' camps in outback areas for railway construction, road maintenance and building pipe-lines are ideal opportunities for day or night programs. Workers are mostly tolerant to the gospel, and if the approach is friendly and reasonable, more often than not they will be prepared to listen. They welcome diversion and will readily accept well presented outdoor programs, particularly films at night. They will probably smoke and drink while listening and often applaud a 'no-holds-bared' gospel message. They may be wary of responding publicly, but will do so in personal conversation afterwards.

The working man's closest friend is often his glass of beer, so he and his mates spend as much free time as they can with their special friend in saloons, bars and hotels near their places of work. Whenever there is a work break, the bars are full, providing the more venturesome evangelists with opportunities for lively kerbside gospel programs. There is seldom a problem in getting an audience, and despite potential difficulties some exciting results have been obtained for Jesus Christ in this way.

One large brewery in the Tasmanian city of Launceston allowed a group of OAC staff members to take a specially equipped vehicle into an outdoor enclosed bar area where employees enjoyed free drinks after work. For about 45 minutes fifty or more employees relaxed, drank and listened to music, singing, personal testimonies and how Christ could supply them with everlasting refreshment. During a time of personal sharing one man clutched his glass and wept. He wanted Christ to break the power of alcohol, but lamented he didn't have the moral courage to make the change. These men were not church goers, but welcomed the informality and variety of an open air approach.

Another team of evangelists was working in the city of Gladstone in Australia's State of Queensland during a crippling strike at the world's largest aluminium refinery. The pickets which barricaded the road to the main gate, changed every four hours, giving the evangelists a continually changing audience. The morning on which a vital union meeting was to be held, a specially equipped trailer unit was opened close to where the unionists planned to meet, and a well-attended gospel program was held up to the commencement of the union meeting. The families of people contacted in the town said the men had shown considerable interest in the gospel.

Some countries have seasonal sheep shearers, tobacco and hop harvesters, stone, berry and pip fruit pickers, and vegetable and wheat summer workers. These people who move from district to district and even country to country offer the open air preacher continuous opportunities.

3. Where people are educated.

Playgrounds of primary and secondary schools, and open spaces for relaxation in technical colleges and university campuses are ideal. While many students play sport or use the gymnasium during the midday break, there are always many with nothing to do. The challenge of these young people is exciting, but permission must be gained from the authorities. In some cases music will attract an audience, but so will sketched messages, visuals, object lessons, the ventriloquist doll, questions and answer sessions, controlled debates or straight preaching. When such outreaches are co-ordinated with Christian groups within the institution the Christians get stimulated, and their assistance is invaluable.

4. Where people go for relaxation

a. Shows and fairgrounds in developed countries

Amongst the most popular outdoor gatherings are fair-grounds with their agricultural and pastoral exhibits, sporting events, parades of livestock, industrial displays, and the usual side-show alley. They usually last for days and attract great crowds of city and country people. The outdoor evangelist could be forgiven for feeling they were being held just for his benefit!

Working alone or with a team, using a specially equipped vehicle, a stage, or just standing on the grass, workers usually run out of energy before running out of listeners. A series of 30-minute programs with music, singing, a clear personal testimony, and a brief gospel message is ideal. This should be followed by personal work with those showing interest—and a rest break before re-commencing. With good weather thousands can be reached, and many won for Christ. Additional coordinating ministries include a book stall, a tent for personal work, special hourly childrens' programs and daylight films for adults.

b. Sports gatherings.

Weekend matches between neighbouring sports teams have a magnetic attraction for their fans, all hoping for a win. No-one would think of preaching during a game, but why not afterwards? It takes time for patrons to get away, and some will always listen if what they hear is interesting and to the point.

Then there are the big-time sports fixtures when lines of people camp overnight at the entrance to the sports field or stadium to make sure of the best seats when the gates open. An interesting gospel program, especially if accompanied by a free hot or cold drink is sure to be well received.

But what about the largest of all sports gatherings such as the Olympic Games, the World Cup soccer finals, or the various British Commonwealth Games? YWAM's enthusiastic teams have opened up a new dimension in open air evangelism by presenting Christ where the major events are held. By mime, drama, singing and testimonies, thousands have been reached and some won for Christ. Informality, sincerity and personal warmth are the keys. If individual churches are refused permission to work, then the Church must rise to the occasion on a person-to-person basis. Christ should never be allowed to be fettered in the open air while buskers are given freedom to do their thing. The traditional Sunday hours for preaching at 11 a.m. and 7 p.m. are no longer relevant. The gospel belongs to every place at any time.

c. *Beaches, rivers and swimming pools.*

These opportunities should make every evangelist drool with delight! People who would spurn an invitation to attend an indoor crusade will lie in the sun without a protest, listening to every word of an open air program and afterwards freely admit to having enjoyed it. When street clothes are exchanged for relaxing gear or swim-wear, it seems that business worries, the cares of tomorrow, and often anti-religious attitudes are given a rest. Doctors, white and blue collar workers, Supreme Court Judges, politicians and the unemployed all look alike, and that's the time when informally dressed preachers can win their confidence, friendship and response.

d. *Parks and reserves.*

The wide open spaces have a special appeal to children living in postage stamp sized rooms, city apartments with stair wells as their only playground or who race up and down the walkways of high rise tenement buildings hundreds of feet above ground level protected by wire grills like so many animals in a cage. No wonder they love to get out. When they meet young people who enthusiastically share Jesus and his love, puppets, a good story-teller, and good singing, the scene is set for time of reaping. If there are no nearby reserves, any open space where children play with do—even side-walks. Few children hear the gospel at home or at church and unless it is taken to those leaders of tomorrow's generations, their slide into paganism may never be stopped.

e. *Camping grounds and trailer parks (Western style)*

In many countries people take vacations by towing caravans or house trailers long distances, staying overnight at places where special facilities are available. Managers of transit or holiday caravan parks and camping grounds usually welcome Christian groups willing to show films and present well balanced gospel programs. Clocks are never a rule of life on vacation and people have time to sit and talk about the gospel.

f. *Where people wait for public transport.*

Bus stops and railway station platforms are usually places where each minute seems to last 90 seconds, punctuated by sighs, much shifting of feet, and checking of watches. While the open air evangelist may not be able to operate in every railway station, bus stops abound. A friendly smile, a warm greeting, a short interesting message and the offering of suitable literature is usually well received. During Chicago's snow season, one OAC evangelist uses his outdoor approach on the platforms of the underground where people are waiting for trains. They willingly listen, and some respond to the gospel. Many years ago an open air personal worker used to stand at one of the bus stops in downtown Sydney. He wasn't waiting for a bus, but for those unfortunate enough to have missed theirs. Time and again a bus would pull away leaving some late comer frustrated. The personal worker would then say how sorry he was, give the time the next bus was due, say a few words about how tragic it would be to miss God's opportunity of salvation through Jesus Christ, offer a well chosen gospel booklet and bid them good-day. He sowed, trusting God to give the increase. Many years later a conference speaker was passing through a Third World country and a missionary shared how he happened to come to Christ. 'I had just missed a bus in Pitt Street, Sydney', he said, 'when this man . . .' You guessed it. The speaker was so struck with the story that he retold it in another country, and one of the audience came up and said, 'Thank God for that man, whoever he may be, that is how I came to Christ.' It happened a third time, so he determined to find that open air bus-stop missionary when he came to Australia. After much enquiry he found a very old man who had no idea that God had blessed his efforts so abundantly. Who said that open air evangelism had to be done with a team?

g. The streets of shopping centres.

This is probably the most popular place for open air evangelism. The type of people may change from shoppers, businessmen, commerce and trade employees in daytime, to window shoppers, and those on their way to theatres and entertainment at night. Select the right places and times, and your audience is ready-made.

The stories of how God has met people's needs in these places are legion. People with theatre tickets in their pockets have paused to make fun out of an outdoor preacher and have been unable to leave because they found their greatest need met in Christ.

Would-be suicides have stopped and found a new life someone else died to give them. Men on their way to commit a crime have been arrested by Jesus Christ instead of the law. One man said 'someone' turned his feet down a side street when he was intending to walk straight down the road. He met that 'someone' after listening to the gospel. The tears, the confessions, the tangles and the tragedies revealed are heartbreaking. But the cleansing, release, joy and new life that Jesus ministers is beautiful to see. Some very ordinary slabs of concrete sidewalk have become doorsteps to heaven.

- *The shopping centre plazas and reserves*

  Listeners will include mothers and children taking a rest from shopping, professional and business people soaking up fresh air and sunshine, typists and their friends enjoying a sandwich lunch on the grass, paper sellers, odd-ware vendors, the lunch-hour forty winkers, and the trash-can diners, but each one a person for whom Christ died. A gospel preacher's delight! For some, the only gospel they may ever hear. If this challenge is taken up, don't expect everyone to look approvingly, and offer congratulations. In fact, preachers may think they are being totally ignored, but when a reader does not turn the page of his newspaper or book for 10 minutes, it's not because he's paralysed—he's listening. And the man on the grass under the tree watching the birds is hearing you very clearly like that lady who has been staring at a book she has been holding upside down for ages. Preachers who walk around and dialogue with the people when finished, will be glad they didn't let the opportunity go.

- *Outdoor shopping malls*

  Thank God for modern architecture and the wide open spaces which now surround many shops and business premises. They provide seats, trees, fountains, walkways and a lovely atmosphere to preach Christ in a personal way. No shouting, just heart to heart sharing.

  Many cities have turned mid-city streets into malls and thrown them open to buskers, cults, politicians and the like. Others have regulated the type of activity permitted, and preaching sometimes comes at the top of the list of banned events.

  In Launceston Tasmania, the Mall Board refused to allow preaching for fear it could affect the surrounding retailers. A visiting evangelist happened to be in the city during preparations for a Leighton Ford Reachout, and offered to use some object lessons during a time of publicity for the Crusade without offending the no-preaching rule. He not only got the interest of the crowd but wove the gospel into his explanations so that the people got the message while the retailer's cash registers continued to ring. Among the large crowd that morning were members of a local motor-cycle gang, obvious by their leather gear. They had no intention of going to the Reachout, but they are just as accountable as if they had, they had heard the gospel that morning.

  Indoor shopping centre malls are another matter; they are privately owned and controlled. However, by special arrangement they can provide opportunities for drama and good gospel music with singing and appropriate comments and testimonies. Direct preaching is almost always banned.

- *Lines of theatre patrons*

  A regular Sunday evening open air program has been held at a reserve in the centre of Wellington, New Zealand, for more than 25 years. In the early years a picture theatre opposite the reserve commenced Sunday evening screenings and there was always a line of people waiting to buy tickets while the gospel program was being held. The patrons couldn't help but hear the gospel as the line very slowly snaked its way past the ticket box. Some never made it inside. Those who did will never be able to plead spiritual ignorance at the Day of judgment.

  In tropical climates, open air programs can be held with theatre patrons waiting outside in the cool evening air before the films commence.

  h. Even in the most unlikely places

  In the Northern Australian State of Queensland, floods are frequent during the holiday monsoon season. One Evangelist found himself stranded for hours in a line of about 70 cars. He walked up and down speaking about the Lord, distributing tracts to drivers and passengers. Later, when he was marooned at a railway siding with a freight train and crew, transporters, and more cars, he conducted evening programs with gospel films, sketching and preaching with both acceptance and response.

An aircraft had just landed on a water-logged grass landing strip on an island in Vanuatu. The only sign of civilisation amongst the coconut trees was a thatched grass hut—the terminal building. After unloading, the plane took off in heavy rain leaving eight nationals and one Western evangelist in the open-sided shelter. Half an hour dragged by, interrupted only by the occasional crackle of the radio, the constant drumming of the rain and a little quiet conversation. Suddenly, the evangelist realised what an opportunity was being missed, so taking some object lessons out of his bag he shared the gospel with the group in English, asking a national pastor travelling with him to conclude in the local dialect. He did, and tracts were given out. Finally a jeep squelched its way to the shelter and somehow all managed to squeeze in. The pastor was very quiet during the lurching drive through the plantation. He later confessed he had learned a valuable lesson in using every available opportunity for sharing the gospel.

A program siting and timing ready reckoner.

The following suggestions come from experience to assist:

1. The solo open air evangelist.

	SITING	AVOID	TIMING
STREETS	Wide footpaths (sidewalks) Openings to arcades, rest areas.	Congested places. Shop doorways. Clerical workers.	Mid-morning, mid-afternoon shopping hours. Late night shopping.
PARKS	Close to where shoppers, office, or industrial workers relax.	Playing areas. Large open spaces where voices are lost.	Lunch hours during weekdays 12.30–1.30 p.m. Children daylight hours.
PLAZAS	Where most people can see and hear.	Long programs. Loud amplification. Shouting.	Shopping and lunch hours. Some at weekends
BEACHES	On the sand or nearby grassed areas. Shade on hot days.	Long programs. Anything one person can't handle.	Mid-late mornings and afternoons.

	SITING	AVOID	TIMING
CAMPING GROUNDS	In open space away from tents or trailers. See caretaker.	Hours of sleep and rest. Be considerate with noise.	10.00–11.00 a.m. Late afternoon Early evening
HOUSING AREAS	Grass verge in front of houses by permission. Play areas.	Sports areas. Loud amplification. Handling children	Sat. Sun. 10.00–12.00 noon 2.30–4.00 p.m. Holidays

2. For the evangelist operating with a team of supporters.

	SITING	AVOID	TIMING
STREETS	As above, and near places of night entertainment or window shopping.	Places where drink affects patrons, rough areas.	As above, and 1 hour before and after theatre opening time.
PARKS	Same as above. Also weekend programs with children— families.	Entertainment and sports areas or near main roads.	As above. Weekend—warm daylight hours. Night-time if parks floodlit.
PLAZAS	Where most people can see and hear.	Programs longer than lunch hours. Better to do personal work.	Shopping and lunch hours 12.30–1.30 p.m. Late night hours.
BEACHES	As above but for larger audiences.	Danger from sports, rising tides, kicking sand etc.	Mid-late mornings and afternoons.
CAMPING GROUNDS	As above. Organised programs may be held.	Swimming— sport, eating and rest hours.	As above plus evening programs by arrangement to 9.30 p.m.

HOUSING AREAS	Grass verge outside houses by permission. Play areas.	Sports areas. Loud amplification. Handling children.	Sat. Sun. 10.00–12.00 noon 2.30–4.00 p.m. Holidays

3. For evangelists with equipped vehicles and team support.

	SITING	AVOID	TIMING
STREETS	Choose wide streets—paths. Some city hotels with workers.	Being near pedestrian crossings. Loud amplification.	10.30 a.m.– 3.00 p.m. Night time 7.00–9.00 p.m.
PARKS	If people can be reached park on edge of park.	Loud amplification. Known rough areas at night.	As above. 12.30–1.30 p.m. 7.30–9.30 p.m.
PLAZAS	Generally not suitable for vehicle use. If so, as above.		
BEACHES	Only on grass areas. Permission may be needed.	Consider others, watch noise level, avoid sun exposure.	As above, also early evenings if people around.
CAMPING GROUNDS	As above	As above	Ideal 6.00–7.45 p.m. children's program. Family program with films, music, preaching etc. 8.00–9.30 p.m.
HOUSING AREAS	As above	As above	Regular Sunday school programs fine weather— vacation time. Times as above.

i. Special opportunities in developing nations with suitable climatic conditions.

During visits to the Christian Leaders Training College in the highlands of Papua New Guinea, the writer and pastors taking refresher courses drew up a list of opportunities for open air evangelism which apply to many other so called Third-World countries.

• *Markets*

From early morning to late afternoon markets are filled with vendors, buyers, lookers, and socialisers (the common pastime).

Market day is the red letter day of the week; all feet and vehicles are pointed in the same direction. Vendors mostly sit, buyers stand or squat, and time is measured by the length of the shadow rather than hours and minutes. Anytime during the day, except when the sun is at its hottest is the time for open air evangelism. There is always plenty of time for personal work, follow-up and counsel—the rest of the day if necessary.

An indigene well-known to the local police for his crime record was aimlessly wandering around the weekly market in Mt Hagen in the highlands of Papua New Guinea. He heard someone playing a trumpet, so headed in the direction of the sound and found that it came from a lone Swiss missionary who, when he had finished, spoke of the amazing things Jesus Christ could do in people's lives. The black man wasn't interested in religion, or church, but because of his continual trouble with the Police knew he was overdue for a change of life style, so he trusted Jesus as Saviour on the spot. The subsequent change in this life impressed everyone including the police, and many came to Christ. A thriving church soon began through his testimony and preaching. All this because of one missionary, a trumpet, and Jesus Christ.

• *Trade stores*

Country villages are often one-street affairs with the trade store the centre of attraction, providing ready-made crowds for the open air preacher. The larger towns with more shops, provide even bigger crowds, often blocking the footpaths and filling areas of grass. All ages are there from the tiniest babies to the highly respected older people, with the family's most valuable asset, a pig often squashed in the middle. Between the noise of shuffling feet, the buzz of conversation, squealing pigs, and loud greetings, there are great opportunities for preaching.

• *Hospitals*

Hospitals are strictly a family affair in developing countries, with the sick inside and the rest of the family living outside. Apart from preparing their simple meals, waiting relatives don't know what to do with their spare time, but personal workers and preachers should have some ideas!

• *Prisons*

What an opportunity for a captive audience with no chance of the congregation walking out if the preacher goes too long! In the larger cities chaplains visit prisons but the smaller prisons do not have this service, so the right type of open air preaching is generally welcomed.

• *Funeral feasts*

After the funeral comes the feasting. After the feasting comes the speeches, so why not some preaching? Everyone forgets the calendar at such times. Some of them may well have come great distances on foot, so no-one is in any hurry to leave.

- *Plantations*

Although working hours are generally long, Sunday is usually free, and families love to sit around and listen to gospel songs, sing hymns, and be impressed by a good speaker. The writer has had some of them respond to Christ. Christian workers who invest some of their weekends preaching and teaching plantation workers will reap a rich harvest of souls. So next time you pass a coffee, tea, coconut, rice, banana, sugar cane, or cocoa plantation, start praying about taking the gospel to them where they feel most at home—just sitting around in the shade.

- *Outside courthouses*

Wherever there are people, there are law breakers to be dealt with and disputes settled. Judicial systems usually operate slowly and much time is spent waiting around. Another ready-made audience.

- *Hotels*

Whatever good Westerners have done for developing nations, there is often an ugly blot caused by alcohol they have also introduced. This social cancer consumes individuals and families alike. Hotels are so often crowded by addicts and waiting dependants, but outdoor programs can be effective in winning some for Christ. The enemy often protests noisily but power belongs to the people of God.

- *Villages during the day*

The opportunities vary with the culture. Some women spend their working days in the gardens, some do handicrafts around their thatched huts, while others just look after the children and keep house. Where women remain in their villages, open air evangelism is certainly possible during the daytime.

The writer remembers a number of occasions in the Philippines when after advertising by amplifier from a car, or by door-to-door personal contact, very worthwhile programs were held outside homes, sometimes in the middle of little-used roads.

- *Villages after dark*

Where there is a lack of electricity, it is early to bed and early to rise. But before bed, there is always time to talk and relax, and that is an ideal gospel time.

An African leader told the writer during the Lausanne Congress that if he had his way he would do village open air evangelism at 4:30 in the morning! He reasoned that villages would be quiet, sound would travel, people would just be wakening and their minds would be clear to listen to the gospel message before rising!

- *Festive—tribal—sports gatherings*
These are sure winners as tourist attractions especially when feathers, head-dresses and tribal regalia are involved. There is always feasting, much entertainment, squandering of time. What about open air evangelism?

- *Feasts*
A good feast is an essential way of life in many cultures. In Papua New Guinea hundreds of pigs are barbecued for sing-sings, and when the logs beat out the news, the mountains swarm with people on the move, drawn by the irresistible desire for feasting. The diet may vary around the world, but the happening doesn't. Should not Christ be heard there? The devil makes enough noise!

- *Washing places*
Rivers, streams, lakes and ponds are the laundry sites of the under-privileged. This is an ideal place for a woman-to-woman ministry.

- *Marriage feasts* are another good opportunity to share the gospel. They are traditionally times of feasting and speech-making.

- *Medical clinics* are again family affairs where time does not matter.

- *Community building* projects bring families and tribes together.

- *Fishing communities.*
Many are isolated and can only be reached by a four-wheel drive vehicle or by boat for community outreaches. Christian indigenous fishermen sometimes join the crews of larger fishing boats where they can profitably use spare time in dialoguing the gospel.

- *Vocational Schools* have resident students who have a lot of spare time. Favourable principals sometimes permit outdoor gospel programs during school hours.

- *Community schools*
Daytime visits can usually be arranged, and whole schools reached with the gospel.

- *Roadside groups*
In countries where people walk by foot from place to place there are well beaten trails, and recognised rest places ideal for the outdoor preacher.

- *Wharves.*
Shipping is important to many developing nations. Labourers either wade into the sea to carry merchandise ashore on their backs, crew barges which carry cargo from ship to shore, or work on the wharves. Western style unionism sometimes complicates an approach, but generaly speak-

ing the writer has found that open air evangelism during the lunch break is well received.

Obviously this list of suggestions cannot be exhaustive, but it should open up something of the vast potential for open air evangelism. When eyes with 20/20 evangelistic vision are focussed beyond the four walls of a building, the possibility horizon never ends.

	Markets and Bazaars	**Villages**
Siting	Keep in the shade if possible. Keep near the main flow of people.	Obtain permission from head man, or leader. Be as central as possible.
Avoid	Excessive amplifier volume. Criticising other religions, churches. Having your listeners stand in the sun.	The same as markets and bazaars.
Timing	Preferably early. No problem at night.	Morning, afternoon, or evening.

Suggestions on the conduct of these programs will be given in later chapters. Meantime, avoid having the sun in the eyes of listeners. If listeners are to sit on the ground, select a comfortable place, use the wind to carry your voice if possible, and pick up discarded literature afterwards.

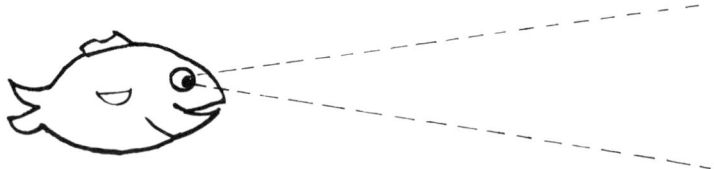

Chapter 3

SOME ANSWERS TO QUESTIONS ON OPEN AIR EVANGELISM

Prejudices try every possible survival tactic to prolong their miserable existence. They will even sneak away and hide in terror at the very suggestion of a decent burial, eventually regaining strength to reappear by living on a mean old diet of negativity and biased thinking. They breed in closed minds, and hide from the light of truth. This chapter is aimed at the eradication of prejudices against open air evangelism. The following questions and answers are drawn from past conversations and are by no means fictional.

Question 1
'Times have changed. Open air evangelism is a primative method of reaching people who are media conscious and have high standards of entertainment. Can you expect anyone to be sufficiently attracted by outdoor preaching to want to stop and listen?

Answer
Changing times have brought some excellent methods of communication which have considerably updated open air evangelism. It is true that people expect a high standard of entertainment today, but an outdoor preacher is not there to entertain, just to preach Christ. The preacher and his team have one big advantage over media and entertainment personalities. They are right on the spot, can be spoken to, and their personal warmth can be felt. People will stop and take notice when they hear and see how the gospel has answered inner frustrations, burdens, and heart

longings in other people's lives. Just as a hungry man finds it hard to resist the smell of good cooking, so an empty, lonely and sin-weary person is attracted to the forgiveness, love and peace others show and offer in Jesus Christ.

Question 2

'Isn't it arrogance to expect jet-age man to have time to stand around listening to some ancient religious history, or scare talk about future judgment and all that nonsense?'

Answer

Living in a jet age doesn't mean that everything is done at jet speed or with Star Wars fantasy. Everyday living is very different to screen or comic book fiction. We cannot escape planet Earth with its limitations and problems. With unemployment and shorter working hours, people have more time for outdoor living so the open air evangelist actually has more time to reach them. The gospel is not past history, it makes history by changing lives. It is right up to date, meeting the needs of today's generation, and for those interested in checking history it will found accurate in every detail.

Fears of future judgment are deeply embedded in many people's hearts, and only Jesus Christ is able to deliver from that bondage. The gospel is in fact so powerful that people who have heard only a few words when hurrying past an open air program have had no peace until they have made further enquiries and found new life in Christ.

Question 3

'But aren't all open air preachers crackpots, fanatics? Aren't they people who can't get on with anyone else, and enjoy the exhibitionism of outdoor preaching?'

Answer

Not at all. Some may have given that impression, but it doesn't take long to identify them. They bear no resemblance to the self-controlled Christ-exalting Spirit-filled preacher.

Question 4

'Open air preaching is an aggressive method of trying to force religion on people who have rejected the church. Shouldn't they be left to themselves and not be pestered with the gospel?'

Answer

When sportsmen head out for a day's fishing, they don't toss a notice over the side of the boat warning the fish to keep away. They use every method they know to entice the fish to bite. If the fish don't like the look of the bait, that's it. It is the same with outdoor evangelism. As one evangelist used to tell his listeners—'There is no glue on the sidewalk, you are free to go whenever you wish'. Churches which have been faced with closure because of dwindling members, have come alive by taking the gospel outside to the people.

Question 5
'Doesn't having to shout above traffic noise tend to drive people away, rather than attract them to the gospel?'

Answer
Open air preachers don't have to shout. By applying principles of voice production they can project their voices without harm to themselves or offence to their listeners. John Wesley said that on one occasion when he thought his voice was likely to be drowned out by the roaring of the sea whipped up by a north wind, 'God gave me so clear and strong a voice that I believe scarcely one word was lost'. (John Wesley's Journals Page 243.) Where amplifiers are permissible, voices may be lifted to a comfortable listening level without discomfort or embarrassment.

Question 6
'Isn't it too dangerous to preach outdoors today?'

Answer
*And when has it not been dangerous? Preaching outdoors challenges the devil on his own territory. Jesus Christ is always there and he has **all** power in heaven and earth to protect those who do his will. Experienced preachers testify freely to special protection in situations out of their control. Outdoor preachers should be careful not to stir up trouble, then expect protection, or claim to have been persecuted if their lack of common sense has been the cause. Known danger spots and potential areas of high racial or religious intolerance should be avoided.*

Question 7
'Couldn't interjectors (hecklers) interrupt proceedings and leave a preacher so discredited that no one would want to listen to him?'

Answer
This is a mental hazard of open air preaching, a fear which is insignificant in experience. No open air preacher should ever give the impression he is a 'know-all', and there is no disgrace in admitting to having no answer. Any preacher who chooses to ignore interruptions, or who politely explains that he is not conducting a public-discussion exercise but explaining the meaning of the gospel will never finish with 'egg on his face'. A warm smile, a polite answer, a sense of humor, an unruffled manner, and a quiet determination not to be side-tracked will keep a preacher in credit.

Question 8
'How would you deal with drunks, and people intent on interrupting preachers in public places?'

Answer

Do what Jesus did. Show them courtesy, Christian love, and dialogue so that they forget their intentions. Team members should be trained to entice them aside and talk with them quietly so that their conversation doesn't disturb the program. Sometimes humour will prick their little ego balloon, but aim to make friends with them if possible.

Question 9

'Isn't open air evangelism a very undignified method of presenting the gospel that discredits the church?'

Answer

Why should it be thought undignified to do what Jesus did? The gospel is God's good news for sinners and they need to hear it. The Great Commission was given to people for people. Churches were never licensed as authorised stations. The gospel adds dignity to a preacher, and every outdoor preacher should preach with dignity.

Question 10

'Isn't open air evangelism a hit-and-miss method because of the unreliable nature of the weather?'

Answer

Believe it or not, outdoor evangelism is adversely affected more from uncertainty as to what the weather is likely to be, than by bad weather itself. A pastor of a downtown church in Newark, New Jersey, who didn't think too highly of open air evangelism saw an open air program being held in the snow. He was asked to take part, and reluctantly did so. When he saw how the people stood with such interest, he couldn't help but wonder what could happen in summer conditions. He found out by having to look for a much larger church building to accommodate the increased members who had come to Christ through his church's open air programs! When God is at work, the weather isn't important. Shop verandahs (canopies) offer shelter in wet weather, but many times people have stood in the rain listening to OAC programs with, and even without umbrellas. William Booth considered that fair weather open air preachers were lacking in concern and Christian charity for the lost. Charles Haddon Spurgeon once told his students that John Livingstone delivered a famous discourse in the yard of the Kirk of Shotts when not less than 500 of his hearers found Christ though it rained in torrents during a considerable part of the time. (Lectures p. 239.) Billy Graham knows that experience only too well. Adverse weather conditions never dampen a heart hungry for God.

Question 11

'How can open air preaching be effective when environmental noise creates anything but a spiritual atmosphere?'

Answer

A spiritual atmosphere is the work of the Holy Spirit, not the result of surroundings. A person may sit inside a consecrated church building which has everything going for a spiritual atmosphere, and be resentful, spiteful, depressed, engrossed with personal or family worries, and not really hear a word said. The prayers of team members can cause the Holy Spirit to create both the inner and outer atmosphere favourable to people responding to Christ. Of course preaching sites should be chosen carefully to avoid as much interference as possible.

Question 12

'How can you claim the gospel ought to be preached outdoors when people may not be able to stay long enough to hear sufficient to make an intelligent response. Is that responsible preaching?'

Answer

All Christ-exalting preaching is responsible preaching. Each portion heard and understood has an accumulative effect, until finally it all adds up and a response is reached. The writer has known people to have heard something of the gospel in passing an outdoor gospel program, and to have been troubled for up to two years before returning to enquire further. Every time the gospel is heard it can produce a twinge of conscience particularly to those who are running from God. Passing a church door may not challenge a sinner, but hearing the gospel when it is least expected can be un-nerving. OAC has even been accused of following people around because they have heard the same challenge from city to city, even country to country. As some fish fight for hours before being netted, so some people resist for a very long time. It is not the time which counts, but the eventual landing of the fish!

Question 13

'Is it right to preach the gospel where people may trust Christ as Saviour, but walk away without contact and follow-up?'

Answer

Christ must be preached regardless of results. Not all those responding do so outwardly. The Holy Spirit who alone regenerates the person repenting and trusting Jesus Christ for salvation, will bring the newly born child of God to the maturity of discipleship if personal follow-up is not possible. When the Ethiopian eunuch believed in Acts 8, he asked for baptism in a pool beside the Gaza highway, then went on his way rejoicing, obviously filled with the Holy Spirit. Although Philip was not allowed to do any follow-up, the history of the growth of the church in Ethiopia proves that the eunuch was well instructed. Open air preachers should aim for personal follow-up where responses are indicated, and trust the sovereignty of the Spirit of God to ensure that a complete work is done where contact is not possible.

Question 14

'Are the results of open air evangelism sufficient to justify it?'

Answer

Visible results alone never justify any preaching of the gospel. The Great Commission makes it very clear that every person in the world is to be given the good news (Mark 16:15). Should a trustworthy servant re-write his master's instructions to suit himself? Missionaries don't rush home because they see no immediate results. Adoniram Judson laboured twenty years in Burma before seeing souls saved, despite the loss of his wife and family. Preaching the gospel is warning the lost to flee from the wrath to come. God alone does the head count. The writer is convinced that the numbers reached by open air evangelism as compared with traditional indoor preaching overwhelmingly justify the method.

Question 15

'Are there not better methods to reach people than open air evangelism?'

Answer

Probably so. It would be foolish to claim that this is the best method, but if people are not being reached by other means it may be the only one to succeed. Methods should be used as a fishman selects his gear—what is most suitable to attract and handle the fish. Be assured, open air evangelism is no worn-out discarded piece of fishing gear.

Question 16

'But what about problems with the Police and local authorities?'

Answer

Right public relations should prevent that. Local authorities won't want to hinder a work that potentially assists them with their social problems. Locally-elected officials will be careful about opposing permits requested by, or with the backing of churches full of voters! Common sense and a little local knowledge should stop permit applications being made for sites which would obviously be refused, or disputed. A spirit of co-operation with Police and local bodies is a good safeguard.

Question 17

'Should open air evangelism be conducted if it is not church-sponsored?'

Answer

The ideal is for churches to conduct their own outdoor programs amongst the people who know and accept them. Full follow-up is then possible.

Alternatively, a local church may sponsor a visiting open air preacher using an identifying sign or suitable publicity. If sponsorship is not available, open air programs should still be held without causing any embarrassment to local churches by preaching content or conduct. Those responding should be introduced to an evangelistic church as soon as possible afterwards. Lay foundations for future bridges of friendship.

Question 18

'If open air evangelism is as important and as effective as you say, why aren't more churches doing it?'

Answer

A good question. Some think it is out-moded. Some feel that what they have seen is unimpressive, or that their church already adequately caters for the gospel needs of locals.Others believe that their services are given sufficient publicity, and that because they pray for God to bring the people in, they have no further responsibility. Other churches again believe that their programs are so full they could not handle one more method. Country churches may also be very hard pressed to gather a crowd in sparsely populated areas. Doubtless many would like to, but don't know how to. C.H. Spurgeon told his students, 'No sort of defense is needed for preaching out of doors' but it would need very potent arguments to prove that a man had done his duty who has never preached beyond the walls of his meeting-house. A defense is required rather for services within buildings than for worship outside of them.' (Lectures 11,123.)

Question 19

'One doesn't lose respect by going to church, but whatever would my friends think of me if they saw me standing with a street preacher?'

Answer

To be ashamed of Jesus Christ is to be unworthy of him. To confess him, not only honours him but strengthens spiritual character. The Lord Jesus promises to bless those who confess him. (Matthew 10:32–39.)

Question 20

'What if I made a bad show in front of other people, or forgot what I was going to say?'

Answer

Why not practise first? Try speaking in front of a mirror. Write out what you want to say and memorise it. Don't be too tough on yourself, others will not be as harsh. Commit your way to the Lord and expect him to help you and don't be discouraged by your first effort. Many who have begun hesitantly have developed into powerful preachers.

Question 21

'How can I overcome a fear of people laughing at me and thinking I am odd?'

Answer

They laughed at Jesus Christ and he said we would get the same treatment. If non-Christians do not look on believers as 'odd' there is surely something to be concerned about! The facts are, very few people ever laugh; they are generally interested. Don't confuse a stranger's smile of encouragement with one of derision. The few who do laugh have probably had too much liquor, or are trying to smother guilty consciences. Laugh with them and show that you do not take yourself too seriously.

Question 22

'What could I do? I dont' have gifts and abilities like other people?'

Answer

That's the devil's lie, ignore it. You could start by praying during the program. Then there are always pieces of equipment to be put away, and discarded literature to pick up. Sooner or later someone is bound to ask you a question about the gospel and you will be able to share what you know about Christ. Step by step you will gain courage, and begin to use ability you did not realise God had given you. Say with Paul 'I can do all things through Christ'.

Question 23

'If I were asked to preach or lead an open air program, how could I keep going long enough?'

Answer

That is another subtlety of the devil. Who said sermons or outdoor programs had to last a long time? A preacher who says all that is on his heart with conviction then stops, is appreciated. It is also better to conduct a number of short programs than one tediously long one, making more time for personal work with interested people.

Question 24

'What would I do if the unusual happened and things didn't turn out as I expected?'

Answer

The Lord knows and he promised never to leave you. Rely on him, and he will show you what to do. Personal inferiorities and fear of the unexpected are probably the two greatest potential mental hazards. They arise from an inadequate appreciation of the Deity of Jesus Christ and the power he can exercise in a believer's life. When we realise who we are because of who he is and what he did for us, we will relax and let the Lord's wisdom and authority flow through us.

One simple answer to all the potential problems and fears expressed in this chapter is the constant filling and control of the Holy Spirit.

Chapter 4

LESSONS FROM THE PAST

How accurate is the saying, 'If we learn anything from history it is that we learn nothing from history'. The Word of God confirms this.

Wise open air preachers should therefore endeavour to apply some obvious principles of outdoor preaching established during four important Biblical occasions of outdoor preaching.

1. Ezra and the great gathering at the Jerusalem Water Gate (Nehemiah 8)

God had stirred the hearts of two kings of Persia to facilitate the rebuilding of Jerusalem. Cyrus, the temple, and Artaxerxes the wall. Then he gave the people a hunger for his Law and caused Ezra the priest to make preparations in advance to minister to the people's needs. From the huge outdoor gathering which followed we learn:

(i) When choosing a site, aim for as much free space as possible (v. 1)

When there is a choice, the site for outdoor evangelism needs careful planning with Ezra's two objectives in mind. The first was to bring the greatest number together in the smallest area possible so that all could see and hear, and where they would not be disturbed by passing people and animals. The water gate which led to the Gihon Spring was not a general thoroughfare, so the large open space in front of the gate was ideal. Secondly Ezra instructed his carpenters to build the platform where the people would not have to look into the sun for the eight-day series. The need for safety and personal comfort are still essential to listeners, particularly when there is no obligation to stand and listen.

(ii) Don't forget the children (v. 3)

Ezra's crowd was mainly made up of adults, but obviously many children were with their parents, as 'others who could understand'. Ezra knew that if he aimed his teaching at the adults, the children would miss out, but by making sure the children could understand, everybody would be reached. The *Readers Digest's* high circulation has been built on the same principle by selecting a literary style appropriate to the 11-13 year old age bracket. A simple style of communication will reach all ages, and in any case children need God's Word as much as adults.

(iii) Give the people God's Word (vv. 1, 2, 7, 8)

Today's crowds usually want everything but God's Word. They enjoy a good compere, singing, personal testimonies, visual aids and object lessons, but preach on sin, righteousness and judgment, and many will walk off. Ezra's crowd were hungry for God's Word and asked for it. Today's crowds know little about, and couldn't care less for God's Word, but their cry for reality and help can only be satisfied from God's Word. Give them what they need, even if it is sugar-coated by what they like.

(iv) Speakers need to be seen to hold attention (v. 4, 5)

Ezra must surely get the credit for constructing the world's first outdoor preaching pulpit. It was high enough for Ezra to be seen above all the people who were all standing out of respect for the Law. It was also big enough to accommodate the whole of his platform party. John Wesley considered he honoured his father's grave by standing on it to preach. Others have used walls, tree stumps, tailgates of vehicles, stepladders and boxes, to be seen by all the people. One special feature of OAC vehicles is a slide-out platform to do just that.

(v) If a speaker can't be heard, people won't stop and listen (v. 3)

Ezra lived thousands of years PA (pre-amplification) so he used the backdrop of his platform as a sounding board to project his voice. The people gave attention because they heard and understood every word, and Ezra aimed for attention, good hearing and an appropriate response. Maybe this is where George Whitfield got his design of a portable platform and sounding board through which he was able to reach tens of thousands and be heard up to a mile away!

(vi) Ezra believed in team work (v. 4)

He shared responsibilities and invited 13 well-known and respected men to join him in the platform party. Their presence added dignity and weight to the already solemn occasion. Even today, people who tend to reject a lone preacher will stand and listen readily to a group gospel presentation.

(vii) Words without meaning are a waste of time (v. 8)

Ezra knew a thing or two about getting through to people without the benefit of such modern helps as the psychology of communication. He selected an additional 13 men whose sole responsibility was to read the Law clearly and distinctly, and explain it so that everyone knew their personal responsibility to obey all it required. Modern 'verse shouters' and 'judgement thunderers' would benefit from studying Ezra's approach and remembering what Jesus said about understanding being the key to results (Matthew 13:23). Meanings, not words alone bring understanding.

(viii) Doing things God's way produces best results (v. 9)

Ezra's faithful preaching and teaching produced conviction, repentance and a willingness to obey God. Unless these steps are evident in any experience that a person claims to have had with God, the results will not be those of the new birth.

2. Jonah and his lone crusade in a very large city (Jonah 1-4)

Nineveh was one of the world's great cities. Great in importance and size, great in population (there were 120 000 babies and small children quite apart from adults), and great in wickedness. Then God stepped in and we learn:

(i) A lot about the character of God.

• *No-one can sin and get away with it.*

As in Genesis chapters 3 and 6, so in Jonah chapters 1 and 2. No nation, no city and no individual may sin in private or public and expect to get away with it. God sees and knows all. No sin can be regarded as trivial because it is a violation of God's holy will and deserves immediate punishment. Because God is merciful he warns people prior to judgment. The story of Nineveh reveals a caring, merciful but unchanging God.

• *God did not choose an angel, but used a man.*

Angels warned righteous Lot of coming judgment, but God sent a man by underwater express delivery to warn the Ninevites. From Genesis to Revelation, God has warned every generation prior to judgment by a person who pleases him. And when he does so, the key factor is not the number or importance of the people to whom the message is sent, but the authority and power which rests upon his messenger. The writer firmly believes God longs to anoint many more to the warning and calling ministry of open air evangelism in the closing years of the 20th century.

• *Class distinction counts nothing with God*

Jonah didn't begin by asking his way to the palace. He trudged through the city for a day without saying a word and was probably near the city centre when he began to thunder a call to repentance. The news soon got around and although Jonah gave a command performance before the king, he began with the average man about town. It is true that a man's gift will make room for him before great men (AV Proverbs 18:16), but it is also true that many of today's best known preachers and evangelists began with open air preaching. Please note the foreword.

• *Smooth words don't impress God. He requires changes*

Those who heard Jonah were deeply moved by his authority. Business dried up, laughter vanished, banquets were cancelled, fine clothes and jewellery were put away, and sackcloth supplies quickly sold out. When God saw that cries for mercy were backed by genuine evidences of amended life styles, he postponed judgment for around 150 years and spared that generation.

(ii) Much about what God expects from His chosen messengers.

• *Immediate obedience—there is no guarantee of a second chance*
Jonah had a rough journey getting back into God's directive will. Some don't have a second chance like Jonah, and settle for God's second best which brings nothing but sadness and regrets. God may still use an open air ministry to teach his chosen servants.

• *Small mindedness blinds spiritual vision of the glory of God*
(Chapter 4)
Jonah was big in courage but small in compassion. He cried out of self-pity, not for the people, and he was more concerned about his comfort than God's glory. Open air preachers are really God's front window display to the non-churched world and if people do not like what they see, they are not likely to want what they hear.

3. The apostle Peter and the great outdoor meeting following Pentecost (Acts 2)

The Lord Jesus left clear instructions about the strategy of world evangelism before the Holy Spirit gave the needed ability.
The power . . . the Holy Spirit
The purpose . . . to make disciples
The pattern . . . in Jerusalem, then in Judea, and in Samaria
The perimeter . . . to all the ends of the earth.

The disciples carried out the instructions to the letter. They gathered together for prayer and fellowship in excited anticipation. They waited in unity, no-one trying to go-it alone. But immediately they had received the power of the Holy Spirit nothing could hold them back. Acts 2 is the story of their partnership with the Holy Spirit and what they began to do together.

• *Peter showed a boldness which could only have come from God*
Peter's leap from pre-crucifixion cowardice to post-pentecostal boldness is surely a testimony to the power of the Holy Spirit. He turns weakness into strength, emptiness into fulness, and empowers faltering lips to speak without apology. Peter was the first, many others have followed him. Will you join them?

• *Peter declared a message which could only have come from God*
Peter's recorded sermon is obviously incomplete, as verse 40 points out. It may have been a Greek translation of what was said in a variety of tongues, but at least it was remarkable for its content, being the first of a new type of message centred around the completed work of a glorified Christ. Sermons provided by the Holy Spirit often defy homoletical analysis as their results defy human explanation. Open air preachers still need Peter's boldness and effectiveness.

4. The Apostle Paul and his open air address to the Greek philosophers at Mars Hill (Acts 17).

In the opinion of the Athenians, Paul was nothing more than an itinerant religious rabble-rouser. The intellectuals considered him fair game, so with tongue in cheek invited him to declare his views before the councillors of a criminal tribunal which met on the Areopagus (Mars Hill), a bare rocky outcrop to the south of the Acropolis. Despite being incensed at the gross idolatry he saw in the city, Paul approached the subject wisely, and modern open air preachers could well learn a lesson or two from him:

(i) Paul made a careful approach which attracted interest (v. 22,23)

He kept his feelings well under control and didn't accuse his hearers of idolatry. Instead, he commended their religious zeal, then aroused curiosity by saying he represented the very God to whom they had erected a spare altar in case one may have been overlooked. As an opener it was a sure-fire interest getter! Dale Carnegie, later verbalised the principle Paul used this way: 'If you want honey don't kick over the beehive'.

(ii) He glorified God without making fun of their mythological deities (v. 24-28)

Preachers who rubbish revered heathen gods only succeed in causing their hearers to hate themselves and the gospel. Modern mission researchers contextualise the message by showing how it can take people from the frustrations of their religious philosophies to fulfilment through Jesus Christ. Paul bridged the gap between the Greek mythical gods and his God in verses 26-28. His God was not 'up there' but 'down here', very much involved in human affairs, and approachable. He even referred to their own poets to support his thesis, a point which must have been well taken. Paul's logic was unanswerable.

(iii) The climax was well-timed and effective (v. 31,32).

Paul carefully planned the timing of his trump card, the resurrection. He kept it until the final challenge, knowing full well its explosive potential could end their tolerance. It happened just as Paul had expected, and the council broke up immediately.

Even today's reactions to open air preaching are similar. Some jeer, some want to talk further but some will believe.

(iv) Paul didn't wait around to argue (v. 33).

He simply walked away when he finished. No speech of thanks from the council, no gift for expenses, no shaking hands all round. He didn't give anyone a chance to spoil the effectiveness of what he had said. He had delivered his soul, the rest was over to God.

(v) The success of such a ministry lies in quality of response not in quantity (v. 34).

Those few who did respond to Paul's gospel didn't keep it to themselves. Theirs was a response of discipleship which they showed by joining Paul. Obviously a gentleman and lady who responded were well known for their names to have been left on record. According to church history, Dionysius later became Bishop of Athens.

Summary
Be a worthy member of the genealogy of God's open air preachers by learning from the living dead who still speak in the power of example:

- Ezra and his desire to communicate effectively to all ages by paying attention to details of importance.
- Jonah and his personal process of subjection to God's will so that God could be merciful to a repentant city through the ministry of his servant.
- Peter and his power and authority in preaching through the fulness and control of the Holy Spirit.
- Paul and his wisdom and effectiveness in preaching Christ in the face of skepticism and intellectualism and nationalism.

Chapter 5

GETTING IT ALL TOGETHER

Having established the validity of present day open air evangelism and noted some well established principles which never date, it is time to consider the content and conduct of programs. But first there needs to be an explanation as to why the word 'program' is used instead of 'service' when speaking of preaching in the open air. When the gospel is taken outdoors it needs a non-church look and sound to attract and hold the outsider's interest. Because of the informality of proceedings the word 'program' seems more appropriate. There is also an absence of community hymn singing, Bible readings, collections, public prayer, announcements, benediction and church language associated with church services. A program also suggests five points which need to be considered:

1. Leadership
2. Likely audiences
3. Reaching the objective in the available time
4. Program suggestions
5. The part of voluntary helpers

1. Leadership

When two or more people are working on a mutual project one person needs to assume leadership by agreement, appointment or election if confusion is to be avoided. The leader of an open air evangelistic team should ideally be able to put together and present a gospel program of variety, interest and challenge. He or she should not act the big boss, have authoritarian attitudes or expect to be in the limelight all the time. A leader needs to be filled with the Holy Spirit, able to give gracious, wise, positive and helpful advice as well as guidance and leadership. Also to discern, encourage and blend the personal gifts and abilities of voluntary helpers into a well coordinated team. Encouragement needs to be shown to those who lack confidence and gracious restraint to those who display over-confidence. A good leader should always encourage and actively assist the development of others who show leadership potential, and be quick to show appreciation and generously commend a job well done.

Leaders should not show favouritism, but aim to be impartial in judge-ment, warm in personal relationships, capable of respecting confidences, studious of the Scriptures, fervent in prayer and submissive to the sovereign Holy Spirit. He or she should be inoffensively firm in standing by decisions made and in carrying them out, willing to apologise when wrong, able to arbitrate amongst team members, and sensitive in human relation-ships to know when someone is hurting. Leaders should also be able to handle and adjust grievances on a Biblical basis.

Such job specifications may appear unrealistic when looking for leaders, but are biblical ideals and should be kept in mind as objectives. Candidates should be chosen on the potential they already show in character, ability and inter-personal relationships and encouraged, prayed over, and guided so that they reach their full potential in God.

Leadership responsibility also includes:

(1) The control of open air programs. The leader needs to be on hand at all times to assist any person who gets into difficulties such as losing con-fidence, suffering a lapse of memory, or being unable to handle a heckler (interjector), a drunk, or other interruptions. Should someone unexpected-ly 'run out' of words the leader needs to take over immediately to keep the program alive.

(2) Ensuring that team members know the place and time of open air meetings, transport arrangements and details of what they will be ex-pected to do.

(3) Making sure that someone is responsible to see that equipment and literature are ready for each program. This includes sketchboard and nameplate, paper and clips, paints or chalks, amplification equipment (if permissible), lighting (if needed), basic follow-up materials and tracts for general distribution.

(4) Adjusting the microphone to its correct height for each user and keeping the amplification volume at a comfortable listening level.

(5) Choosing the most appropriate time to make a challenge to repent-ance, faith and discipleship and doing so personally or requesting the speaker to do so. The leader also needs to see that personal workers con-tact people responding to invitation.

(6) Giving voluntary helpers as much advance notice as possible so that they can prepare adequately for the part they are expected to play.

(7) Training team members in effective communication. Program critiques should be held to improve standards but evaluations must be kept objective. When it becomes necessary to speak to certain helpers about their conduct, attitude or contribution to a program, it should be

done privately in a spirit of love and humility. In cases where the whole team would benefit by sharing the evaluation, it would be wise to obtain the consent of the individual concerned before sharing.

2. Likely audiences

Open air audiences differ greatly. The locality, time of day, weather, site and the class of audience will have considerable bearing on the type of program.

- With an audience of children, program content needs to be planned to gain interest with variety and appeal.
- With an audience of teenagers, prepare for questions, dialogue, humour, simple apologetics and vital testimonies from young people. Messages should be short, well-illustrated and to the point. Visual aids and object lessons will be well received. Be prepared for noise and interruption.
- With an audience of mature adults, well-informed and thought provoking messages are needed. Sketch messages, visual aids and object lessons will also stimulate interest and hold attention.
- If the audience is to be Jewish, Roman Catholic or Muslim, careful attention needs to be given to the message content and the Scriptures quoted. The gospel is God's power to save, not offend.
- If the people are likely to have had no religious background or Bible knowledge, messages need to be simple, carefully explained and well illustrated.
- If rough elements are likely to be present ladies may need protection, and care needs to be taken not to provoke trouble by showing wrong attitudes.

3. Reaching the objective in the available time

The chief objective of evangelistic open air programs must always be to bring people to a saving knowledge of Jesus Christ. The program content needs to be blended wisely so that this objective can be reached within the time available. The following diagram outlines this process. The point of commencement is at the bottom, each phase moving upwards towards the goal of challenging people to repentance, faith and discipleship. Suggestions are for an average program. The Holy Spirit can prompt a challenge at any stage, and the leader should be sensitive and follow this.

- The first column shows the steps which lead to an increasing awareness of the need of Jesus Christ as Saviour.

- The second column offers suggstions for solo and team program items which will accomplish this.

- The third column suggests times for each phase. (Principles only can be given as each program varies.)

PROGRAM CONTENT

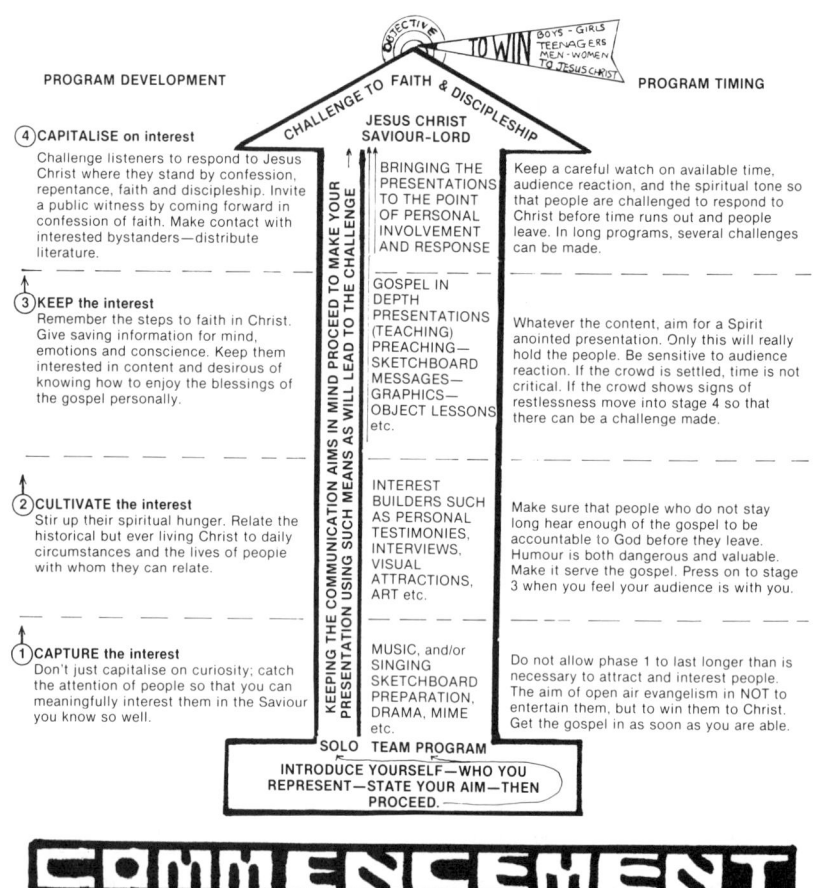

PROGRAM DEVELOPMENT

OBJECTIVE TO WIN — BOYS - GIRLS, TEENAGERS, MEN - WOMEN, TO JESUS CHRIST

CHALLENGE TO FAITH & DISCIPLESHIP

JESUS CHRIST SAVIOUR-LORD

PROGRAM TIMING

(4) **CAPITALISE on interest**
Challenge listeners to respond to Jesus Christ where they stand by confession, repentance, faith and discipleship. Invite a public witness by coming forward in confession of faith. Make contact with interested bystanders—distribute literature.

BRINGING THE PRESENTATIONS TO THE POINT OF PERSONAL INVOLVEMENT AND RESPONSE

Keep a careful watch on available time, audience reaction, and the spiritual tone so that people are challenged to respond to Christ before time runs out and people leave. In long programs, several challenges can be made.

(3) **KEEP the interest**
Remember the steps to faith in Christ. Give saving information for mind, emotions and conscience. Keep them interested in content and desirous of knowing how to enjoy the blessings of the gospel personally.

GOSPEL IN DEPTH PRESENTATIONS (TEACHING) PREACHING— SKETCHBOARD MESSAGES— GRAPHICS— OBJECT LESSONS etc.

Whatever the content, aim for a Spirit anointed presentation. Only this will really hold the people. Be sensitive to audience reaction. If the crowd is settled, time is not critical. If the crowd shows signs of restlessness move into stage 4 so that there can be a challenge made.

(2) **CULTIVATE the interest**
Stir up their spiritual hunger. Relate the historical but ever living Christ to daily circumstances and the lives of people with whom they can relate.

INTEREST BUILDERS SUCH AS PERSONAL TESTIMONIES, INTERVIEWS, VISUAL ATTRACTIONS, ART etc.

Make sure that people who do not stay long hear enough of the gospel to be accountable to God before they leave. Humour is both dangerous and valuable. Make it serve the gospel. Press on to stage 3 when you feel your audience is with you.

(1) **CAPTURE the interest**
Don't just capitalise on curiosity; catch the attention of people so that you can meaningfully interest them in the Saviour you know so well.

MUSIC, and/or SINGING SKETCHBOARD PREPARATION, DRAMA, MIME etc.

Do not allow phase 1 to last longer than is necessary to attract and interest people. The aim of open air evangelism in NOT to entertain them, but to win them to Christ. Get the gospel in as soon as you are able.

(vertical text) KEEPING THE COMMUNICATION AIMS IN MIND PROCEED TO MAKE YOUR PRESENTATION USING SUCH MEANS AS WILL LEAD TO THE CHALLENGE

SOLO   TEAM PROGRAM

INTRODUCE YOURSELF—WHO YOU REPRESENT—STATE YOUR AIM—THEN PROCEED.

COMMENCEMENT

An explanation concerning the challenge to respond to Christ

If the meeting is not a long one, it should be concluded after the challenge to respond to repentance, faith and discipleship. When a longer program is planned and more than one challenge can be given, the interest and spiritual level should be rebuilt after the challenge with music, further testimonies, and one or more gospel messages.

The following diagram shows three different types of outdoor program, the spiritual tone reached, and challenges made.

98

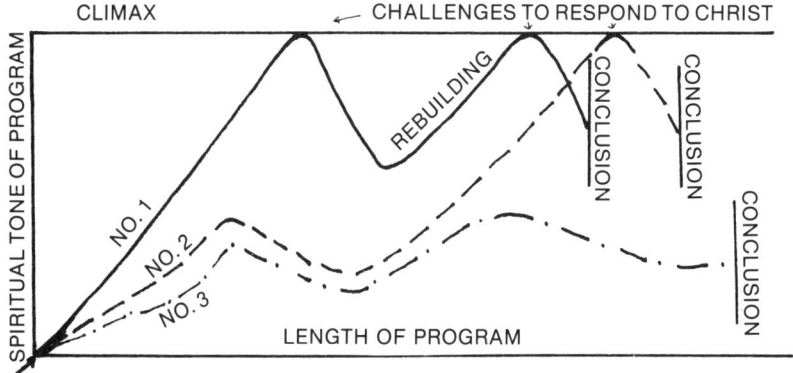

No. 1 shows two spiritual climaxes were reached and two challenges to respond made before the program concluded.

No. 2 shows that is was difficult to build the meeting to a climax caused by the time taken to build a small crowd from passers-by. Finally, the spiritual level reached the point where a challenge could be made. The meeting then concluded.

No. 3 shows that the atmosphere never rose to a high level. There were numerous interruptions, the crowd continuously changed and finally, interjectors (hecklers) prevented a challenge being made. The program concluded with an explanation of the way of salvation and personal counselling.

The manner in which a challenge to respond is made will be dealt with later under the title 'net results'.

4. Program suggestions

The leader of an outdoor team has the responsibility of compering the program or appointing a compere. He should prayerfully select the theme, and plan each contribution to build up to the challenge to respond to Jesus Christ. When others are being given experience, they should follow the leader's suggested format.

The leader makes or breaks a program. Too much talking between contributions will overshadow what others have said or done, and focus attention on himself. Too little causes the program to lack cohesion. He needs to speak clearly, be warm and friendly, have the right words to 'glue' contributions together and be sensitive to the Holy Spirit. When groups have not worked together, and there is no recognised leader, pray and select the team member who appears to have ability and who has the confidence of team mates, and ask that person to try. By honest evaluation, trial and error, prayer, encouragement, and trying different people in leadership, the Lord will put his seal on the most fitted person.

Program content of sketchboard sermons, visual aids and object lessons has been covered already. Extra materials are in Part 6. In addition there are a number of other options which will give leaders wider freedom of choice.

1. Drama

As people have become used to street-theatre, mimes and similar forms of street entertainment, drama is ideal for drawing crowds and preparing them for a program of singing, testimonies and messages. Drama can also be a powerful means of gospel witness by itself.

2. Question and answer contributions

Some people are too shy or nervous to speak publicly. This can be overcome by one or two question and answer sessions. Within a short time most people become confident to testify without prompting.

There are also times when a speaker can question a team member whom he knows has had the type of experience which would emphasise a point he wishes to make.

3. Panel testimonies

Instead of asking team members to share their testimonies individually, the leader invites two, three or four of them to form a panel. The questions asked, the answers given, and the comments made, make up an interesting gospel presentation. Here is a suggested panel testimony in which the leader asks the panel certain questions, each person answering in turn.

Leader: *'At what age did you ask Jesus Christ to be your Saviour?'*

Answers: 25,18,7,31.

Comment: *'Obviously age is not an important factor in commitment to Christ.'*

Leader: *'What made you want Jesus Christ as your Saviour?'*

Answers: 'Because I was desperately lonely.'
'Because I was frightened of death.'
'Because I wanted my sins forgiven.'
'Because I saw such a change in my friend who became a Christian.'

Comment: *'There are obviously many causes of people being drawn to Christ as Saviour.'*

Leader: *'Did you find that Jesus Christ was able to give you what you longed for?'*

Answers: In each case the answer will be personal and warmly positive.

Comment: *'It is obvious that Jesus Christ is able to answer every need and fulfil every longing.'*

Leader: *'Where were you when you invited Jesus Christ to be your Saviour?'*

Answers: 'In church'
'At a youth camp'
'At home'
'Sitting in my friend's car.'

Comment:	*'Well, the place of commitment is obviously not important.'*
Leader:	*'What does Jesus Christ mean to you now?'*
Answers:	'These will vary but will all glorify Christ and show something of the peace and joy of sins forgiven, the assurance of eternal life, the blessing of Bible reading, answers to prayer, guidance etc.'
Final comments:	*Attention may be directed to the difference of age, sex, place and motivation, but the cause of the change of life is obviously Jesus Christ alone. A challenge to respond to Christ may well follow this.*

This format is very flexible and may be expanded to include other features of the pre and post new birth experience. Members of the audience often identify with those testifying.

4. Favourite gospel verses

Many voluntary helpers do not consider themselves speakers, but if asked will gladly quote their favourite gospel verse and give three reasons why it appeals to them. These explanations become in effect mini-sermons and encourage team members to analyse a verse and speak clearly logically.

5. Several people sharing one subject

When a supporting team is inexperienced, the preaching responsibility falls on the leader. One way for helpers to gain experience is for the leader to invite two or three people to share on such subjects as:

• **Sin**

1st person to speak on 'What God thinks of sin'.

2nd person to speak on 'What God did about sin'.

3rd person to speak on 'What God expects us to do about our sin'.

• **Salvation**

1st person to speak on 'Why man can't save himself'.

2nd person to speak on 'What God did for our salvation'.

3rd person to speak on 'How can we receive God's salvation'.

In both examples the leader introduces the topics and speakers and concludes with a summary and application.

6. The support of artistic ability

Some people cannot preach but have artistic talents which can supplement the preacher's message. Suggestions include:

• Drawing a scene illustrating the sermon subject.

• Sketching a scene of the cross as a background theme.

• Illustrating some truth of the message highlights.

- Artistically printing the gospel text on which the message is based.

7. Hanging loose

A lot has been said about structured programs and it is right to be orderly, but the Holy Spirit must always direct the format. He also uses unstructured groups of young people filled with joy and enthusiasm for their Lord and equipped with little more than a guitar or two. They pray, share, preach and do whatever comes naturally to them, attracting crowds and often see souls won for Christ.

Voluntary helpers need to be shown how to evaluate their contributions and continually reach for higher standards. They need encouragement and help from those who are experienced to reach maximum effectiveness and develop their own type of approach. Some good suggestions for program evaluations are:

- Does our presentation encourage people to stand and listen?
- Does it communicate the gospel effectively?
- Are people being led to Christ?
- In what ways can we improve to reach and win more souls?

Finally, a good leader will be able to 'hang loose' when things don't turn out as planned. Be prepared for the following things to happen: A key musician or singer is late, has forgotten to come or fallen sick. Transport has gone haywire; no-one thought to bring the paints or tracts; and the person rostered to preach says he hasn't had time to prepare a message. Maybe two of the team have had a tiff and won't talk; some essential person has to go early. The generator won't start and to top it all off, some noisy teenagers come around and refuse to turn their radios down. So be inflexible and enjoy your breakdown or, rest in the Lord and give that grinning devil a knockout blow. Let the Spirit of God take charge of you and your resources and rejoice as you see what victories God will give through your faith. Open air evangelism sure is a great training ground!

5. The part of voluntary helpers

Open air evangelism is one of the greatest outlets for young people desiring to reach others for Jesus Christ. The by-products include more intense discipleship and growth in spiritual maturity, a greater love for the unsaved, lives being given to the ministry, missions or other types of fulltime Christian service.

Helpers need love, understanding, encouragement, protection from themselves and others, confidence placed in them, a shoulder to cry on, laughter and approval. They also need to learn how to blend themselves and their gifts into team work, to know how and when to do their thing and to realise what is expected of them as team members:

1. Helping the team leader:

- By willing co-operation, doing what is requested promptly.

Grievances should be settled privately after the program. Co-operation also means doing exactly what is asked, such as not preaching when a testimony is required. This also means keeping to the subject and staying within the time allowed.

- By staying close by the leader to do anything he may ask such as distracting the attention of an interjector (heckler), or speaking to an enquirer.
- By listening intently and prayerfully to the speaker, and resisting the temptation to wander around or talk to other team members.
- By avoiding anything which could spoil the Christian witness in the eyes of onlookers, such as obvious pettiness, disinterest, or even affection towards other team members.
- By not talking to people or counselling those around you. Move out of the crowd if necessary and counsel where others will not be disturbed.
- By not preaching obviously to only one person in a crowd. Look around, making everyone feel comfortable and welcome.
- By removing sunglasses before speaking. Eyes communicate.
- By speaking as if your listeners have never heard the gospel before. Make it news, good news, exciting news, urgent news, personal news.
- By speaking slowly and clearly when not using a microphone. The devil wants you to mumble and gabble.
- By not laughing at drunks or those who scoff, heckle or throw off at the gospel. Laughing only encourages them.
- By not carrying a large Bible. A pocket version can be used if necessary without turning off young people who think a large Bible is a sign of a bigoted and closed mind.
- By not chewing gum, having hands in the pockets or jingling coins.
- By using simple words which will not complicate the gospel. Peter said 'Lord save me', the thief 'Lord remember me', and the publican 'God be merciful to me'. Each was heard and saved.
- By being honest in what you say and owning up to what you don't know. It is never a disgrace to admit you don't know. People admire openness.
- By helping to unpack and pack equipment and clearing the area of discarded materials afterwards.

2. Learning the principles of where to stand during programs.

• Street programs

Pedestrians must be able to walk through at all times during programs held on footpaths (sidewalks). This is one condition enforced by Police officers who have authority to close down a program if access is blocked, even if a permit is held. One voluntary helper should be detailed to keep people moving so that access is kept open.

Voluntary helpers tend to form a spectator gallery along a window or wall at the back of the footpath like so many sparrows on a fence.

This area should be kept clear for interested people who want to hear from what they feel is a 'safe distance'. When people pack around, the helpers should form a semi-circle in front of the speaker or platform to keep drunks and problem people away (see the dots in the diagram which follows).

When few people are in the streets and a crowd has to be gathered, team members have a very important part to play. Shown by the letter 'H' in the diagram, they stand up to several metres from the leader as the program begins. They act as decoys and passers-by will stop and stand behind or near them where they feel a little more secure. As the crowd builds, the helpers slowly move toward the tight circle position and those who are standing behind them will automatically follow. A compact crowd is more personal.

The positioning of the two literature distributers 'LD' is important. No literature should be given to anyone joining the listening crowd, only as they leave. The arrows which indicate the outward movement of the audience indicate this. People will stand without feeling threatened when they are not approached. In this next diagram please notice that the program is not being held opposite the doorway of business premises.

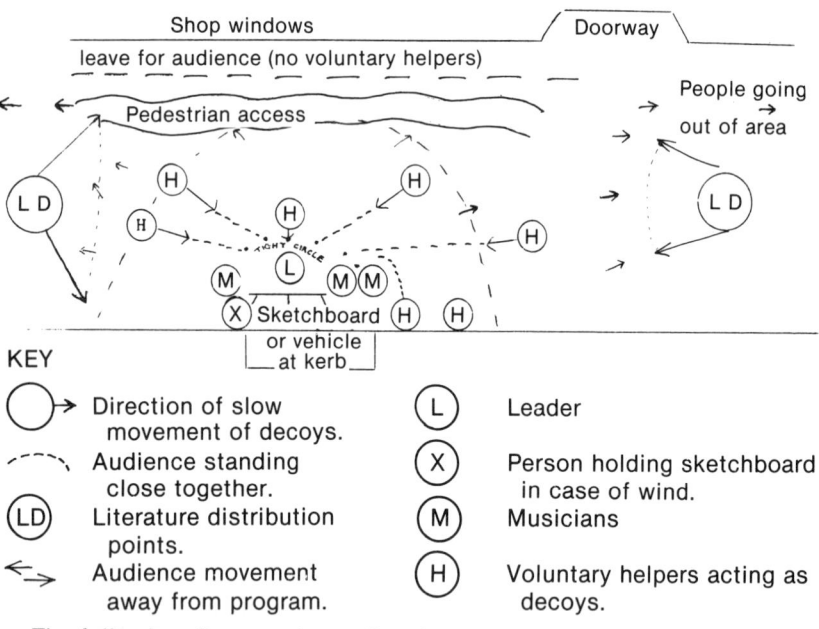

KEY

◯→ Direction of slow movement of decoys.	Ⓛ	Leader
⌁ Audience standing close together.	Ⓧ	Person holding sketchboard in case of wind.
ⓁⒹ Literature distribution points.	Ⓜ	Musicians
⇆ Audience movement away from program.	Ⓗ	Voluntary helpers acting as decoys.

The following diagram shows the places where voluntary helpers stand during adults' programs in a park or open plaza. Helpers should work to consolidate a crowd in a similar manner to a street meeting. In this diagram a sound system is in use. Note the relative position of the sun and the direction of the wind.

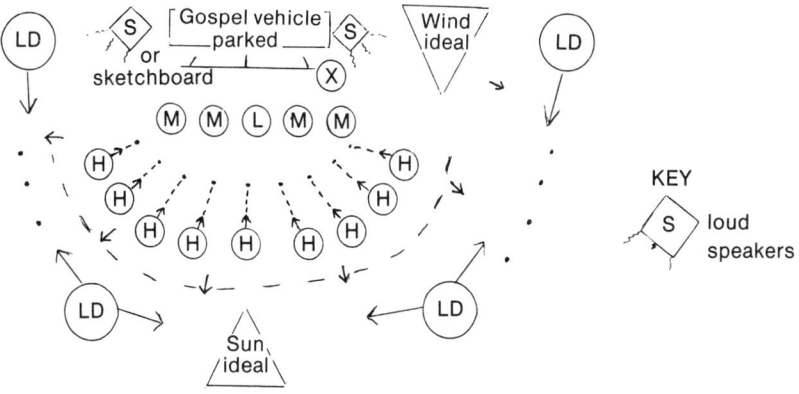

3. Learning to speak to the best advantage

• By the use of a microphone

A hand held microphone should be close to the mouth even when the head is turned. If the microphone is being held by someone else, or is on a stand, swivel your head around the microphone as this diagram shows.

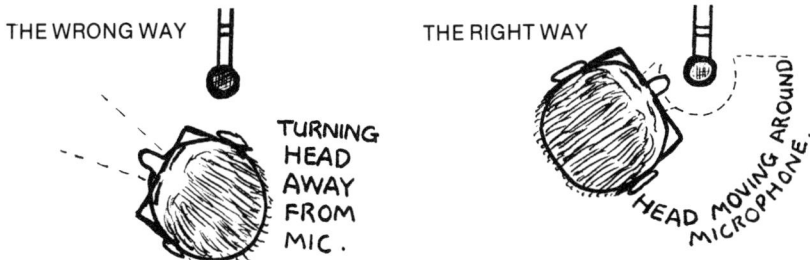

Learn to sense the volume level and adjust your voice to give better listening. If you have a strong voice, speak more softly. If a soft voice, speak up. If you are a loud or forceful speaker back away from the microphone when you are approaching the sound barrier. In fact, a variation of soft and loud preaching will add emphasis and impact.

• Developing a non-shouting, penetrating tone of voice.

Shouting turns people off and does terrible things to the voice. By experimentation and practice it is possible to project the voice at a volume which really carries and may be maintained without damaging the voice. A good open field is the best place to practice, not the bathroom. Follow these steps illustrated by the diagram:

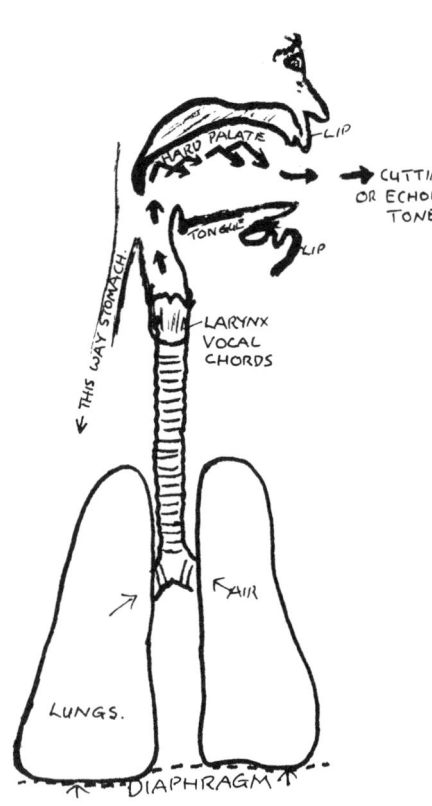

1. The diaphram should be tense so that the air is expelled under control in 'word-gusts'.
2. The neck and throat muscles are tensed.
3. The sound is thrown in a controlled tone off the hard palate of the mouth.
4. The words are expelled with penetrating clearness.

- Use the hard palate of your mouth as an echo chamber by tensing the muscles of your throat and mouth.

- Eject the breath from your lungs by tensing the diaphram and expelling the words by bouncing them off the hard palate of your mouth so that they sound sharp. (This does not come from the vocal cords.)

- Reduce the highs and lows from the range of notes in your normal speaking voice by using the middle register only which has the clearest sound. The best way to find the cutting tone which echoes is to cup an ear with the tips of the fingers of one hand and speak sharply in different tones into the hollow of that hand. When you find the note which echoes and pierces your ear, remember it and practise.

- **Take advantage of the wind**

    Where possible have the wind behind the speaker to carry the words as far as possible. But do not have an audience looking into the sun to do this. Remember, speak slowly and DIS—TINCT—LY.

- **Use the sounding board principle for clarity of hearing.**

    Because high vaulted structures cause voices to echo, many ancient cathedrals and churches had a circular piece of wood suspended above the pulpit as a sounding board to deflect the preacher's words down toward the congregation. There is a simple but most effective experiment by which anyone can prove the sounding board principle. Speak at your normal level then walk backwards into a corner of any room. Your voice will immediately be reflected by two walls and without having raised your voice, the volume will appear to have increased and the words will be heard more clearly. Now apply this principle to open air preaching:

    - When a speaker stands with his back to a wall, the wall throws the voice forward. It may be advantageous to ensure that the wall does

106

not contain a window from which a non-appreciative hearer is tempted to dampen proceedings!

- Voice-reflecting canopies can be attached to cars, station wagons and vans for use in outdoor preaching.
OAC uses such canopies.

- When speaking in open spaces stand in front of a sketchboard and let it project the voice.
- When speaking in the streets of shopping centres, project the voice toward a store window and this will deflect the sound in both directions.

Finally, a few do's and dont's

- Do display the name of your church or group in some way. It will warm the hearts of those who know you and encourage them to pray for you. Strangers will not avoid you thinking you are a cult. A name plate on the sketchboard is ideal.

- Respect private property. Where possible, obtain permission before using vacant blocks of land. Some parks and reserves have regulations against any form of public meeting. Enquire at the Town Clerk's office.

- Darkened areas such as recessed doorways or openings to shopping arcades are ideal for night programs. People are more likely to listen in unlighted areas or where they are not being jostled by shoppers. However, speakers and singers need to be clearly seen and spotlighted where necessary.

Some suggestions for making simple equipment and the adaptation of sketchboard messages in non-Western cultures may be found in chapter 10.

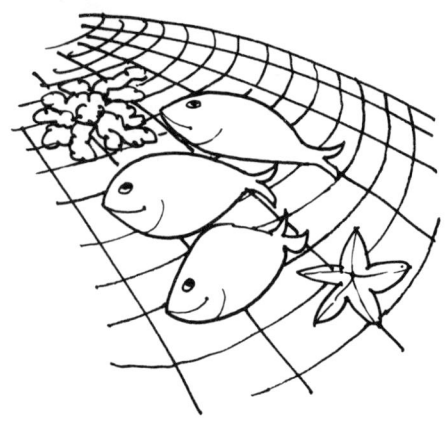

Chapter 6

NET RESULTS

Open air evangelism could well be called 'Operation Rescue'. People who come to Christ either 'hooked' by the bait of the gospel, or 'netted' by the challenge to respond, need to be lifted out of their old environment of sin and into the fullness of new life in Christ. Of course, God's hook and net can be avoided at will, but people need to be faced with the urgency of personal response for important reasons.

- To counter common beliefs:
  'If you're not a heathen you must be a Christian.'
  'This is a Christian country so I must be OK.'
  'If you're sincere in the way you worship God, that's all that matters.'
  'I'm a churchgoer and a good citizen, I don't need anything more.'
  'I've got my own religion.'
  'I've done a lot of good things in my day, and nothing very bad.'
  'God is supposed to be loving so how can he send his children to hell?'
  ... and so on.

- To make it clear that God has placed a time limit on his offer of salvation. He alone knows the expiry date.

- To make the gospel so clear that people who do not immediately respond will go away knowing exactly what they have to do to receive eternal life. The Spirit of God can prompt a response later.

- People are so used to the self-help principle that they must be warned that this doesn't work with God. The truth of the supernatural nature of spiritual re-birth must be laid on the line.

- The explanation of action rather than attitude may stir Christians in name only to seek a heart and life experience. Many good church members have no idea of the new birth experience.

Many people would like to have a relationship with Christ that does not involve a public confession or change of life style—a kind of eternal life insurance policy which comes into effect at death. But that is not what Jesus taught. He expected a visible response. The man with the withered hand had to stretch it out. The blind man had to wash his eyes. The lepers had to go to the priest. Faith must be active, it is not just an attitude. People who come to Christ outdoors have an excellent opportunity of showing their faith by their actions. For this reason OAC has encouraged people to make a public declaration of their faith.

The timing of a challenge to repentence, faith and discipleship. This can be made:

1. When the audience has shown prolonged interest, and the gospel has been preached in sufficient detail and clarity for a meaningful response to be made.
2. When a song, testimony or gospel message has lifted the spiritual tone to a level where it is right to make a challenge to response. This may happen at any time before the end of a program, which is quite different to an indoor service where the challenge normally comes at the end of the message.

In the OAC ministry the leader of each program is responsible to decide when a challenge should be given. It has been found that preachers are not always able to discern the right time to make the invitation, but a leader can sense if people are ready for a challenge or when a preacher has reached the peak of his message. Timing is important. Preachers who don't know when to stop will anti-climax, and the best time for making an effective invitation will have been lost. The crowd will often confirm this by drifting away, while the preacher continues with his last points and wonders why the crowd has gone. The writer knows—this has happened to him!

The standard OAC practice has been for the leader to hand to the preacher a pre-arranged booklet or card when he wishes the challenge should be given.

The manner in which a challenge is given

The speaker, or the leader of the program if the speaker has not had the experience, begins:

1. **by saying that Jesus Christ may be trusted as Saviour, just where people stand.** Not only does Jesus want to save people where they are, but as they are. The time will never be more appropriate than that very minute. Listeners have every decision making faculty with them as they stand, and all that is needed is that inner green light of mind–heart–will. Few will have ever heard it so clearly and the urgency of using the opportunity to get right with God should be stressed. Even if people do not respond immediately, they should go away knowing how Jesus Christ can become their personal Saviour. A clear explanation will also help to

stop people coming forward with the best of intentions, but for the wrong reasons.

2. **by telling them what it will cost in terms of practical living.** The Lausanne Covenant makes this important point: '... in issuing the gospel invitation we have no liberty to conceal the cost of discipleship. Jesus still calls all who would follow him, to deny themselves, take up his cross, and identify themselves with his new community'.

Some of the 'costs' of discipleship are:

- being genuinely sorry for self-centred living and the practice of sin, and whole-heartedly turning away from it. In other words, repentance.
- submission to the standard of holy living the cross of Jesus demands, yet makes possible.
- embracing a new life style in which Jesus Christ is glorified in habits, morals, conduct, plans, time, finance and friendships.

3. **by explaining how people can put their faith in Jesus Christ.** Faith must be in the person and work of Jesus Christ, not in praying or repeating a prayer to him. Faith believes God and does what his word says. 'Anyone who *calls* on the name of the Lord shall be saved', (Acts 2:21), and 'If you openly admit by your mouth that Jesus Christ is the Lord, and if you believe in your own heart that God has raised him from the dead, you will be saved. For it is believing in the heart that makes a man righteous before God, and it is stating his belief by his own mouth that confirms his salvation' (Romans 10:9,10 JBP).

Encourage people to speak to God silently in their hearts no matter how few and simple the words may be, confessing and forsaking their sin, asking forgiveness, placing their trust in Jesus Christ alone, receiving him as Saviour. The wording of a simple prayer may be helpful to some:

'Dear God,

'I confess I have disobeyed you, broken your laws, and lived to please myself. I deserve your punishment and I thank you for allowing your Son Jesus to be punished instead of me.

'I am truly sorry for my sin and wrongdoing—(pause to name sins)—and I turn from them to ask for your forgiveness; Please make me clean inside through the blood of Jesus.

'Thank you Lord Jesus for dying for me, I trust you only for my salvation, and invite you to become the Lord and Saviour of my total personality. Please live your life in me and make me the person you want me to be.

Amen'

Sincerity of heart counts more than words, and while faith is expressed in words, words without faith cannot save.

4. **by inviting those who have trusted Christ as Saviour to indicate this openly:**

- that they may be strengthened by their confession of faith in Jesus Christ (Matthew 10:32).
- that their level of understanding and sincerity may be evaluated and further counselling given where necessary.
- that counsellors can give immediate spiritual guidance to those who have entered into life in Christ.
- that workers may obtain names and addresses for follow-up and local church notification.

The Method

The preacher, (or the leader of the program) should take a pre-selected gospel booklet in his hand and extend it at arms length toward the people. The booklet should be offered from side to side covering the whole group while the invitation is given to those who have trusted Jesus Christ as Lord and Saviour to declare this publicly by stepping forward and accepting the gift booklet.

Nothing needs to be said as people respond. If responses are slow, or if there is no response, one or two things may be added while the book is being offered, such as:

- 'There is no significance in the book itself, and coming forward does not make anyone a Christian. It is an outward evidence of inner sincerity.'
- 'By taking this booklet you are not expected to join us, help us, or give us money. You are merely making your first witness to Jesus as your Saviour.'
- 'You are not being asked to change your church, but simply to confess that Jesus is now your Saviour and that you intend to follow him all the way.'
- 'You are under no obligation to give us your name and address. If you do so, we will only use it to send you some helpful literature on how to live the Christian life.'

The booklet should be extended as long as people respond, or until it is obvious that no one is prepared to make a public stand. Lack of outward response does not mean that people have not come to Christ.

- **Note:**

Outward indications of response in developing countries such as the raising of hands, or the taking of booklets should be regarded only as interest in the Christian gospel. Most of these people will need to do a correspondence course on basics of the Christian faith and have some form of counselling before experiencing the new birth.

Dealing with those who respond to a challenge of faith and discipleship

As each person steps forward, the speaker should shake their hand and ask if they have just placed their faith in Jesus Christ as Saviour. A born again person will openly confess this (Romans 10:10). Each person who makes a profession should be given a booklet and asked to remain for a minute or two for a further talk or be introduced to a team member for counsel. When a crowd is scattered over a large area, suggest they raise their hands, or those in cars turn on their parking lights if they have trusted Christ as Saviour, then voluntary helpers should move around speaking to those who have responded.

People also come forward for other reasons:

- Christians step forward to witness for Christ. They should be thanked, and the challenge restated with an emphasis being placed on a response by those who have not previously received Christ as Saviour.
- Some come forward because they admire your stand for Christ, or who are moved by what they awkwardly call your good 'speech'. Thank them, and if possible introduce them to a personal worker.
- People often respond just to get the literature. It is wise to give them a copy, or they will think you have broken your word. It should then be made clear to the rest of the crowd that literature will be available at the end of the program, but that the particular piece of literature offered is for those responding to Christ.
- Sometimes people ask questions during a challenge to respond. They should be politely asked to wait until the challenge is completed. Those who are genuine will gladly wait, but those who are insincere will not do so, and can ruin the atmosphere unless they can be stopped. A good rule is—no questions during a time of challenge.

Public challenges to respond should never be automatic. There are times when they would be inappropriate, such as:

- When there has been persistent heckling or noisy opposition. The devil often oversteps the mark, and through it someone does respond to Christ. Personal workers should be observant and move in to speak to people obviously interested, on a one-to-one basis. Avoid exposing sincere people to ribald laughter or rude comments.
- When bystanders have been arguing amongst themselves and tempers have become a little frayed, it is better to close the program and look for opportunities for personal work.
- When there has been too much humor from the preacher or crowd. Humor is a valuable aid to a good atmosphere, but, hilarity and laughter won't win souls. Salvation is not a fun experience.
- When the final stages of a message and challenge are continuously interrupted by some person or people under the influence of alcohol. The devil always knows when to send his followers in to break up an effective gospel message and challenge.
- When the listening audience is obviously disinterested.

In such instances listeners should be told how to exercise faith in Christ as Saviour, and urged to take this step. The challenge to respond publicly should be avoided in favour of person to person dialogue and challenge.

USING THE HAND NET

Frequently, more people are brought to Christ through personal work at the end of the program than respond to invitations.

Voluntary helpers need to be sensitive to what God is doing among listeners as the gospel is being preached. This is evident by the interest shown, the length of time people listen, attitudes toward any who try to take them away or distract them, or questions asked. Should one leave before a challenge is given, a counsellor should follow and speak, once away from the crowd.

Sometimes people walk forward, take the booklet and leave without waiting for counsel. They too should be followed and spoken to. If there is evidence of new life, simple follow-up advice should be given, and if possible the name and address obtained for follow-up purposes.

During programs, questions sometimes indicate a sincere interest in the gospel. In order not to stop and speak to only one person, the leader should introduce the questioner to an experienced helper, and suggest they move a little further away for discussion. The same can be done with groups. Many have come Christ this way. All team helpers should be trained thoroughly in leading souls to Christ, counselling backsliders, answering common Bible questions, and in follow-up procedures. All who respond should have personal counsel. Responses need to be checked for sincerity, and classified for appropriate follow-up steps.

Good open air teams need the support of experienced personal workers. Mature Christians can have a very profitable ministry by talking to those who have been listening to outdoor preaching.

Finally, gospel tracts should be offered to those who remain when the program ends.

Some may want to argue, and the devil likes to stir up Christians to defend their faith so that interested people are not approached. Helpers need sensitivity as to whom the Holy Spirit would have them speak. A good rule is—if you don't find genuine interest within the first minute or two, move on.

In the parable of the fishing net (Matthew 13:47–50), the baskets full of good fish represent the righteous at the end of the age, and the bad fish thrown away are the wicked. Angels will then do the sorting. Open air evangelism similarly sorts people, and one way to prepare 'good fish' for final sorting is by effective follow-up.

Follow-up is a sensitive issue in all evangelism. Discipleship is the objective of the Great Commission. There are sometimes practical difficulties in open air evangelism when people leave before being counselled, or when there are insufficient counsellors to cover all interested people. Some Christians use this as an excuse for non-involvement, but it really should stimulate people to fill the need and get involved. Have you ever asked yourself this question: 'Whose responsibility is follow-up?'

1. Follow-up is the responsibility of the Holy Spirit.

Preachers only point the way to Jesus Christ. The Spirit of God alone convicts and brings a person to repentance, faith and regeneration. He alone enlightens, cleanses, teaches and guides the believer. The salvation of the Ethiopian eunuch in Acts 8:26–39 illustrates this process.

2. **Follow-up is the responsibility of the person who leads a soul to Christ.**

The Apostle Paul showed this during his three missionary journeys:

Firstly, by personal visitation. Before returning to Antioch at the end of the first outreach, Paul and Barnabas retraced their steps and checked out the converts, strengthening and exhorting them. (Acts 14:21–22.) Paul's first move in his second journey was to revisit the believers won to Christ previously (Acts 15:36), and the third missionary journey was a partial repeat of the same principle. Those who counsel people won to Christ outdoors, should aim to have personal or telephone contact with them as soon as possible and as often as necessary to help them get established.

Secondly, by writing. During the third missionary journey, Paul dictated five follow-up letters to the converts—three at least from Corinth. They have since blessed countless millions.

Every open air preacher needs to have carefully chosen and suitably graded follow-up materials.

3. **Follow-up is the responsibility of the local church.**

Wherever Paul won people to Christ, he formed them into local churches, then appointed suitable believers as spiritual shepherds to watch over them (Acts 14:23). His letters to Timothy and Titus are full of personal counsel, and follow-up advice to those in their care. Local churches are God's follow-up centres and open-air workers should aim to link those they counsel as quickly as possible with warm Bible-believing churches where they can receive all the Christian love and care they need. For survival, even newly hatched fish need fine food and protection from predators!

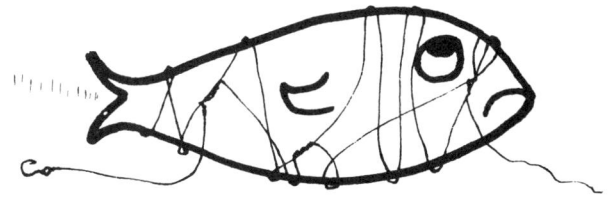

Chapter 7

PERSONAL WORK ... UNTANGLING THE LINE

Fishing often turns out to be an addiction, rather than a sport. The addict braves all weathers, put up with all conditions, denies himself all comforts, and still loves it. Among the things that trouble the fisherman most, must be a tangled line. He will take every care to keep this from happening, and spare no effort in untangling the mess should it occur.

Personal workers sometimes need untangling from ideas and attitudes which hinder good communication. Two problems come immediately to mind. The first is believing that certain soul-winning booklets are inspired, and that no-one could be saved without them. Indeed? The Holy Spirit managed exceedingly well before they came into existence. The Holy Spirit certainly blesses and uses them but it is not his will that a personal worker should be unable to lead a soul to Christ without a counselling booklet. A personal knowledge of God's way of salvation should be a counsellor's top priority. From this, a flexible counselling plan should be prepared for use with people of all ages and needs, and then—and only then—should there be freedom to use an appropriate counselling booklet. A background plan of salvation has been included in the resource section, Part 6, Chapter 3.

The second problem is that some people have inflexible attitudes about how a person should come to Christ, and what the experience should be called. New converts are often subjected to detailed questioning not unlike a vehicle check-list, and finally judged as genuine, questionable, or phoney, solely on the basis of the questioner's own personal experience. Nicodemus, Saul, the Ethiopian eunuch, and the Philippian jailor all came to Christ through different experiences. The first sought a personal interview with Jesus. The second was knocked down by the glory of God and heard the voice of Jesus. The third had a man run up and ask him a question about what he was reading, and was led to Christ in his chariot from Isaiah's gospel. The fourth was scared to die and asked for counsel. Each experience was different.

And what about the variety of words used for the life-changing encounter with Christ in the New Testament? It is called salvation—the new birth—regeneration—to be in Christ—newness of life—redemption—becoming a child of God or a Christian—passing from death to life—being justified—made righteous—becoming a member of the Body of Christ—having one's name written in the Lamb's Book of Life—and being reconciled to God. Each term describes one thrilling aspect of the same miraculous experience. Everything God does shows his touch of beauty and variety.

Personal workers would be well advised not to fasten on to methods and name tags, but to commence counselling the contact where he or she is at spiritually, not necessarily at some spot marked 'GO' on a printed route map to a goal marked salvation. This calls for careful listening with the outer ear to what the contact says, and with the inner ear to what the Spirit says. He will sort out the priorities and show where to begin. Some people will be like fruit, ripe for picking, and may be led straight to Christ. Others may need questions answered, words explained, attitudes re-shaped, or misunderstandings corrected. The whole process of counselling needs to be Spirit-guided.

1. The personal worker's preparation

The University of Hard Knocks has a world membership. Everyone learns in it, but not all graduate. The Professor of the Soul Winning Faculty is the Holy Spirit. He actually goes with his students into the fields of experience to give them constant guidance and assistance. He requires his students to:

- **be humble, sincere and open.** Pride in any form is forbidden. Family background, wealth, university degrees, social standing, Bible knowledge, and even church positions may be helpful in identifying with contacts or establishing credibility, but must never become a barrier to communicating the gospel (Philippians 3:4-8). Humility is the door to openness, sincerity, patience and self-control. The Golden rule of personal work is found in James 3:17.

- **be realistic.** Going beyond your depth will only get you into difficulties and won't help your counselee. Commence with someone of your own age and sex if possible, and call for an advisor at the first sign of inadequacy.

- **be willing to identify.** Barriers may go up unless personal workers identify with their contacts. God did this in Jesus Christ. Paul did this. Great preachers have done this. Personal warmth, empathy, tolerance and genuine interest in people are evidences of the Spirit at work.

- **keep cheerful.** Counsellors should ask for grace to keep their cool and remain polite in the face of indifference of opposition. A sense of humour is a valuable asset in counselling.

- **pray for discernment.** It is important to be sensitive as to whether people wish to listen. Unwise persistence may be taken as religious harassment and could spoil a personal friendship, or harm a contact's attitude to the gospel. Don't be mistaken. Some people appear to listen politely, but underneath they may be seething with opposition. Others passively agree with everything the counsellor says and unless they are asked to express their feelings in their own words, they could be pressed into a false decision.

- **be well prepared.** Before counselling make sure you have a small Bible or New Testament, a notebook, ball-point pen, gospel tracts, follow-up materials and something to keep your breath sweet.

- **be one-tracked not side-tracked.** Some unbelievers enjoy the mental stimulation of a good religious conversation, but look out, the devil will be out to steer that conversation far away from the gospel. Always keep your goal in view of leading people to Christ.

- **don't be a steamroller.** Be courteous and don't flatten the other person with a volume of words. Cults have a name for doing this. Be winsome, to win some and aim to leave the fragrance of life behind you, rather than a fragrance of death (2 Corinthians 2:14–16).

- **don't let fear cripple you.** It is natural to feel inadequate for the task, but never fear it. Claim your spiritual authority in Jesus Christ and take your stand against any feelings which come from the devil. 'For God did not give us the spirit of timidity, but a spirit of power, of love, and of self-discipline' (2 Timothy 1:7). Isaiah's wonderful Counsellor is with you, so what is there to fear?

- **personal appearance is important.** Be sensitive to personal appearance. Personal workers should be neat and tidy for the gospel's sake, and have clean clothes, shoes, nails, handkerchiefs, and please oh please, a clean breath. (Carry a breath refreshing agent.)

2. Speaking to the contact or enquirer

Personal workers should listen for the spiritual heart-beat of a counsellee or contact and not be guided only by what they hear. The reasons for this are:

1. **Regeneration should never be presumed because the contact uses language which sounds genuine. It may be a sheep skin to hide a wolf.**

On one occasion the writer counselled a man who seemed to be very familiar with the experience of new birth. He agreed with everything said, giving the right answers at the right time. Throughout the conversation the writer had no soul witness that he and the contact were one in Christ. After praying for wisdom, he was prompted to ask—'If I were in hospital with only a few minutes to live, and you came to visit me, how would you help me obtain peace with God?' Within the next thirty seconds the man's true spiritual condition came to light. His heart was far from God and in fact he was in bondage to spiritual error, obviously in the grip of a deluding religious spirit.

2. **A genuine experience of regeneration should not be overlooked because the contact does not know how to express it.**

Some young Christians asked the writer to speak to a young seaman they did not think was born again because his experience of Christ seemed unorthodox, and he could not give the day and date of his experience. When asked what Jesus Christ meant to him, the man brightened immediately and replied, 'I used to curse and swear, but now I love reading the Bible, praying, and singing hymns. He has entirely changed my life.' He showed the fruit of a changed life, the only evidence which really counts.

3. **Regeneration should never be presumed because a contact seeks counsel on difficulties in living the Christian life.**

When unbelievers are counselled as believers because they claim to be believers, they will become more deeply deluded. If there is any doubt, ask the counsellee to tell you how they know they are saved (1 Peter 3:15). A lady visited the writer and asked for help to make her prayers more enjoyable and rewarding. She complained of a lack of real communion with God although she said she prayed frequently. It was soon evident that she was praying the Lord's family prayer, as a non-family member. She turned out to be a religiously respectable Rosicrucian, deeply involved in its mysticism but obviously in need of being born again.

4. **Regeneration should never be presumed because a contact claims to be a Christian.**

Many people genuinely believe a Christian is one who believes in God, goes to Church, or shows social concern for people in need, as Jesus did. Some confidence tricksters also claim to be Christians. They know all the right spiritual language, and even use the names of well known Christians as part of the act to get money from those they deceive. A direct question such as 'Who is Jesus Christ to you personally?', will quickly strip a person back to the bare boards of reality.

- **Some have decided to follow Christ, the Great Leader.**

They do so to the best of their ability, but the essentials of discipleship are missing. There may be self-denial, but there is no sign of the cross in personal sanctification and discipleship. Transformation is the requirement.

- **Some have accepted the Bible's ethical teachings as a personal moral code.**

The rich young man in Mark 10 was very moral, and while it earned him a 'Highly Commended' award from Jesus Christ, it wasn't what he asked for—eternal life. He refused to climb off the throne of his life and offer it to Jesus Christ, and went away unsatisfied.

- **Some say they have given themselves to God.**

In salvation, God does the giving, we do the receiving. King Solomon said that the sacrifices, the ways, and even the thoughts of the wicked (uncleansed by blood sacrifice) are an abomination to the Lord. (Proverbs 15:8,9,26). A young married woman said to a counsellor 'I have done it all before'. When asked exactly what she had done, she replied 'I gave myself to God, and it didn't work'. When it was explained that Christ is received as Saviour she followed the counsellor's advice, and later said 'I feel as if I have just been plugged into life'.

- **Some claim to have had a special spiritual experience and feel right with God.**

  A woman involved in mysticism claimed to have had an experience of light and warmth while listening to an open-air preacher. She returned to the open-air program from time to time looking for another experience as her acceptance with God, but continually refused to reject Buddha and receive Christ.

- **Some believe their relationship with the Church assures their acceptance with God.**

  Some people believe that confirmation, baptism, partaking of the sacraments, and church membership prove that a person is a Christian. The Lord Jesus clearly teaches in John 3 that being 'born from above' is the only means of entering the Kingdom of God.

- **Some base their claim on believing in God and the Bible.**

  If this is merely an attitude of mind without Jesus Christ being received as Saviour, it cannot save. Without active trust, belief is only a piece of unproductive knowledge.

5. An experience of regeneration should not be suspect because it does not fit our understanding of the working of the Holy Spirit.

God's Spirit will never be limited to our counselling patterns. His diversity of ministry in the first century is the same in the twentieth. Starr Daily, the renowned and hardened American criminal had a blinding revelation of Jesus Christ while semiconscious, tied to a beam by leather straps around his wrists with his feet dangling just above the floor. He was cut down a transformed man, and others were transformed both spiritually and physically through his ministry.

Most people are led to Christ through some pattern of counselling, but there are others who do not experience identifiable stages of entering into life in Christ.

- A young lady born to devout parents could never remember a time when she did not believe that Jesus Christ had personally died for her sins. She testified to the assurance of divine life by the witness of the Spirit in her heart and her experience of prayer and Bible reading. She could not remember a point of decision, but she was sure she belonged to the Lord. Just as night turns into day silently, so some people are not consciously aware of a climax in entering into spiritual life during childhood.

- Another young lady found herself mixed up with alcohol and men. Realising she was unable to straighten herself out, she asked help of a God she was not even sure existed. A little time afterward she attended a Billy Graham Crusade meeting, and envied the life in Christ which the evangelist spoke about, but did not commit herself to Jesus Christ. She then began to attend church and the grip of sin's power weakened. She joined the church and this seemed to bring her into the fullness of life in Christ.

- A semi-illiterate drunk was camping out in the bush in Queensland, Australia. One night as he walked out of his tent and threw his empty bottles into the scrub he looked up and saw the stars shining brilliantly in the clear country air. The sheer beauty of it gripped him and he stood there for a while thinking that a God who made stars must have a better way of life than drinking bottle after bottle. Then and there he prayed asking that he might know that better life. God heard him. As he moved around the countryside, he started attending church and learned about God's love in Jesus Christ, and responded to him.

- During World War II an American naval serviceman had the misfortune to be stationed with professing Christians whose lives did not measure up to what they professed. Although an agnostic and a sceptic, he bought a copy of the Bible intending to find the truth in it, and in his own words 'to ram it down their necks to silence them'. He began reading at Genesis chapter 1, and by chapter 6, the wickedness of man and God's determination to punish everyone except those who had found grace in his sight convicted him of his own sin. He cried out to God to save him from the punishment he knew he deserved. God heard his prayer, and saved him. He then grew into the knowledge of Calvary and Christian living.

6. Sadly a few people are so unsure of their salvation that they make repeated professions of faith in their search for assurance.

Some professing Christians (fortunately a small minority) respond repeatedly to gospel invitations, talk with every preacher who visits their church, and have more highs and lows about assurance than variations of a weather chart. It is difficult to pinpoint their true relationship with Christ, and to keep them stable. One way the writer has found helpful is to lead them once more through the progressive steps to Christ and to record the decision in writing in such a way that it becomes a solid foundation for future trust.

Should spiritual insecurity remain after counselling, release from the rejection syndrome should be sought from those experienced in this field of ministry.

7. Some have not fully experienced new birth because of lack of understanding.

The writer was visited by an alcoholic who had asked God to forgive his sins while sitting in a chapel with an open Bible. He was sure his sins had been forgiven, but he had no relationship with Christ. He readily placed his trust in Jesus Christ as Saviour when this was explained to him. His church had presumed his salvation.

8. Faith in Jesus Christ must include cleansing through his shed blood.

The writer has found that so many people who are professing Christians are just that—professing Christians, but not possessing Christians. To them, Jesus Christ is a friend, guide, helper, example, but never Saviour. It follows there is little or no conviction of sin, no repentance, therefore no cleansing or salvation. Faith in Jesus Christ as a person, without his vicarious sacrifice is meaningless.

'In him we have redemption through his blood, the forgiveness of sins in accordance with the riches of God's grace . . . (Ephesians 1:7).
'in whom we have redemption, through his blood, the forgiveness of sins' (Colossians 1:14).
'and through him to reconcile to himself all things . . . by making peace through his blood shed on the cross' (Colossians 1:20; see also Hebrews 9:26; 10:19; 1 Peter 1:19).

The following illustrations show the genuine basis of salvation through blood, as compared with the false.

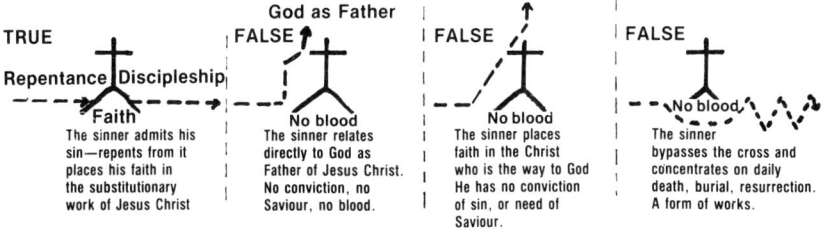

TRUE	God as Father FALSE	FALSE	FALSE
Repentance Discipleship Faith	No blood	No blood	No blood
The sinner admits his sin—repents from it places his faith in the substitutionary work of Jesus Christ	The sinner relates directly to God as Father of Jesus Christ. No conviction, no Saviour, no blood.	The sinner places faith in the Christ who is the way to God He has no conviction of sin, or need of Saviour.	The sinner bypasses the cross and concentrates on daily death, burial, resurrection. A form of works.

Chapter 8

PERSONAL WORK ... USING THE RIGHT BAIT

Anglers generally spare no time, effort, or expense in preparing for that tug on the line. The struggle of man against fish calls for total dedication. Nothing but the best in equipment is good enough, and nothing but the freshest bait will do. Fish ought to be flattered that the fisherman is more satisfied with the thrill of landing the big one, than getting a return on his investment of money for fishing gear.

It is the same with the soul fisherman. The joy of leading a soul to Christ far outweighs anything else. In the study of spiritual appetites and appropriate baits, the personal worker needs to know a little about what he is liable to encounter. For example:

1. **Indifference.** Lack of interest or spiritual lethargy is sometimes caused by prolonged exposure to lifeless church life, or by taking personal offence over some difference with the church or a professing Christian. It may also be the result of an over strict childhood. Social and economic standards also effect attitudes as may be seen when business is poor and unemployment is high. These people need to meet Christians who have a contagious personal excitement about the gospel to really understand what Jesus Christ can do with lives committed to Him.

2. **Unbelief.** Some people won't believe because they cannot see sufficient evidence to cause them to believe. If an agnostic is genuine, he should be prepared to believe when given reasonable cause, and Christian apologetics should help him.

Others have made up their minds that they have no intention of believing, facts or no facts. This is usually a cover up for deliberate sin. They claim to be atheists to smooth over their guilty consciences. Genuine athiests are rare, but God rejecters who claim to be athiests are plentiful. The Bible calls them fools (Psalm 14:1). A few really want to believe, but just can't. Their problem is demonic, and their minds need to be freed from the bondage of unbelief (2 Cor 4:4). The writer knows of, and has personally experienced times when victory has been gained by the use of the name of Jesus Christ and the power of his blood. People were then able to trust Christ as Saviour.

3. **Playing for time.** When some people come under conviction of sin they look at their watches and make some lame-duck excuse about being late, or having an appointment. Felix tried it on Paul, promising to listen again at some convenient time. People should never be detained against their will, but should be reminded of the shortness of this life, and their accountability to God.

4. **The peacock display.** You know the type. He fans out the feathers of his own self-esteem and points to all the good points he has, the commendable things he has done, and how much better he is than some of those church 'hypocrits'. He is full of pride, doesn't believe his sin is very great, and feels no spiritual need or concern for the future. Unless he repents, God will pluck his self-righteousness. The story of the publican and the tax-gatherer in Luke 18 may be helpful.

5. **Love of sin.** Some love their sin so much they mock the gospel, others would like to be saved, but are shackled by sin and can't let it go. Others again would be happy to accept the gospel as long as their personal living was un-affected. Many are convicted by the moral standard of the gospel, so attack it to divert attention from themselves. It is the writer's opinion that when it becomes obvious that a contact is involved in deliberate sin and is unwilling to repent from it, counselling should cease until there is evidence of genuine repentance. Jesus Christ will not save a person who regards his sin more highly than the one who died to redeem him from it. On one occasion two young people being counselled for salvation admitted they were living together. They were told to consider whether they were prepared to separate before further counselling. They returned agreeing to separate, and were led to Christ. On another occasion a man stood with his back to a store window, weeping. He said how much he wanted Jesus Christ to be his Saviour, but he knew he couldn't be because he was being unfaithful to his wife and did not have the will-power to stop.

Never let people see how shocked you are by the sin they confess. The heart of man is capable of the vilest evil, but God can, and will forgive. Let God's love flow through you; it will influence souls when nothing else will.

6. **Self-condemnation.** Many people have convinced themselves they are beyond hope of salvation. Their understanding of the nature of God is pathetically inadequate, and their inflated guilt complex grossly over-

sized. They need patient re-education to be able to grasp the greatness of God's love and mercy, and should be encouraged to reach out and take God at his word. Others believe that their sin automatically shuts the doors of God's forgiveness, and so fall into a state of despair. They also need encouragement to grasp the forgiveness and cleansing God offers through Jesus, his open door.

7. **Religious prejudices.** 'I have my own religion' may be a lie for self-protection, or for fear of offending a church which demands exclusive loyalty. Members of the Masonic Lodge also claim to have their own religion, unaware that their religious rites are both blasphemous and idolatrous in God's eyes. A vital personal testimony may win through where the gospel would be rejected.

8. **Self-gratification.** Those living for pleasure, social prestige, sexual indulgence, or intense business activities usually have no desire for gospel dialogue and little sense of need. Approaches are often met with ridicule or rejection.

9. **Demonic opposition.** People involved in occult practices, witchcraft, or the obviously demon possessed will often strongly oppose the gospel. Soulwinners should make a habit of wearing the spiritual armour of Ephesians 6 and seek the wisdom of God in discerning the difference between the voices of their contacts, and those of evil forces controlling them. Demonised people may be wanting help, but don't know how to ask.

10. **Distractions which hinder people from grasping what the gospel will do for them.** There are occasions when people are so taken up with what is happening to them, or around them that they cannot fully understand the gospel, or respond to the claims of Jesus Christ. These situations include:
    * times of personal sorrow, such as a death, divorce, separation, or marriage breakdown.
    * family worries over finance or sickness problems with children.
    * business or job difficulties which threaten living standards.
    * those who suffer continuous wearing pain, or whose minds are dulled by drugs either medically prescribed or self-administered.
    * people who keep themselves in a twilight zone of consciousness through alcohol.
    * mothers whose concentration needs to be upon their children or people who are engaged in something which demands their full attention.
    * times of watching special TV programs or listening to favourite music are never ideal for soul conversation.
    * people who are physically exhausted or those who have not eaten for a long period have no powers of concentration.
    * times of shock such as diagnosis of terminal disease or news of a tragedy.

11. **The influence of friends.** If strangers could influence Peter to deny his Lord, how much more will unbelievers be swayed by the opinions of their families, friends, business associates, and peers.

12. **Strong religious or philosophical attitudes.** Dr Francis Schaeffer has a good word of advice in suggesting that these people be asked to tell how their beliefs could help you in your desire for the best in this world and the next. When their best falls far short of what Jesus Christ has done for you, show them the difference and share Christ.

Making contact with people with a view to leading them to Christ.

Some people find speaking with strangers 'as easy as falling off a log', but others can't even climb up on the log. Both types need the power of the Holy Spirit to be effective. Some suggestions are:

1. **always obey the Spirit's promptings.** The story is told of a man who settled his account at a large city hotel. As he was walking out the door he felt the Holy Spirit prompt him to go back and speak to the cashier about his soul, but he left without doing so. He felt badly about it as he walked down the road. Eventually he went back to the cashier's desk but no-one was there. When a flustered manager finally came out he asked to speak to the cashier. The manager said 'Sir some thirty minutes ago, shortly after you left the lobby that man went into a back room and shot himself. He is dead.'

   The inscription on a large statue in a public concourse in Athens has a message to everyone interested in soul winning:

   'What is your name O statue? . . . My name is Opportunity
   Why are you standing on your toes? . . . I shall not remain for long.
   Why do you have wings on your feet? . . . To show how quickly I pass by
   Why is your hair so long on your forehead? . . . That men may seize me
   when they meet me
   Why is your hair so close cropped behind? . . . Because once I have
   passed no one can lay hold of me.'

   A lost opportunity in soul winning may mean a lost soul for eternity.

2. **accept a natural turn of conversation.** Personal fears, the death of a friend, the prospect of war, financial uncertainty, family unhappiness, life after death, the search for reality by such means as transcendental meditation, and a host of other subjects common to so many conversations are ideal to introduce spiritual seed thoughts which may open up an opportunity for in-depth sharing.

   Some people make the weather a commencing point. Others will flash a smile and make a cheerful remark which makes people ask the reason for such unusual cheerfulness. Those who pray over every daily detail will be sensitive to the openings the Holy Spirit provides, and will not alienate people.

125

3. **take advantage of any situation which opens up the way for spiritual conversation.** Times of sickness, bereavement, family upheaval, and accidents may do this. The writer was in a Jumbo jet from Sydney to Hawaii via Fiji when the captain came on the intercom to say he had a problem and that it was necessary to return to Sydney. An hour later when in sight of Sydney, the captain broke the news that the problem had been a bomb scare, but that he, the company and the police felt reasonably sure it was a hoax and that the plane would proceed to Nadi airport at a reduced altitude as a precaution. The lady in the adjoining seat immediately said 'Oh well, I suppose if your time has come to die you may as well be blown up in the air, as die in any other way'. This immediately opened up a sharing session on the assurance of life everlasting.

4. **lay bait.** Soulwinners need to be as wise as serpents and as harmless as doves. An unusual lapel badge will often stimulate the question you are waiting for.

   An open Bible, New Testament, or a Christian book in a train, bus or aircraft will not only attract the curious, but also classify the reader. The writer has had in-depth conversations on various kinds of transport because of reading material.

5. **identify yourself.** Christians who love souls should carry gospel booklets. Every pleasant contact during the day is an opportunity to pass one on. When it strikes a responsive note it is a natural opener for sharing the gospel.

6. **take the initiative by asking a question.** Few may wish to follow the example of Mr Fredrik Franson a noted soul-winner and founder of the Evangelical Alliance Mission. One of his favourite methods was the use of a direct question. On one occasion his train stopped for 10 minutes in Buros, Sweden and he hurried across the road to greet a friend who owned a store. A lady was leaving just as he entered, so he held the door open for her. She thanked him, and the following conversation then took place. 'Madam are you saved?', 'Saved?', 'Do you know Jesus Christ?', 'Yes, he is the Son of God', 'Do you love him?', 'I'm afraid not', 'Don't you think you ought to?', 'Yes', 'Well if you do be rapid about it. My train leaves in five minutes'. The two then knelt on the floor and the lady was led to Christ in about two minutes. Years afterwards the store keeper testified that the lady was a sincere healthy Christian.

   Use the approach which comes most naturally to you. The following three methods may be helpful. In each, a well received leading question will open up others and will soon show whether the contact is open to further counselling.

	Method 1	Method 2	Method 3 (The late Dr Paul Little)
Leading question	'May I ask you a question?'	'Are you interested in spiritual things?'	'Do you know Jesus Christ as Saviour or are you still on the way?'
Second question	'If you were to die tonight, where do you think you would go?'	'Can you say that you know for certain where you will be in the next life?'	'How far are you on the way?'
Third question	'Would you like to be sure you will go to heaven?'	'You hope to go to heaven don't you?'	'Would you like to know and be sure?'
Fourth question		'What makes you think that God will let you be there with him?'	

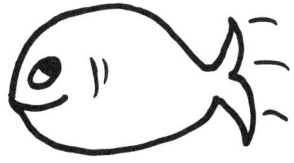

Chapter 9

BEING PREPARED FOR ANYTHING

The writer regrets that total success in open air evangelism can't be guaranteed even if all the recommendations to this point have been carried out to the letter. Unexpected situations do arise, and the leader's ability to handle them will often determine the result. Some suggestions for handling them may be helpful.

1. When programs are interrupted by law enforcement officers

Open-air preachers should expect police, wardens and security officers to look in on them from time to time. After all, they are responsible for maintaining law and order and preserving public safety and the rights of citizens. Care should be taken to gain the confidence of local authorities by the way in which outdoor programs are conducted.

Firstly, aim to avoid confrontation

(1) by obtaining permits required by local government or Police regulations. An enquiry at the Town Hall or Police headquarters will clear this. When applying for permits:
  - If you are not known locally it will be helpful to take a local pastor or well-known Christian business man with you on your first contact as evidence of character and church support.
  - Avoid requesting permits for sites which you know would be questionable or refused. These include those close to bus stops, pedestrian crossings, entrances to public buildings, and narrow or congested streets.
  - Request a temporary permit for a site which the authorities con-

sider doubtful to give them time to evaluate a trial program. This attitude makes friends and often secures permits.

- Assure them that there will be no appeals for finance and that obstruction, nuisance, or annoyance will be avoided. These are always major concerns.
- Apply for permits progressively. Use the camel's-nose principle.

Just in case you don't know that story it is said that one freezing night a camel driver built a fire in his tent in the desert telling his camel it had to stay outside. The camel shivered then gently pushed its nose through the tent opening. The driver shouted at it to get out, but finally gave way provided the nose only shared the warmth. Soon the head followed and more arguments, the camel winning by a short head. Hardly had the driver turned to the fire again when two front legs and shoulders came through the opening making the driver really mad. The camel spoke tearfully of their long friendship and won the day. In the end of course, the tent was filled with camel and the driver slept outside in the cold.

The moral is—apply for permits gently, one or two at a time until you have all you need. OAC staff used this principle when they first applied for permits at the City Hall in Chicago. Despite twenty city attorneys being against them initially, they ended up with all the permits they could handle.

(2) **by wise siting and conduct of programs** where formal permits are not required. In the United States of America the Constitution and Bill of Rights guarantee freedom of speech to open-air preachers. Wisdom is still needed to avoid locations which would antagonise authorities and cause congestion or danger to listeners. The exceptions are parks and recreational areas which display notices prohibiting public speaking.

Secondly, aim to co-operate fully with the authorities

(1) Always obey instructions given by law enforcement officers. Close up if ordered to do so, then take the matter up with the officer concerned or his seniors. No permit or statutory right can prevent the Police exercising their authority to close down a program if in their opinion this is advisable for public safety reasons. Law enforcement officers include beach inspectors, park rangers and security officers.

There are occasions when people in authority allow their own personal religious prejudices to override their professional judgment to the preacher's disadvantage. They should be treated with respect so that he gospel is not discredited and the matter taken quietly to higher authorities.

(2) Written permits should always be carried and shown when requested by authorities.

2. When interjectors (hecklers) interrupt the program

Fear of interruptions and program disruptions is rather like a mirage which looks so real at a distance, but the closer one gets the more it disappears. With patience, humour, courtesy, honesty, tact, and the wisdom of the Holy Spirit most situations can be turned into spiritual profit. From experience it has been proved that:

(1) some interruptions may be ignored
Develop a 'deaf ear' and a 'blind eye' for people who pass snide remarks, ask irrelevant questions or just try to interrupt. Sooner or later the person will get the message and will either stay and listen or move off in search of fun elsewhere. Where voluntary helpers feel that the interruptions may be a cover-up for a spiritual need, one of them should quietly draw the individual out of the crowd and dialogue with him.

(2) other interruptions may be used to advantage
Sometimes questions, dialogue and even passing remarks open up profitable opportunities to apply the gospel. Ignore the irrelevant to prevent being sidetracked. Occasionally it is advantageous even necessary to answer interjectors when:

- An opportunity opens up for the gospel to be explained more fully. Sincere questions and genuine problems give preachers worthwhile opportunities to explain aspects of the gospel which answer personal needs. Of course any question or statement which turns out to be unduly provocative or to have a sexual motive should be ignored. A well-known OAC evangelist thanked one regular interjector saying, 'every time you open your mouth you put a sermon in mine!'

- When it helps attract a crowd.
A lively exchange with an interjector can attract people just as much as a fire or an accident. Some preachers have even prayed for an interjector, and after one has built a crowd then become a nuisance, suggested that he transfer his skills elsewhere. With good humour, most of them oblige. Stubborn types should be given the 'deaf-ear' and 'glass-eye' treatment.

- When it is the only way to quieten a persistent interjector.
The interjectors who won't respond to 'move on friend' or the 'deep freeze' treatment, are usually those who want to do all the talking and use your crowd to air their own views. Their constant interruptions become very wearisome to preacher and crowd alike. Sometimes it is better to allow them to speak, then reply point by point. The more sincere will respond to this but there are always persistent types who maintain their verbal barrage. By this time your voluntary helpers should be exercising 'Operation Relief'. One of them should edge up to the interjector and distract his attention by saying something like: 'That speaker is not interested in hearing you, but I'm interested in what you've got to say, why don't we go over there and you tell me?' With a nod in one direction he should move away and mostly he will be followed. At a safe talking distance the worker should give his name, shake hands and then

direct the conversation toward Jesus Christ. There is nothing like genuine Christian love and friendship to quieten opposition and prejudice.

- When there is a danger of losing face with a crowd.
  Gospel preachers who ignore every question may run the risk of being discredited particularly if the crowd assumes they are unwilling to face basic issues. These include the supposed evil which has been done in the name of religion: holy wars; the inquisition; persecutions of religious minorities; church wealth and property ownership etc. The outdoor preacher is a natural target for protest. It would be foolish to deny history, but it is also fair to ask how many wrongs were done by Jesus Christ, whom the preacher represents. No one ever accuses him.

- When it is necessary to clear up misunderstandings.
  Open-air preachers may run into flak from those who think preaching should be kept inside churches, or who see 'religion' from a very twisted point of view. Some of the misconceptions, misquotations of scripture and opinions given are often very humorous. But the world's maxim 'If ignorance is bliss, 'tis folly to be wise' should never be applied as eternity may be at stake for the hearers. Explanations may not change the prejudices of the questioners, but will put things in the right perspective for open-minded listeners.

Even experienced outdoor preachers need to constantly remind themselves that attempting to answer interjectors without the power of the Holy Spirit can be disastrous. The devil has one well-worn but highly successful trick he tries on outdoor preachers regardless of experience. He well knows that pride can be a preacher's weakness so he aims a fiery dart of temptation smack into the preacher's heart. 'Show that pip-squeak you are much smarter than he is, make him look ignorant and stupid in front of all those people. Blind him with theology. Wither him with rhetoric. Vent a bit of righteous anger for your Jesus, he's not here to defend himself!' If the preacher does, the devil chalks up another victory. The answer in the flesh always rebounds, the preacher becomes discouraged, the gospel discredited, the listener disillusioned and the devil delighted. Only the Spirit-filled speaker can resist that.

3. Classes of interruptions which may be expected in open air evangelism.

Although most programs are conducted without any interruption, certain types of people may turn up in large city outdoor programs. The devil has a special anti-gospel commando force:

(1) those under the influence of alcohol.
Whether the light-headed party goer, the common drunk, the inebriate or the alcoholic, his interruption can be very disruptive. The light-hearted happy ones are out for fun and usually argue that Jesus Christ is the patron saint of drinkers because he turned water into wine. The in-

coherent and unsteady are often argumentative, but usually controllable. Unfortunately, some are aggressive, nasty and spoiling for a fight. Avoid dialogue and touch contact.

Because alcohol is a socially acceptable drug, drunkenness is often excused. People attending open air gospel programs are usually tolerant toward people affected by alcohol, until they start to interfere with their listening. Then they will tell them to be quiet and if they are not will often push them out. The program leader can do little more than good-naturedly put up with the interference, but team helpers can assist:

- By standing in a semi-circle around the speaker so that the drunk cannot push through to the speaker or equiment.

- By surrounding the drunk and gently manoeuvring him out of the crowd and down the street. Care must be taken not to take hold of him by the arm or shoulders as this is technical assault. Those under the influence are very sensitive to being pushed around and will often react violently.

- If the drunk is able to talk reasonably coherently, a worker should engage him in conversation and try enticing him away by moving slowly out of the crowd and down the street. The aim is to turn his attention elsewhere.

(2) The bucket-mouth brigade

These characters are against anything you might be for, and for anything you might be against. Generously endowed with loud voices and inflated egos, they wander around arguing with one another until they come across their favourite target, a gospel preacher. Then begins the constant needling, the barrage of sarcastic comments, ill-mannered remarks, unanswerable questions, filthy language, and a variety of antics aimed at distracting the crowd. They may handclap, blow whistles and shout remarks to one another across the crowd. Fortunately this type breed mainly in large cities and are largely nocturnal. Patient, unruffled preachers surrounded by praying helpers can control them, but personal workers would be better to speak with them individually rather than challenge the whole group.

(3) The person with a chip on his shoulder

Sometimes the sight and sound of an open air preacher is all that is needed to change an apparently respectable person into a noisy and often unreasonable one. The cause may be a grudge against a church, or a minister for something he has said or done or even against God for allowing wars and injustices. Some don't have a reason but just react. A man once tried to attack the writer as he passed an open air program. He was restrained by bystanders and later explained that because he was deeply grieving over his wife's death, he suddenly got mad at God when he heard preaching.

Others give an open air preacher a rough time either out of self-justification, rebellion against an overstrict religious upbringing, or as a defence for running away from God. These people need genuine Christian love and understanding.

(4) The over-full garbage cart

People whose minds constantly feed on a filthy diet of sex and perversion often delight in off-loading some of their mental and moral refuse where the gosepl is being preached outdoors. Nothing is sacred or clean, and the virgin birth of Jesus Christ is a prime target for their mockery. Those whose minds are permanently located at gutter level are in urgent need of spiritual deliverance before the gospel will make sense to them. Demon bondage of this nature can only be broken by spiritual warfare under the anointing of the Holy Spirit. Degraded women are very much more offensive and difficult to handle than men.

(5) The attention getter

If teenage years can be dramatic in a Christian home, how much more for those who have never experienced real love, understanding and attention. Some of them delight in empty questions, stupid and sometimes offensive remarks, childish pranks with equipment and general loud laughter. They need to be handled patiently and sensitively, and if possible dealt with individually.

(6) The budding university Professor

. . . the self-image projected by some university students. Living in a world of the deified question mark, the open air preacher and his message may come in for some pseudo-intellectual analysis. The critique is usually verbal and occasionally strident. Once 'Mr Intellect' feels he has demolished both preacher and message he usually moves on surrounded by his own halo of self-esteem. What this type actually knows about the gospel can usually be written on a postage stamp. What they think they know would fill a college library. Counteract error with truth and look out for the person who is really searching. Genuine personal warmth, humility and openness can disarm and win this type to Christ.

(7) Worshippers at the shrine of the goodness of human nature

No humanist wants to hear the gospel. Why should he? He believes that from man and in man and for man are all things. Against all evidence to the contrary he believes mankind will yet reach the very heights of perfection by human resources alone. The man Christ Jesus doesn't figure in this process. The humanist may listen quietly, smile to himself, shrug his shoulders and saunter off. He may also express his self-satisfaction openly and scoff at the gospel. Patience, courtesy and the Word of God are needed.

(8) The smart Alec opportunist

He loves the sound of his own voice and refuels his ego with the laughter of those he amuses. An open air preacher's crowd is his delight, so with patter and humour he puts on his own vaudeville act. An OAC preacher effectively handled one of them by saying, 'Sir, you have just made two mistakes.' then carried on preaching. Curiosity soon got the better of the man and he demanded to know what were the two mistakes he was supposed to have made. The reply finally was, 'First of all, clowns are usually in a circus and this is not a circus, we are preaching Jesus Christ as Saviour. Secondly, clowns get paid for their services, and here you are doing it for nothing. Man, you want to wake up to yourself!' Non-offensive answers given with a smile are the best defence.

(9) The wolf in sheep's clothing

The cultist will sometimes prowl around open air meetings waiting to pounce on any who show interest in the gospel and offer his own literature. It is sometimes advisable to ask listeners not to receive written materials from anyone who is not identified as one of your group. Be careful of the cultist who tries to entice preachers into a doctrinal debate over selected verses upon which their particular heresy is based. Resist that at all costs and refrain from expressing opinions about churches or religious groups. Stay with the gospel and the truth of the Word.

(10) The anti-God fraternity

Atheists, sceptics, scoffers and some agnostics are part of this brotherhood. They are bound together by a rejection of God rather than disbelief in His existence. They are mentioned in the Psalms as fools and are usually quick to prove it. One OAC evangelist has a sermon entitled 'The atheist is God'. He rightly claims that any person who authoritatively declares that there is NO evidence of God, must himself have ALL knowledge and have visited ALL space and searched ALL exisitng matter to be so sure. Only God Himself could be so positive. Resist the temptation to argue. Let the Word speak for itself and fair-minded people in your audience will accept the truth particularly if it is confirmed by your gracious attitude.

(11) The political campaigner

Don't be drawn. The pharisees tried to catch Jesus the same way but he wouldn't be trapped. Just smile and say 'I'd rather have dog ticks than politics, at least they can be cleaned up!'

(12) The funny man

A humorist in a crowd is a potential three-way hazard. Firstly, by clowning he may ruin a spiritual atmosphere. Secondly, if the speaker has no sense of humour and gets angry or sarcastic he will lose the respect of the crowd. Thirdly, if the speaker has a good sense of humour and tries to match or surpass the humorist he may entertain the listeners but will quickly lose all spiritual impact. Like fire, humour spreads quickly, can be very destructive, and is hard to extinguish.

(13) The sincere enquirer (including genuine agnostics)

Answer as fully as possible for the enquirer's benefit and for others who may have similar thoughts. If possible, challenge these people to respond to Christ.

4. Some suggestions from experience

(1) Don't be sidetracked

The Gospel may be likened to the action of a wagon wheel. The hub stands for Jesus Christ; the spokes stand for the variety of gospel expressions used; and the rin stands for effective communication with people. If the function of that wheel is to be effective from hub to rim each spoke must be firmly and accurately in place. The leader must construct the wheel carefully and accurately.

(2) Depend upon the Holy Spirit

The manner in which interjectors (hecklers) are handled should depend on their sincerity. The Lord Jesus knew instinctively who were sincere and who were not, and answered them accordingly. Some interjectors will not hide their attitudes. Some will lie, and others will be honest. Listen to what the Spirit tells you.

Try this simple test which will indicate the sincerity of a questioner. Ask for the question to be repeated. The first time, to be sure you have heard it correctly; the second because of background noise; the third so that the people on the edge of the crowd can hear. Finally, a fourth time for someone at the front whom you suspect may be hard of hearing. If the question is a phoney, with each repetition it will lose impact until finally it probably won't need an answer, the questioner having disappeared. As a bonus, the time taken will help the preacher prepare an answer if the question is an awkward one, or the question is sincere and the questioner is still waiting.

(3) Remain courteous even in the face of abuse

It is spiritually profitable to stay courteous even if pride suffers. The writer has learned that when interjectors have been handled discourteously, other listeners have been turned away from the gospel. Genuine courtesy will have the opposite effect.

(4) Don't pretend to know more than you do

You never know how travelled, educated and knowledgeable some of your audience may be. The wise preacher will avoid making dogmatic statements beyond his knowledge and expertise. More people are won to Christ by honesty and godly example than by theory and argument.

(5) Honesty pays off

Knowledgeable questioners sometimes set traps for unwary speakers. If the answer is beyond you then say so; you will receive credits. There are no prizes for dummies.

(6) Keep control of the program

The speaker alone should deal with an interjector (heckler). Team

135

members should be supportive in prayer but not answer for the speaker. They should only speak out when invited by the leader or privately for the purpose of distracting an interjector's (heckler's) attention and persuading him to leave the crowd as previously outlined. Should a speaker be unable to answer an interjector or maintain control, the leader should take charge.

(7) Be prepared

All open air workers should read the apologetics contained in Josh McDowell's books and J. Edwin Orr's *Answers to 100 Questions.*

(8) Finally, be one jump ahead

Sometimes a listener will want to ask a question. If you are not sure of the questioner's sincerity, ask with a smile, 'How many sir?', or 'Do you wish to ask a question or volunteer information?' It won't affect the genuine but will gag the insincere.

5. When unavoidable events interrupt the program

(1) The Hari Krishna devotees

There is little else to do but wait until the saffron-robed chanters and din-makers jump and jerk their way down the road.

(2) Fire trucks, police vehicles and ambulances

From experience it is advisable to continue preaching. Once a crowd leaves it is most difficult to get it back. Voluntary helpers should be trained to keep their eyes on the speaker and ignore the sirens, bells, or flashing lights of passing vehicles.

(3) Mob violence

Leaders should protect their voluntary helpers as much as possible and take all precautions to prevent injury or damage to vehicles and equipment. Urgent prayer and a swift exit has kept workers from dangerous situations in some of OAC's activities.

Chapter 10

CHILDREN'S OPEN AIR EVANGELISM

The children of Jerusalem were a great concern to the prophet Jeremiah. They were war refugees, innocent victims of their parents' sin. He dedicated this prayer to them:
> 'Arise cry out in the night, as the watches of the night begin; pour out your heart like water in the presence of the Lord. Lift up your hands to him for the lives of your children, who faint from hunger at the head of every street' (Lamentations 2:19).

These words have lost nothing of their impact with the passing of the centuries and Jeremiah's five concerns for boys and girls should be ours today.

1. Children are important

'Arise cry out . . . pour out your hearts . . . lift up your hands to him . . . for the lives of your children.'

Children are the 'us' of tomorrow. Their salvation is of top priority:

(1) to God
'It is not the will of your Father which is in heaven that one of these little ones should perish' (Matthew 18:14).

(2) to Jesus
The disciples of Jesus Christ overstepped their authority and grossly underestimated his love for children by refusing them access to him. 'But when Jesus saw [it], He was indignant and pained, and said to them, allow the children to come to Me—do not forbid or prevent or hinder them—for to such belongs the kingdom of God' (Mark 10:14 Amp.). '. . . and He took [the children up one by one] in His

arms and (fervently invoked a) blessing, placing His hands upon them' (Mark 10:16 Amp.). '. . . and whoever receives and accepts and welcomes one little child like this for My sake and in My name receives and accepts and welcomes Me' (Matthew 18:5 Amp.).

(3) To the world of today and tomorrow
At least 44% of the population of Africa is under 15 years of age.
At least 43% of the population of Asia is under 15 years of age.
At least 42% of the population of Latin America is under 15 years of age.

And these percentages are steadily increasing. It has been estimated that 75% of known Christians come to Christ before they reach 17 years of age. Child psychologists estimate that 80% of a child's character and brain capacity is formed by the 8th year. These figues should provide the greatest incentive for giving top priority to child evangelism.

2. Children have great potential

- Jonathan Edwards came to Christ at the age of six years and became a mighty preacher.
- Matthew Henry met Christ at 10 years of age. He wrote a Bible commentary which is still widely used nearly three centuries after his death.
- Bishop Taylor Smith, one time Chaplain-General to the British armed forces, was converted when 11 years of age.
- Frances Ridley Havergal, well-known as a hymn writer, found Christ at nine years of age.
- Graham Scroggie, a great preacher and teacher, was converted at nine years.
- Mary Slessor, a famous African missionary, was saved at seven years.
- Count Zinzendorf, founder of the Moravian Missionary Society was born again at four years.

These names are only a few of so many whose lives confirm the saying: 'an adult saved is a soul saved, but a child saved is a life saved'. C. H. Spurgeon wrote 'the capacity for believing and faith lies more in a child convert than an adult convert. Children often provide the key to other members of the family and fulfil the scripture 'a little child shall lead them'.

3. Children are in danger

'. . . for the lives of your children . . .'

(1) Even the most innocent looking child has a sinful nature.

God said: '. . . every inclination of his (man's) heart is evil from childhood' (Genesis 8:21).

Isaiah said: 'You were called a rebel from birth' (Isaiah 48:8).

King David said: 'Surely I have been a sinner from birth, sinful from the time my mother conceived me' (Psalm 51:5). 'Even from birth the wicked go astray, from the womb they are wayward and speak lies' (Psalm 58:3).

The Apostle Paul said: 'There is no one righteous, not even one' (Romans 3:10). 'All of us also lived amoung them at one time, gratifying the cravings of our sinful nature and following its desires and thoughts. Like the rest, we were by nature objects of wrath' (Ephesians 2:3).

Every-day living confirms this. Despite being shielded from the evils of the world, the children of Christian parents show exactly the same tendencies to wrong-doing as other children. Every sweet, innocent looking new-born baby already has a nature fully stocked with the seeds of sin just waiting for the chance to develop and blight its life.

(2) Children are eternally lost once they become accountable for their own conduct and sin wilfully.

In Matthew 18:12–14 Jesus tells a simple story of one sheep lost out of a flock of 100 to illustrate that children can be lost spiritually. The farmer didn't write the animal off to stock losses by natural causes, but penned the 99 securely, and set out to find the lost one. The shepherd's disregard of time, comfort and safety indicates the priority Jesus gave to the salvation of children. The punch line comes in the last words. 'In the same way your Father in heaven is not willing that any of these little ones should be lost'. The significance of the Greek word 'appollumi' translated 'lost' or 'perish' (KJV) is explained by W. E. Vine's Dictionary of New Testament words as meaning 'to destroy utterly, not as in extinction, but ruin, loss of well being'. The value God places on every child is shown by the severe punishment reserved for anyone who entices one to sin (Matthew 18:6). 'When a child is old enough to sin knowingly, he is old enough to believe savingly' C. H. Spurgeon.

4. Children are persons who should never be overlooked because of their age.

'... that faint for hunger ...'

It is little wonder they 'faint for hunger' for acceptance, identity, recognition, understanding, companionship and love. They are so often left to console one another because they are:

- passed over or ignored because of their size. (Hence they can't be blamed for also feeling unimportant.)
- got rid of because they interrupt what 'grown ups' want to do.
- told to keep quiet because they are making too much noise.
- sent out to play so that adults can talk.
- packed off to bed so that the people can have 'fun'.
- called 'kids', 'brats', or a lot of other demeaning and hurtful names.

What so many lose because of broken homes and a secularised teaching system, Jesus Christ is able to provide, and many of today's generation will only hear that through open air evangelism.

'See that you do not look down on one of these little ones' Jesus said (Matthew 18:10). 'A soul's price does not depend upon its years' (C. H. Spurgeon).

5. Children are everywhere just waiting for recognition

'... at the head of every street ...'

A street without children is as unnatural as a bird without feathers. In good weather children can be reached with the gospel as they play outdoors from early morning until dark, seven days per week. They are in school grounds before lessons begin, during the lunch break, and even after school before making for home. They gather at parks, reserves, recreational and sports areas, beaches, rivers, swimming pools, caravan parks, fairgrounds, places of entertainment and generally on the street outside their homes. They have more time to spare than adults, accept Bible truths with less prejudice, and have greater imaginations which make it easier to hold their attention.

Children's outdoor evangelism has so much to commend it. For example:

- Children can be reached who don't go to Sunday school, or who would not be allowed to.
- They enjoy the informality.
- The freedom to come and go as they wish is attractive.
- Those who miss Sunday school because of family outings to beach and picnic areas can still be reached.
- Since outdoor evangelism is not a formal classroom situation, the boys and girls are relaxed and learn more easily.

There are five well-defined steps in bringing boys and girls to a saving knowledge of Jesus Christ. These are:

Children have time to spare, little prejudice and respond quickly to genuine friendship.	Children readily give attention and suffer few mental distractions when the presentation is alive and kept moving.	Children can grasp theology and deep truths with simple and effective illustrations. They need to be taught before they are wrongly influenced by others.	Children have the capacity to learn and retain because this is a daily school discipline.	Children are sincere and spontaneous in response. Emotional responses should be discouraged and follow-up work commenced as soon as possible.

The place of contact	The means of attraction	The teaching segment	The learning-memory experience	Objective reached
Open Air Programs: Beaches Parks Reserves After school Housing areas Streets Swimming pool Rivers Caravan or trailer parks	**1. Music:** Piano accordians Wind & string instruments. Recorded music. **2. Singing** Choruses **3. Other means** Sketching Puppets Object lessons Ventrillioquist doll, Clowns Crocodile walk Candy chase Personal invitation	**1. Choruses** Teaching theology & doctrine such as explaining the nature of God, sin, redemption etc. Ethics—relationships. Bible content, faith etc. **2. Bible texts** **3. Theological and doctrinal truths** • Storytelling • Sketching stories • Visual aids, object lesson (flannelgraphs, plasticograph etc.) • Drama, mime Bible re-enactments. Daily teaching sessions. • Weekly program contents. • Puppets and Ventrilioquist doll.	**Overall program** • Connected contributions developing a clearly defined & recognisable theme. • Repetition of Bible memory verse. Use of theme choruses • Gospel truths taught from different approaches • Repetition of principles being taught for the day and series at regular intervals • Major on the most important matters if time is limited. Don't forget the value of small rewards for memory work and behaviour etc.	**1. Challenge to Commitment** • Stated clearly. As free of emotion as possible. • avoid group responses. • Without pressure. **2. Responses** • Handled with sensitivity. • Carefully instruct those who respond • Check for sincerity • Follow up responsibly • Pray over regularly

Select according to available time

1. EXPOSURE

Four guiding principles determine the best site for children's evangelism:

(1) Safety

Places should be chosen where programs will not be interrupted, and where there will be no physical danger to the children. Avoid busy roads, noisy factories, distracting play equipment, sports activities and the hazard of flying balls. Even in good locations a sketchboard can be dangerous if caught by a gust of wind. To prevent this, a voluntary helper should be asked to hold the board at all times.

(2) Seating

Avoid places where children have to sit on small stones, prickly vege—

141

tation, or damp ground. A large canvas or plastic square (or strips) will keep the children comfortable and protected. It will also mark out where you want your audience to sit.

(3) Sun

Children should not have to look into the sun. Speakers should suffer this discomfort rather than expect children to sit with eyes screwed up, or shaded with one hand trying to see. Even at personal discomfort, those taking part should not wear coloured glasses while speaking as the eyes are a most important part of communication.

On hot days look for shade so that the children will not have to sit with their backs to the sun for long periods.

(4) Sound

Ideally, select a site where the sun is behind the children, and the wind able to carry your voice to them. If an amplifier is used, keep the volume comfortable for those sitting at the front. It is better to reach fewer people effectively than deafen everyone in sight.

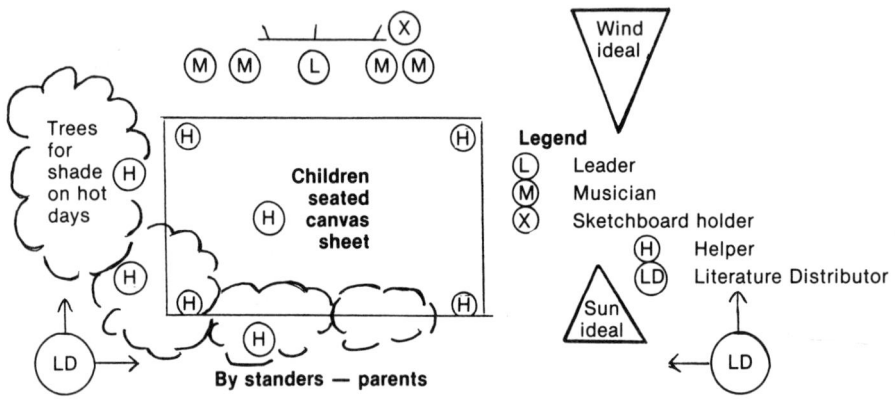

2. ATTENTION

If you want to attract children try:

(1) Music

Piano accordions, wind instruments, guitars and other stringed instruments (particularly amplified) attract children. If none are available, play recorded music and everyone will know that something special is about to happen. Children will soon gather around to find out what is going on.

(2) Singing

Enthusiastic chorus singing by team members, even without music, will soon attract children, and together they will build a bigger crowd. Words should be printed in large letters (suitably illustrated) on durable materials and held high enough for everyone to see. Sheets of good quality paper, light card, pieces of calico, cotton material, sheets of clear plastic overprinted by spirit pens are all ideal. Child Evangelism Fellowship offers a good selection of large illustrated chorus books with music.

Choruses should be selected for their teaching content, musical appeal, and themes to match the program content as closely as possible. Volunteers should be used to hold the words, and a small reward given such as a clip on a card, a piece of candy or a scripture verse card. Everyone will want to help.

(3) Give everyone an enthusiastic invitation

Nothing stirs enthusiasm more than enthusiasm. Whether you personally ask boys and girls to join in the fun, or use a public address system in a car driven slowly around the area, do it with such infectious enthusiasm that the children will sense the excitement, and feel they will be the losers if they don't join in.

(4) Visual attractions

Sketching

The sketchboard can be prepared in a variety of ways to attract attention, such as:

- by drawing a well-known cartoon character from TV or children's books.
- by inviting children (one at a time) to draw marks, lines or squiggles on the board. A team member then turns what the child has done into a bird, fish, animal or cartoon character with a few quick strokes of chalk or brush.
- by drawing a balloon seller holding a handful of coloured balloons showing the coming program content e.g. prizes, stories, singing, competitions, mystery items etc.
- by drawing outlines of a sketch to be used in the program on the sketchboard lying face up, on the ground. The children who crowd around to see what is going on can be sent off to get others. When enough have gathered the board can be lifted into position, the children seated, and the program commenced.

- **Puppets**

  Although it takes time to set up equipment, the children will spread the news, and by the time you are ready you will have an excited audience.

- **Visual aids and object lessons**

  Prepare to do something interesting and it won't be long before some boy or girl will ask 'What are you going to do, Mister?' and you have your first publicity agent. Like the puppet show, your audience will soon be ready-made.

- **The Ventriloquist and his doll**

  If the children are scattered, a doll (dummy) is an ideal 'pied piper' to bring them together. By walking around and using the doll to tell the children what is going to happen, the ventriloquist always arrives back with a happy jostling crowd of children.

- **Life-size comic characters**

  A voluntary helper dressed as a clown, an out-of-space character, a pirate, an animal, or some well-known children's personality should walk around giving out candies, and talking about the program about to commence. He will soon have a fan club following him.

- **A crocodile walk**

  Team members make up the head of crocodile, holding onto one another's hips, inviting the children to tag on behind as they wind round trees, tents, cars etc. to where the program is to be held.

- **The candy chase**

  A team member walks around dropping wrapped candies on the ground. The children soon get the idea and follow him, so he breaks into a run, still dropping candies, and the chase ends at the meeting site where the children are glad to rest and listen.

3. COMPREHENSION

This is the teaching section where the gospel is explained by:

1. Teaching doctrine through choruses

Bible words need to be explained and truths linked to one another, as simply and clearly as possible. Treat your audience as if no-one understands spiritual values.

2. Teaching Bible memory verses

A variety of interesting and stimulating methods need to be used to help chldren learn, understand, and memorise a Bible text. Examples of teaching methods are given in Appendix 'A' at the end of this chapter.

3. Teaching theological or doctrinal truths

Children can be asked to jump from a point labelled 'EARTH' to one labelled 'HEAVEN'. The points are placed further apart than a child can jump to illustrate how impossible it is to get to heaven by self-effort.

- Sin may be taught as missing God's standard of holiness by children trying to hit a small target by firing suction cap darts at a 'safe' distance.

- A reel of cotton thread wound round the arms of a child until he is unable to break free will show the binding power of repeated wrong-doing.

- A flashlight can be prepared to illustrate how sin breaks fellowship with God. Obstructions placed between the batteries will prevent the bulb from lighting up. When the cap is unscrewed to find the cause, a piece of paper with the words 'unconfessed sin' will fall out. When the first battery is removed another piece of paper is found with the words 'disobeying God's Word'. Finally between the second battery and the bulb a banknote falls out, representing 'greed'. When all obstructions are removed and the batteries replaced, the light will function.

- Hold a piece of paper on which names of sins have previously been written in lemon juice, over a lighted candle. The heat makes the words visible, reminding us that God always knows the thoughts of every heart.

- Sin's increasing influence can be visualised by squeezing ink from an eye dropper into a glass of clear water, one drop at a time. The colour is not noticeable at first, but gradually the water darkens. Another method is to blow up a pre-prepared balloon on which names of sins have been written with a spirit pen when inflated. At first, the words can scarcely be read and appear insignificant but become larger with inflation, until finally the balloon bursts, showing the final effect of sin.

- The effect of the cleansing of the blood of Jesus Christ may be shown by using red cellophane to cover the names of various sins written in red on a piece of white paper or card. The words disappear when blending shades of colour and cellophane are used.

- Faith may be demonstrated by trying to open a lock with an assortment of keys labelled 'Good Works', 'Honesty', 'Being good' etc. Only the one labelled 'Faith' will be successful.

- The way of salvation is made clear by the use of the good news glove, the wordless book, or the gospel in a nut, available through Christian booksellers.

4. Story telling

People of all ages love a story well told. Stories should be chosen for the truths they teach, never just for effect or audience reaction. Sources include:

- Bible stories, which provide the greatest resources, including suspense, mystery, and victories against overwhelming odds. And the 'baddies' always get caught. Background materials from Bible commentaries, dictionaries, atlases, and research materials, add to reality.
- History, nature, current events, and personal experiences.
- Novels and consecrated imagination.
- Real-life situations. People's reactions and attitudes.

The speaker needs to be able to put it all together in a captivating manner with a view to impressing truth rather than his story-telling ability.

The story format should follow the same objectives as the overall program, i.e.:

attention.

The introduction should grip attention by being interesting, informative and with the hint of intrigue or excitement to follow.

comprehension

The main body of the story should illustrate a principle, moral or truth, and the Bible memory verse should reinforce this. The teaching should be applied through the story so that if children leave or are taken away before the end, they will at least have heard of the application.

retention

A final summary should reinforce the important memory points, rather like threading a string of truth-pearls for children to take home.

response

The application needs a personal challenge for children to respond to Jesus Christ. Inform the mind, warm the emotions and challenge the will.

Finally, some Do's and Don'ts of story telling:

Do:
- in evangelistic stories, make sure you deal adequately with the death, burial, resurrection and glorification of Jesus Christ.
- be enthusiastic, but controlled.
- forget what adults may think of you, act and dramatise stories for children.
- remember that spiritual life or death may depend on how you present the truth.
- keep both eyes on the time, don't trust one!
- use language understood by your audience age-group.

Don't:
- miss the climax by telling rambling stories, or by giving tiresome detail.
- get carried away by your own enthusiasm, and forget time.
- overdramatise so that the whole point of the story is missed.
- expect children to sit quietly if their interest is not being held.
- speak down to children; speak as one of them.

5. Sketched stories

Sketching strengthens all that has been said about story telling.

Attention is held more easily by seeing the story illustrated. **Comprehension** is better when drawings and words illustrate the message. **Retention** is increased by a message outline being left on the board until the end of the program. **Response** is probably better as the challenge can be made in a quieter and more attentive atmosphere because the interest has been held.

Please remember to:
- do most of your board preparation beforehand if you cannot sketch quickly.

- raise and project your voice into the board when your back is toward your audience.
- keep a paintbrush in your hand at all times to hold interest.
- ask someone to sketch for you if you cannot sketch and speak simultaneously.
- if you happen to relocate indoors, place a sheet of paper on the carpet under the sketchboard. It's cheaper than a carpet shampoo to remove paint stains.
- don't turn your back to the audience for long periods. Paint a little less, more frequently.
- keep your board uncluttered; avoid overcrowding of words or drawings.
- if you want a clean-looking board, use your paints sparingly so that the colours won't run.

6. Visual aids, object lessons

Their sole purpose should be to throw light on truth. Flannelgraph is not ideal for outdoor use, but its plastic counterpart (plasticographe) using reversible figures on a bright background is ideal.

7. Dramas

Dramas, mimes and Bible re-enactments really attract and hold crowds. The gospel comes through without offence.

Consider the following possibilities:
- A robed figure walks past a crowd into the water, dips under the surface seven times and comes out shouting and jumping up and down. On his way back he is stopped and questioned. He turns out to be Naaman, the Syrian healed of leprosy.
- Someone dressed in 'armour' walks around calling for a champion to fight him. A small 'David' comes up, dialogues with his giant, slings a stone. Exit one giant! David is then interviewed.
- Four men carry a man on a stretcher into the crowd. The patient is interviewed. He tells how his friends carried him to Jesus because he was paralysed. How they tore up the roof of a house where Jesus was and lowered him down. How Jesus forgave his sin and healed him. He gets up and carries his stretcher away.
- New Testament characters in appropriate dress can be interviewed as to what Jesus did for them. Zacchaeus, the man born blind (John 9), the ex-demoniac from Gadara, Lazarus, and Barabbas are ideal.
- The Bible is as full of themes for dramas as a garden is full of seeds. Just add the water of imagination and prayer. Sincerity counts more than dramatic experience in presentation.

8. Daily teaching sessions

Where a series of daily programs is being held, a basic teaching session, supported by choruses and a puzzle text, makes an ideal program. A five-day progressive teaching series has been included in schedule 'B' at the end of the chapter. Each day's theme is suitable for separate use.

9. The contents of a week's program

Variety will keep interest at a high level. The core of such programs is the puzzle text and sketch story. In Appendix 'C' a five-day puzzle text and supporting story have been included. A further five-day program appears in the resource section, part 6.

4. RETENTION

The learning-memorising experience is a continuous process rather than a definable stage. The daily themes, teaching, choruses, revision of truths, and the repetition of Bible verses all have the effect of driving truth deeper, as a hammer drives in a nail.

5. RESPONSE

The objective of all outdoor children's programs is to encourage boys and girls to willingly and sincerely respond to the claims of Jesus Christ as Lord and Saviour. The invitation calls for special care.

- Children must clearly understand how Jesus can become their Saviour. They need to be shown what this will mean to them in the future.
- A rush to come forward, or a 'follow the leader' response should be avoided at all costs.
- Avoid a highly emotional atmosphere, or pressuring children to respond.
- The challenge must be adequate, and fair, so that the children know the consequences of neglecting or rejecting Christ, without being threatened with hell-fire. Children need to be loved into the Kingdom of God. Threatening or frightening children has led to sleeplessness and emotional problems. It discredits the Gospel, its Saviour, and children's evangelism.

Several forms of invitation may be used:

1. Ask that heads be bowed while everyone repeats a prayer. To the sincere this is helpful, to the rest it is meaningless. Where children frequently recite the same prayer, there will be no assurance of salvation.

2. Call for a show of hands from those who wish to trust Christ as Saviour, then ask them to repeat silently the words of a prayer. A child making a sincere and uncomplicated commitment will be blessed, but there is no guarantee that those responding will speak to a counsellor. (Wherever possible aim to get the names and addresses for follow-up, and check the responses for understanding and sincerity.)

3. Ask for all heads to be bowed. Invite those desiring to trust Jesus as Lord and Saviour to repeat a simple prayer in their hearts. Then ask the children who have responded to bring a note the next day explaining what they have done. Remember they may not be present again, or may forget to write the experience down and bring it to you.

4. Explain how Jesus may be trusted as Lord and Saviour, using a simple illustration. Three words: **Sorry, Thanks, Ask** in the teaching series, Appendix 'B'. Invite those who would like to make Jesus Christ their Saviour to come and tell you personally at the end of the program. In the usual rush and bustle, most children will run off, but the genuine will wait, or come back. This method is the one the writer used with considerable spiritual success.

Counselling children is similar to adults, but expressed in simple language. Remember:

- children are won by love and understanding. Treat them as Jesus would.
- be sensitive to children who want to be saved but are shy, or don't know how to express themselves.
- use words children understand:
  'Being naughty' or 'doing wrong things' will be more meaningful than 'sins'.
  'Punishment' is better than 'judgment'.
  'Taking our place' should replace 'substitution'.
- when a child understands the Gospel, and is mature enough to pray alone, suggest prayer points leaving them to choose their own words. For example:
  'Tell the Lord Jesus you are sorry for all your wrongdoing. *(Name some.)*'
  'Ask him to forgive you and make your heart clean.'
  'Thank him for loving you and taking your punishment.'
  'Ask him to come into your heart and life as Lord and Saviour.'
  'Ask him to make you strong to live for him and to grow up as he wants you to do.'
  'Thank him for hearing and answering your prayer.'

  For children who do not know what to say, here is a simple prayer:
  'Dear Jesus,
  I know I have done wrong things *(name some)* and I am sorry. Please forgive me, and make my heart clean. Thank you Lord Jesus for loving me, and dying on the cross to take the punishment I deserved. Please come and live in my heart and life as Lord and Saviour. Make me strong to live for you and to become the person you want me to be.
  Amen.'

- check the sincerity of each one responding by asking the question: 'Where is Jesus now?'. The answer should be 'In my heart'. If the reply is positive, ask a second question: 'How do you know?'. If the answer is based on feelings, turn their attention to the Word, and make sure they understand and believe because the Bible says so. (1 John 5:10–11; Rev. 3:20.) If necessary, go over the basics once more. If there is still uncertainty, pray with the child and invite him or her to come and see you again. Don't try to pull unripe fruit from the tree. For those with assurance, explain that Jesus does not leave us if we do wrong things after he becomes Saviour. Sin makes him sad, so we need to tell him how sorry we are and ask his forgiveness. Doing wrong spoils the friendship but doesn't break the relationship. The need for Bible reading and prayer should be stressed and encouraged. Make sure the child has a Bible. If possible, ask for the parents' consent to send follow-up material.

A plan of salvation centred round a shepherd and his sheep may be helpful in dealing with young children.

1. **The Bible likens people to sheep** (Ps. 79:13; 95:7; 100:3).
   Children will see themselves as lambs.

2. **The devil is the sheep thief who stole our hearts from God** (John 10:10).
   Those who do wrong things are following his bad example. That is sin, and hurts God.

3. **When sheep get lost they can't find their way home.**
   Sinners can never find God by themselves (Is. 53:6). Only Jesus can lead us to him. Sheep are the only animals without a homing instinct. They need a shepherd.

4. **Jesus the Good Shepherd came to earth to find all lost sheep.**
   He wanted to find them, make them clean inside, and bring them back to God's true sheepfold—heaven (Matt. 18:11–14; John 10:11).

5. **The Devil who stole God's sheep tried to kill the Good Shepherd.**
   He used Judas to betray him (John 13:2).

6. **God is stronger than the devil.**
   He allowed Jesus to die for our sins before the devil could kill him. He came back to life again so that he could rescue us from the power of the devil, and give us his abundant enjoyable life (John 10:10; John 1:18).

7. **The Good Shepherd will make every boy and girl** one of his special sheep if they ask him to be their Saviour (Rev. 3:20; John 1:12).

8. **The Good Shepherd will keep and protect his sheep from the sheep thief the devil**, for ever (John 10:27–29).

9. **The Good Shepherd promises to look after his sheep.**
   When they die, he will take them to be with him and his Father in heaven for ever (John 10; Psalm 23).

10. **The Good Shepherd expects every one of his sheep to recognise his voice**, follow him, and obey what he tells them. His voice is heard by reading the Bible (John 10:3,4,14,27).

FINALLY, here are some suggestions for the conduct of children's outdoor programs.

Speak of the need to respond to Jesus Christ during the program. Don't presume this can wait for the planned climax. Rain, unexpected interruptions, parents taking children, and distractions may mean you lose your crowd.

- Use language and communication methods children understand, and you will also reach teenagers and parents. Aim for the adults, and you will lose the children.

- Don't overdo action choruses requiring children to stand. If they want to leave, that will be the ideal opportunity.
- Team members should watch the children carefully, and be ready to deal with problems.
- Don't physically touch children or show signs of personal affection. It may be interpreted as a homosexual advance.
- Never tease, or belittle children such as calling a child with spectacles 'four-eyes', or a talkative child 'bucket-mouth'.
- Speak slowly and distinctly if you want to be heard clearly.
- A dog biscuit may be handy bait to lure a playful pup away from wanting to play with the children.
- A sign or banner will keep you from being mistaken for a cult. Parents will trust their children to you if they can trust your group.
- Pick up garbage lying around at the end of the program and retain the goodwill of local authorities.
- Helpers should be on their toes to take part just when they are needed.

Chapter 10

Appendix 'A'

METHODS OF TEACHING BIBLE TEXTS

The picture puzzle

In some cases the drawings will suggest the words, but more frequently letters are added and/or removed to reveal them. Each square represents a word from the chosen text. The squares will vary according to the number of words in the verse. If there is no square available for the Biblical reference, this should be taught separately. Here is an example of this method.

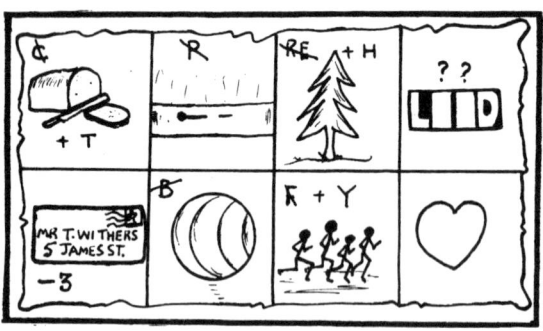

The key to interpretation

Boys and girls are asked alternately to suggest the special word in each square by adding or removing letters from the spelling of the object drawn. Choose squares at random to prevent guessing. The simplest questions should be reserved for the youngest children. From the squares of this text the following words may be worked out:

Square 1 The required word is TRUST
Take 'C' from crust, add 'T'.
Square 2 The required word is IN
Remove 1st letter from 'pin'.
Square 3 The required word is THE
Take 're' from tree, add 'h'.
Square 4 The required word is LORD
What two letters will make a four-letter title for Jesus?
Square 5 The required word is WITH
What word is left when three letters are taken away from the name?
Square 6 The required word is ALL
Remove the letter 'b' from 'ball'.
Square 7 The required word is YOUR
Take the letter 'f' from the number of runners and add letter 'y'.
Square 8 The required word is HEART
This is obvious.

The pie puzzle

Select a text and draw one horizontal mark for each letter of each word, then draw a colourful fruit pie with divisions. Explain that this is to be a competition between yourself and the children. Every time a boy or girl guesses a letter used in the verse, they get a point. Every time they choose a letter not used, you get a piece of pie. Boys and girls are then asked alternately to nominate any letter they believe is in the verse. One mark awarded for each correct answer adds a healthy competitive spirit between girls and boys. When a letter is guessed correctly, fill in each place where it occurs, and credit the winning side with one point. If the letter does not occur, pretend to eat a piece of pie with relish, and block out one piece (as illustrated).

The text used is 2 Corinthians 6:2: 'Now is the day of salvation'. It shows that two correct letters have been guessed, 'o' and 's', and one letter not in the text causing one piece of pie to be 'eaten'.

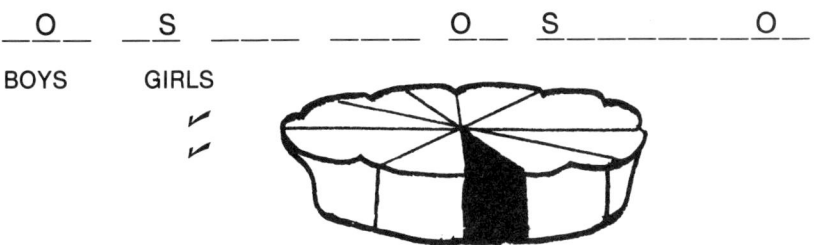

(One incorrect letter, one piece of pie eaten)

The code text

Place all the letters used in the text in alphabetical order, giving each a number. As in the pie puzzle, one horizontal mark is for each letter. Write the corresponding code number above each mark. As the code is broken in competition between boys and girls, the letters should be written beneath the numbers.

The text is Numbers 32:33: 'Be sure your sin will find you out'.

B = 1
D = 2
E = 3
F = 4
I = 5
L = 6
N = 7
O = 8
R = 9
S = 10
T = 11
U = 12
W = 13
Y = 14

1 3	10 12 9 3	14 8 12 9	10 5 7
B E	S U R E	Y O U R	S I N

13 5 6 6	4 5 7 2	14 8 12	8 12 11
W I L L	F I N D	Y O U	O U T

Mystery writing

Parts only of the letters of each word are written (heavy lettering), leaving the balance (showed by dots) to be 'discovered' by someone particularly gifted in languages—yourself of course.

The text is Proverbs 3:5: 'Trust in the Lord with all your heart'.

Th[S]T IN THE L_[R]) ʌ'IH ʌI _ Y[]IP ʜEɅPT

ᴾᵥ3ᶜ ᴣ:ᴣ

The balloon puzzle

Write the words of the text on separate pieces of paper, fold and push each piece of paper into a separate balloon. Ask for volunteers to blow the balloons up until they burst and find the words. Get the children cheering their friends and there will be great excitement. Stubborn balloons should be discreetly assisted with a pin. The words are then recovered, held up, arranged in order, and learned. Balloon blowers should receive small rewards.

154

Jumbled letter texts

The letters of each word are written in the same colour, and every word a different colour. Letters should be separated and scattered in the rectangle. The text is Romans 6:23: 'The wages of sin is death'.

In this example each **word** is made up of the same size and shape of letter instead of using colours. For example, the word 'wages' is comprised of upper-case letters.

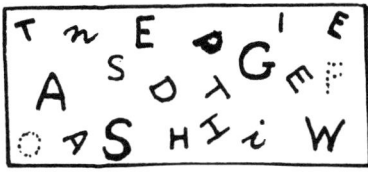

The Martian text

The letters of each word are jumbled. The quickest person to recognise the correct word wins the point. The text is Ezekiel 18:20: 'The soul who sins is the one who will die'.

HET	LOUS	OWH	NISS
SI	ETH	ENO	HOW
LILW	IDE	LEKIZEE	18 SERVE 20

Appendix 'B'

A FIVE-DAY TEACHING PROGRAM
(Credit Mr Philip Edwards)
(Each section may be used by itself)

DAY 1 Subject: Sin

Completed sketches

Progression of teaching—sketching

Commence with a clean piece of paper.

1. Draw Garden of Eden scene—Eve with no skirt. Speak of what was so special about them, NO SIN, and draw a yellow heart.

2. Relate temptation story—shade heart red, and write 'SIN' in black letters. Put skirt on Eve.

3. Speak of God's animal sacrifice—blood shed and sins covered, the skins used for clothes.

4. Adam and Eve put out of Garden. Since then, everyone born has been sinful. Draw a line of identical little figures.

5. Talk about sinful natures producing sinful acts (sins). Ask the children for the names of sins, and write the answers around the heart.

6. Illustrate what sin does to us and God by drawing a high wall with God on one side and ourselves on the other.

7. The Bible tells us about what God did for us—draw the outline of the cross round letter 'I' of the word sin on wall.

DAY 2 Subject: The Incarnation

Crucifixion—substitution

1. Draw in what symbolises a baby basket in your culture. About 2000 years ago angels told some shepherds to go and see God's special Son, a baby in a manger. He was their Saviour named Christ the Lord.

156

2. Draw the cloud and arrow and explain that Jesus was God's Son stepping out of heaven and becoming a baby. His coming was to show how much God loved us.

3. Because he had no sin he was different from us—draw in yellow heart.

4. When he grew up he performed miracles because he was so special. Write in suggestions.

5. The real reason Jesus came to earth was to die on a cross for us. God took our sin, put it on his Son, and punished him instead of us. Draw the cross.

6. Draw in a broken wall showing how the Cross of Christ smashes down the sin barrier so that we can have a new relationship with God.

7. When we trust Jesus as Lord and Saviour he makes our hearts clean like his. Draw in a yellow heart alongside the man.

DAY 3   Subject: Heaven

1. The Bible teaches about a wonderful place of happiness where God and Jesus are—heaven (draw in).

2. The Bible also tells us some of the things which won't be in heaven. Draw each one in turn and explain. The tear—no sadness. Medicine bottle, spoon—no sickness. Grave—no death. The heart with word 'sin'—no sin.

3. Who then will be in heaven? God and his special Son, Jesus, who died for our sins. Draw cross behind heart.

4. Who else? Those people who have made Jesus their Saviour and whose names are written in God's book of life. Draw cross and book.

DAY 4   Subject: Personal commitment to Jesus Christ

1. After Jesus died, he was buried. Three days later some ladies came with spices, found the stone rolled away, and Jesus alive. Draw open grave.

2. Jesus is alive today and wants to come and share our lives like someone coming to live in our house.

3. Draw in a house with a door suitable to your culture. What is missing? A handle on the door. A person who knocks can't get in unless the door is opened from the inside.

4. Draw in letters 'S', 'T', 'A' and a heart with a closed door. Then ask the question: 'If Jesus were to knock on our hearts, how could he get in?'. The answer is: we must open the door from the inside. There are three things that need to be said to Jesus:

   1. **Sorry.** We must tell him we are very sorry for our sin and wrong-doing, which means we turn away from doing these things.
   2. **Thanks.** We must thank Jesus for loving us and dying for our sins.
   3. **Ask.** We must ask him to forgive us and be the Saviour and King of our lives. It is like opening the door of our hearts to him. He will then come into our lives.

DAY 5   Subject: Follow-up, growing in Christ

1. Commence with a clean board. Draw as you speak. When we ask Jesus to be our Saviour we become a part of God's family. Just as we come into our own families by being a baby, we come into God's family the same way. What is important for babies to do? Grow! By reading and feeding on God's Word, we grow in God's family. God also wants to talk to us, so we need to listen to what he has to say as we read the Bible. (Draw Bible-arrow.)

2. Of course we will want to talk to God and tell him we love him, confess our mistakes, ask for forgiveness, and ask his advice. (Draw Prayer arrow.)

3. And what is the place on top of the hill? Yes, a church. We need to go to church or Sunday school to learn more about God and his Bible and find other Christian friends. (Draw Large arrow.)

4. We also need to tell others about Jesus and his love, and ask them to make him their King, as we have done. (Tell Others-arrow.)

Appendix 'C'

STORIES AND PUZZLE TEXTS
FOR A 5-DAY CHILDREN'S EVANGELISTIC SERIES

Puzzle text explanation	Sketch story and sequence

 **DAY 1**

'All ... have (cave) ... sinned (pinned) ... and (candy) ... fallen ... short ... of (1st and 2nd letters) ... the ... glory (ladder letters) ... of (moth) ... God.'

Noah and the Flood

1. God looked down and saw wickedness everywhere.
2. God told Noah to build an ark for himself and family big enough to hold all the animals.
3. When they were inside God shut the door.
4. The wicked were drowned, the righteous saved.

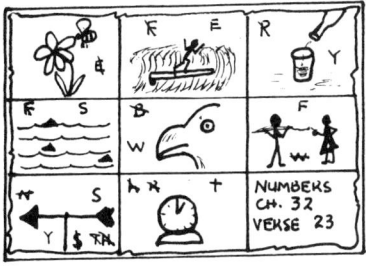 **DAY 2**

Be (bee) ... sure (surf) ... your (pour) ... sins (fins) ... will (bill) ... find (wind) ... you (south) ... out (hour).

Achan's sin at Jericho (Sinners always get caught)

1. Joshua warns the people about taking anything for themselves.
2. Achan steals gold, silver coins, coat, and hides them in his tent at night thinking 'no one sees'.

3. After the defeat at Ai, God reveals the sin.
4. Achan and his family die. Jesus died for us.

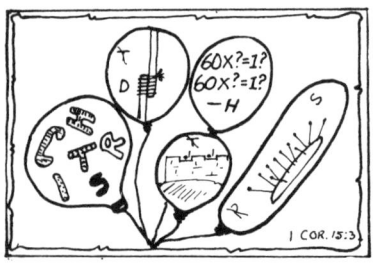

DAY 3

Christ ... died (tied) ... for (fort) ... our (hour) ... sins (pins).

Schamyl, a Russian tribal leader takes the punishment due to his mother.

1. He warns his people of a 50-lash penalty for treason.
2. Is told his mother is guilty. He fasts 3 days.
3. Orders his mother whipped. She takes 5 lashes, he takes her place for the other 45.
4. Jesus Christ took all our punishment.

DAY 4

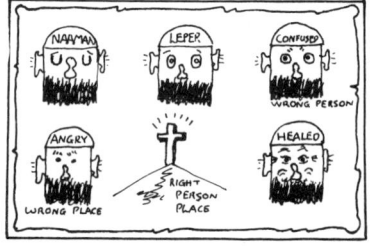

Wash ... me (self portrait) ... and (ant) ... I (lower-case letter) ... shall (shell) ... be (bee) ... whiter (comparison) ... than (only word in puzzle) ... snow (snail).

General Naaman the leper

Prepare the outlines of faces only. Draw the eyes as the story is told.

1. Sad because of leprosy.
2. Hope dawns for a healing by God.
3. Amazement at King of Israel's reaction.
4. Mad at Elisha's instruction to wash in Jordan.

5. Happy after dipping the full 7 times (for sin).
6. The cross of Jesus alone brings us healing.

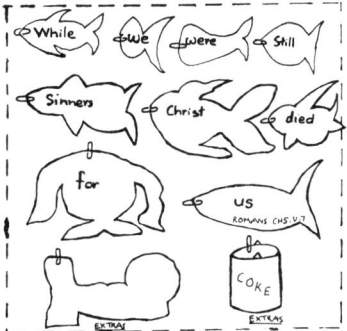

FINAL DAY

(The story of the brazen serpent: Numbers 21:1-9 linked with John 3:14-17)

Light card cut-outs

Write the words on paper and cut out. Attact a paperglide clip. Place behind a screen. A magnet is tied to a 3-ft piece of string attached to the point of an umbrella to make an ideal fishing rod.

As an alternative: Write words on pieces of paper and insert in separate balloons. Select children to blow up and burst balloons. Sort out memory verse.

God must always punish sin. Because of grumbling and murmuring God sent venomous snakes among them and many died. The people confessed—Moses prayed for them—God directed a bronze snake to be make and put on a pole. When people who had been bitten looked at the bronze snake, they were healed.

The Lord Jesus similarly lifted up, and the look of faith will heal all those who suffer the venomous effect of sin.

Family Night

At the conclusion of the five-day children's program, a family night will provide an excellent opportunity for bringing parents and children together. The program should include: the giving of prizes—choruses—a review of puzzle texts of the week—and an illustrated gospel address. Extra items could include a ventriloquial doll used during the week, a film or film strip, graphics, object lessons etc.

An additional five-day program suitable for outdoor or indoor programs has been included in the resources section.

Family-night sketch story of Barabbas

1. Dramatise the arrest of Barabbas for sedition and murder.
2. His preparation for his own cross.
3. The clamour for Barabbas. Jesus to be crucified.
4. The substitution of Jesus for him and us.

Chapter 11

MAKING DO

National workers often lack the finance and equipment of Western missionaries, but experience in developing countries has shown that some pieces of equipment needed in open-air evangelism can be made from local materials at low cost.

1. A portable platform and sketchboard

In Asia there is a lack of Western distinctions between things secular and spiritual. Religious symbols and shrines are everywhere: by the roadside, in public places, factories, and homes. Open-air religious activities are the cultural norm. No-one complains when held up in traffic for some procession of the faithful carrying an icon. It is no wonder that open-air gospel programs do not raise eyebrows as they do in the West. Interest is assured, crowds can be large and normally respond well to learning about life in Christ.

The simple platform shown below has been designed to fit on a car roof rack, or it can be carried by four people into a plaza, bazaar, market or any open space close to a local church. It is lightweight and easy to store.

The sketchboard lifts off the two supports and lies on top of the platform. The two supports also lift out of their wooden sockets and may be carried separately or used as carrying handles for the platform and board through two holes in each side of the platform.

By adding a plywood base to the platform, and making a hinged or lift-off top, the inside may be used to store paints, paper, literature, follow-up material, visual aids and an amplifier.

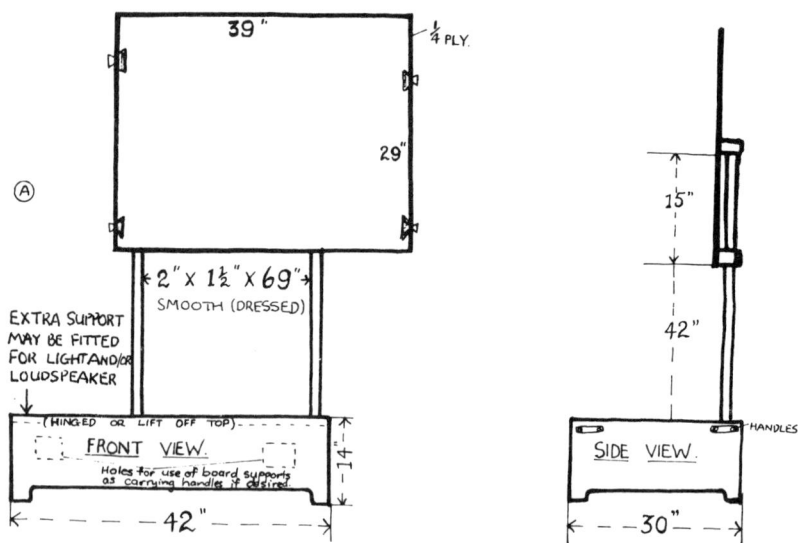

- A nameplate showing your church or mission society should be prepared to fit above the sketchboard, or the height of the board should be increased by three inches to allow for signwriting.

- A third support 2″ x 1½″ x 80″ made to fit into the left front corner of the platform can hold both a loudspeaker and an electric extension light or kerosene lantern for night programs.

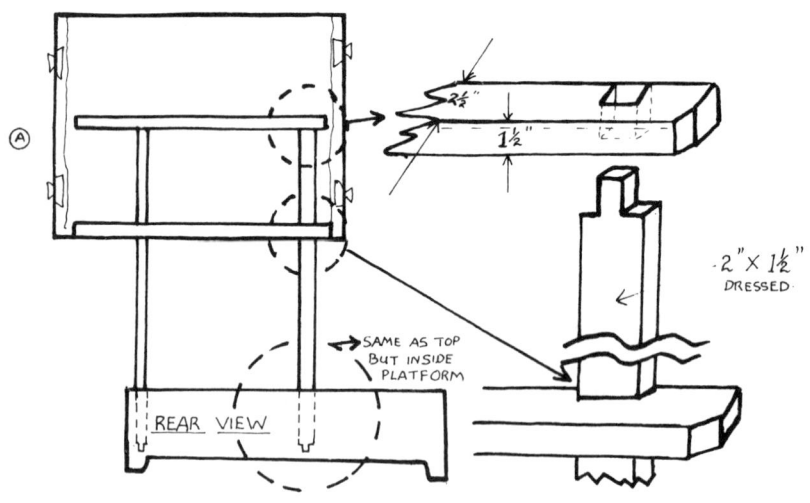

2. Portable sketchboard-and-equipment container

Sketchboards should be varied to suit the size of the paper available. Ideal boards are three feet square, or four feet by three feet, to suit the sizes of the ends of newspaper rolls.

In some countries only offcuts are available. In the Philippines paper is sometimes sized 29″ × 42″, and this limits board size to 29″ × 39″. The construction is simple:

1. Build two wooden frames to the desired size from 2″ x 1″ dressed timber.

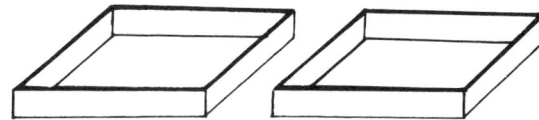

2. Cut two slots in the lower edge of each frame to accommodate the legs. Cover the front with plywood providing for a 1½″ overlap at the outer edges. Drill holes through each leg and frame, in both closed and extended positions, for the insertion of bolts and wing nuts.

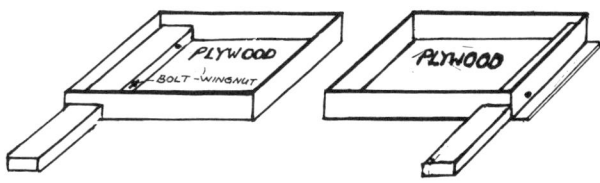

3. Bring the two frames together and join with four small sets of hinges. When the board is closed, fit two catches to hold the two halves together, and a handle for carrying. The inside space is 4″ in depth, and is ideal for carrying paints, chalks and literature.

3. A lightweight timber-canvas combination board

The simplest sketchboard may be made by stretching a piece of canvas over a 2″ x 1″ wooden frame, and nailing it securely on the back of the frame. The supports are held by bolts through the frame underneath the canvas, and secured by wing nuts. The feet are similarly attached and adjusted. Paper is held by clips.

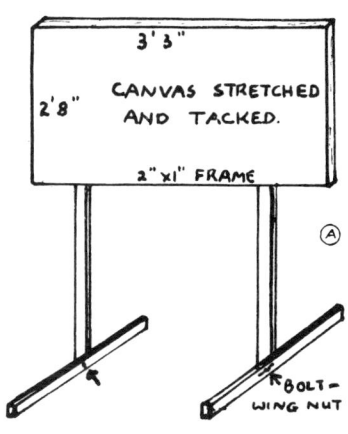

4. Home-made paper clips

An inexpensive paper clip may be made from pieces of masonite, one glass marble, and a strong elastic band. The pieces of masonite are held together with the elastic band twisted several times. A glass marble between the pieces will act as a fulcrum. By applying pressure to the two ends of the clip, the jaws will open to hold the paper securely to the board. Four will be needed for each board.

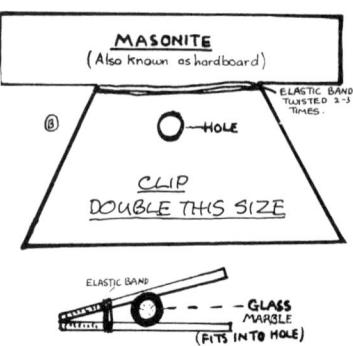

5. Combination chalk and flannelgraph board

Newsprint and paints are not available in every country, but chalks can be found in schoolrooms even in the remotest villages. A simple folder will double as a chalkboard-flannelgraph material holder and textboard.

a. Opened out

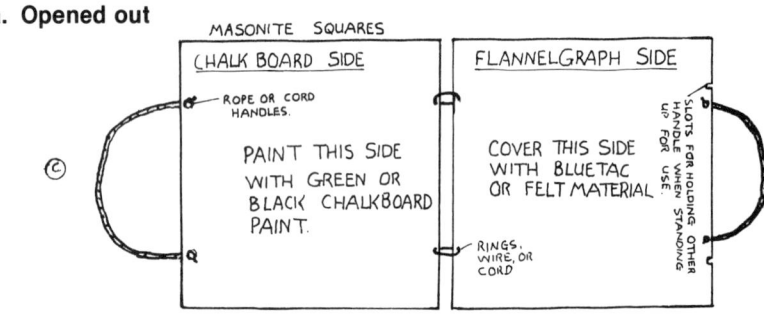

b. Ready for carrying with other materials inside, and text outside.

c. Opened up to stand on a table, chair, car or tree stump, for use as a chalkboard.

166

Acknowledgments:

A. R. Pocklington, OAC—SEND Intl. Philippines.
B. B. W. Tetley, 'Sowers', Philippines.
C. J. Fuller, CLTC, Papua New Guinea.

6. A flashlight battery-operated projector for slides or filmstrips

Before the development of lightweight plastic projectors operated by battery power, this type of equipment was expensive, heavy and restricted to a regular power supply.

Latest developments have changed that. The Crusader Mark 1 projector operates from twelve D-size flashlight cells, has a 25-hour battery life, and may be operated with a daylight screen in the lid of the carrying case. Crusade Mark 2 operates from a rechargeable battery, or from regular car or motorcycle wet cell 12-volt batteries. It uses a quartz-halogen high-density bulb with a projection life of 600 hours and is 5 times brighter than the Mark 1 model.

The equipment is ideal for use in rural, village and mountainous situations. A sheet of white material or paper hung in a tree or attached to a hut wall makes an ideal screen for slide or filmstrip showings. When needed, the projector provides an excellent spotlight for sketchboard messages.

7. An ideal object lesson for the illiterate

Construction details are set out in eight stages using a coconut. The same process can apply to a tin with a lid or a section of bamboo.

Stage 1   Husk the coconut.  Cut it in half and remove flesh.

Stage 2   Burn one hole in each side using a nail or piece of wire heated to red heat.

Stage 3   Cut or burn a slit in the bottom of both halves about 1½ " long and ¼ " wide.

Stage 4   Bend a handle from a piece of wire, or the spoke of a broken umbrella, long enough to go right through the coconut with an extra length to bend the end over about half an inch to keep the handle from slipping out.

Stage 5   Cut strips of coloured ribbon, plastic, or plain coloured material: **Green**—6" x 1"; **yellow, white, red, black**—3" x 1". Attach the colours to one another with cotton, glue, staples, or adhesive tape in the same order. They will then look like this: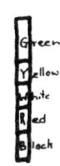

167

Stage 6   Slide the handle through the right-hand half of the nut, and adhesive tape the end of the green ribbon firmly to the middle of the handle. The other colours will then hang down.

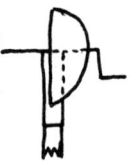

Stage 7   Fit the two halves of the nut together and fasten by means of glue, adhesive tape, wire or string through holes drilled in the edges of the halves. Bend the end of the handle over to hold in place.

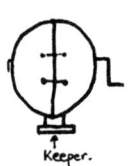

Keeper.

Stage 8   Fix a small piece of wood to the end of the black ribbon so that it cannot be wound inside after use. Wind the colours into the container so that they cannot be seen. Only the wooden keeper at the end of the black should be visible.

To operate

Introduce the subject, then pull on the wooden keeper bringing each colour into view as desired.

Black speaks of the darkness in each heart because of the presence and practice of sin.

Red speaks of the blood of Jesus Christ's atoning death on the sinner's behalf. If animal blood can clean oily and dirty hands, how much more will the blood of Jesus make hearts clean.

White speaks of a cleansed heart filled with the light of the presence of Jesus Christ.

Yellow speaks of the future state of the Christian in glory with his heavenly Father, where there is no darkness.

Green speaks of living and growing, and Christians must grow in Christian experience. Simple illustrations of growth principles can follow.

Even children can make this simple Gospel object lesson. The writer has seen children and adults in the Solomon Islands and India make them quickly with the simplest of materials.

RECOMMENDED READING ON EVANGELISM, COMMUNICATION, OUTREACH

Words on Target, Sue Bartlett
The Gagging of God, Gavin Reid
The Untapped Generation, David & Don Wilkerson (Zondervan)
Living and Learning the Christian Life, G. R. Harding Wood
    (Simplification of Theology etc.)
Taking Men Alive, Charles G. Trumbull (Lutterworth Press)
How to Sin Wouls, Eugene Myers Harusin (Van Kampen Press)

Evangelism and the Sovereignty of God, John Stott (IVF)
The God Who is There, Francis Schaeffer
The Power of Prayer, E. M. Bounds
The Hidden Life of Prayer, D. M. McIntyre
In the Day of Thy Power, A. Wallis
The Kingdom of the Cults, Walter R. Martin
Cults Challenge the Church, James G. Van Buren
The Witness (NT), Kossoff (Collins)
Get Your Hands Off My Throat, David Wilkerson (Zondervan)
Coffee House Manual, David and Ann Wilkerson (Bethany Fellowship Inc.)
20 Ways to Use Drama in Teaching the Bible, Judy Gattis Smith
Who Says God Created, Fritz Ridenour (Gospel Light)
The Christian Persuader, Leighton Ford (Hodder & Stoughton)
On the Other Side, Evangelical Alliance (Scripture Union)
Reaching By All Means (World Wide Publication)
    ICOWE Lausanne
    All People
    All Together
    All the World
    All Power
    All Needs

Open-Air Evangelism

Re-discovering the Open Air, Lt Col Lyell Rader. Ashbury Theological
    Seminary
Outreach (toward effective open-air evangelism), James Northey
    (Salvation Army)
Lectures to My Students, C. H. Spurgeon (Marshall, Morgan & Scott)
Truceless Warfare, W. R. Angus (Marshall, Morgan & Scott) *(Out of print)*
    (The commencement of Open Air Campaigners in Sydney and New
    South Wales, Aust.)
The Truceless Warfare Advances, J. A. Duffecy (Daniels Publishing Co. Inc.)
    (The story of Open Air Campaigners International)

Part 3—INDEX

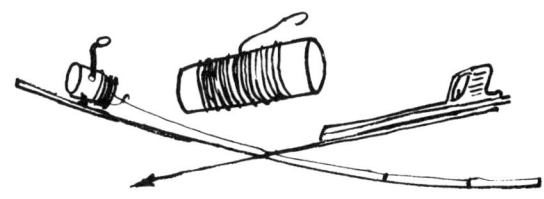

Chapter 1

SPECIALISED PLACES TO FISH

The 'Go' of the Gospel scares many Christians. It is easier to pray with fervour 'Lord bring the people in tonight' than go out and win them where they are. Very few went to Jesus personally, but he went to them where they worked, lived, worshipped, and relaxed. On foot, he criss-crossed the land looking for people who need ministry. He said 'As the Father has sent **me**, I am sending **you**' (John 20:21).

The Gospel belongs to the people. It is God's imperishable food for the hungry, and it needs to be given to them personally, not kept in bulk storage for emergency supply. Open-air evangelism is an ideal way for two or three people or teams to feed the hungry.

1. The evangelistic community religious survey

This is not for church fact-finding or publicity. It opens opportunities to share the Gospel, and is ideal for person-to-person contacts, or for reaching a whole community. When preparing a questionnaire, irrelevant questions about world religions, their leaders and writings, church attendance etc. are better avoided. Those most likely to be answered need to be simple and brief.

Statistics need to be kept for ethical and reference purposes. The word 'survey' suggests evaluation, and local ministers, media representatives and Police may later ask for your conclusions. While these are by-products of the evangelistic objective, they do indicate trends in community attitudes, provide data for outreaches, and comparisons with later surveys.

The final question is designed to open up counselling provided the contact is willing and the time convenient. Four questions which have proved very successful are:

- Do you believe God is personally interested in you?
- Do you believe the Bible has a message for people today?
- Do you believe that Jesus Christ needed to die for the sins of the world?
- Do you know that Jesus Christ is willing to give you a more meaningful experience of life?

The conduct of the survey

1. Place the prepared list of questions on a clipboard together with a sheet of paper prepared for recording answers by a tick under the headings YES – NO – UNCERTAIN for each question.

   A supply of Gospels and literature should be carried, with a notebook and ballpoint pen to record names and addresses of those wanting a further contact, or a visit by a pastor or social worker.

2. As you walk toward your prospective contact, SMILE.

3. Give a friendly greeting, identify yourself by name, say whom you represent, and ask if you might complete the survey by asking the contact four 'yes' or 'no' questions. (This suggests brevity.) It may sound like this: 'Good afternoon, my name is Joe Blow. I represent the local Lutheran Church and I am conducting a community religious survey. May I ask you four **yes** or **no** questions?'.

4. If the answer is 'No', smile, offer a piece of literature and pass on.

5. If 'Yes', proceed with the questions with little or no comment.
   - If the answer to the final question is 'No', ask whether the contact would like to hear what Jesus has done in your life and is willing to do for him or her personally.
   - If the answer is 'Yes' ask when this occurred, and what difference it made. This could lead to counselling for salvation, or discipleship.
   - If the answer is 'Uncertain' offer to share how one can be certain.

   Whenever there is openness or a warm response, proceed to share Christ through your 'evangelistic' personal testimony, and your personal counselling method.

6. If you discern a person is hurting, seek to relate your experience of Jesus Christ to his or her need. Don't forget the follow-up contact.

2. The spiritual opinion poll

This is a free-and-easy evangelistic approach in which people are simply asked for their opinions on three questions. The approach is similar to the survey. The following questions have proved successful:

- 'We live in a so-called Christian country. In your opinion, who or what is a Christian?'
- 'In your opinion, how would a person go about becoming a Christian if he/she wished to?'
- 'Would you mind if I gave you a booklet which clearly shows what the

Bible says about how a person may become a Christian?'

The answer and attitude to the final question may open up an opportunity to share Christ.

3. The door-knock

The Mormons and Jehovah's Witnesses have certainly reaped a huge harvest by this method while the Church has stood idly by. Many Christians will not use the door-knock method of community evangelism for fear of receiving a hostile reception. Actually this seldom happens with the right approach. Many people can be won to Christ and lonely Christians encouraged by door-to-door visitation.

1. **Preparation**

   Obtain all the materials you need for your selected approach such as survey forms, tracts, or counselling booklets. Systematically plan how to cover your target area, then spend time in prayer, claiming protection from all evil, including dogs!

2. **Presentation**

   - If working in pairs, an inexperienced person should learn by going with one who is experienced. Couples may be mixed, but husbands and wives should work together. Taking the paper or milk bottles to the door is a friendly gesture, but avoid touching mail.
   - Knock firmly but with restraint. (Loud and urgent knocking will frighten some women.) Turn and face the street to give the person answering the door the advantage of seeing you first.
   - When you hear the door open, turn, smile, give a pleasant greeting, adding a compliment on the flowers or garden, if it can be genuinely given.
   - Give your name, the group you represent, the purpose of your visit, and if there is no immediate objection commence your survey, poll, or presentation. Don't force yourself on people, leave pleasantly if they object. In some cases you may be invited to return and share with other members of the family. Unless it is obviously a safe contact young ladies should take a male escort with them on a return visit. If the Lord has blessed your time of sharing, or there is an obvious need, pray before leaving. You do not need to close your eyes, in fact in some situations it may be advantageous to leave them open.
   - Take a note of the names and addresses of people who respond to Christ, those who need social help, or those who request a pastoral visit.

3. **Precautions**

   - Be sensitive about keeping a person at the door. Mealtimes, children calling for attention, the conversations of visitors, ringing telephones and whistling kettles are all signs of an inconvenient time to talk. Offer to call again.
   - If you are alone, be sensitive to the witness of the Spirit of God,

and generally avoid being alone in a house with a person of the opposite sex. This may vary with elderly persons.
- Small talk may be useful to establish confidence or friendship. Remember the objective of making Christ known and let small talk be a servant, not a master.

4. Literature distribution

Paul had one motto for all evangelism. 'By all possible means' (1 Corinthians 9:22). Tract distribution may not appeal to everyone, but it sure appeals to those who have come to Christ through its use.

A member of the Mafia was waiting for trial in a Los Angeles hotel room. He decided to commit suicide. He opened the window, then paused, deciding to go for one last walk round the block. Someone pushed a tract into his hand as he passed an OAC street meeting. Back in his room and ready to jump, he remembered the crumpled tract in his pocket. He smoothed it out, read it, then shut the window as a new hope flickered somewhere inside him. The next time OAC was in the street he listened. That night Christ turned him into a new man and at his trial the pastor and members of his church testified to the change in his life. The judge was so impressed he handed down a suspended sentence.

Preparing the literature

Make sure the tracts are easy to read and understand. They should present the way of salvation adequately. Choose those with Bible verses written in full rather than quoting references (for those without Bibles), and that explain what a person needs to do to trust Jesus Christ as Saviour and Lord. Tracts that tell people to have faith, or believe, need to explain these words from a Biblical point of view to be effective.
- Literature should be attractive, neatly folded, clean, and have a contact address for enquiries.

Distributing the literature

The Positives
- Look as if you enjoy being a Christian.
- Look people in the eye as you speak.
- Smile—you can afford to, and they may need it.
- Speak as you offer the literature, something like this:
   'For you, Sir (Madam).'
   'Excuse me, I would like to give you this.'
   'Would you care to accept this?'
   'I'm sure you would like one of these.'
- If people ignore you, refuse, or get cranky, take it pleasantly and keep smiling.
- Pick up any tracts lying around afterwards. It may save problems with local authorities.

The Negatives
- Don't frown or look worried; get right with the Lord before going out.

- Don't mumble or shout; speak pleasantly.
- Don't lunge at people by treating a tract like a sword. Offer it in a friendly manner.
- Don't argue or show resentment if people are unpleasant.
- Don't block people's path in order to force literature on them.
- Don't use the word 'tract'; it sounds religious, try 'booklet' or 'literature'.

People of all ages can give out tracts. Older folk are disarmed when children offer Gospel tracts. They don't like to refuse. The writer's grandmother, in her seventies used to walk to church so that she could put tracts in letter boxes.

Never overlook the potential of a single Gospel tract. A girl once gave a missionary on furlough a penny she had saved, asking him to buy some tracts to take back to his mission field. The missionary bought one good quality tract, with the purpose of giving it to someone special because it expressed a little girl's love and sacrifice. Back on the field a fine young black man with a leopard skin across his shoulder attracted his attention, so he gave him the tract and promptly forgot the incident. Some time later the young man returned, looking for the missionary. He told him he had come to know Jesus as his Saviour through the tract, and as the new chief of his tribe he had come to ask the missionary to visit his people and tell them more about Jesus.

A church bulletin of unknown origin suggests six good reasons for using a piece of literature:

- It reaches the most secluded places and is afraid of no-one.
- It travels cheaply and has few passport or visa problems.
- It usually catches a person in a receptive mood, for it speaks only when he chooses to listen.
- It never gets discouraged and works 24 hours per day.
- It speaks for as long as it exists, and repeats its message over and over again.
- It delivers its message at school, office, factory and home, and disregards jeers and insults.

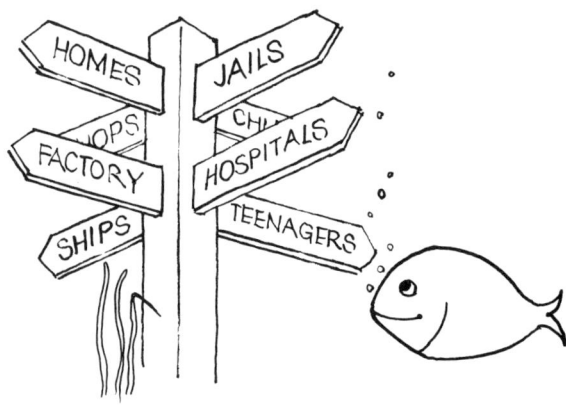

Chapter 2

TRY THESE FISHING GROUNDS

Some fishermen love to fish in a pounding surf, or from a spray-drenched rock. Others like a boat in a heaving swell waiting for the big ones that fight. Others again prefer a restful day on a placid lake where a limit catch is guaranteed in exchange for time and patience. To all types, the sight and sound of water is sufficient to cause them to reach for the rod and reel. In the same way those who have a heart of love and concern for the lost are stirred to want to fish for souls every time they see a group of people together.

The following methods of evangelism may appeal to those who prefer the more 'tranquil' fishing spots to the rigours of the open sea. If these are to your liking, why not try them?

1. Evangelistic home meetings

Much of the early church evangelism took place in private homes. 'Day after day, in the temple courts and from house to house, they never stopped teaching and proclaiming the good news that Jesus is the Christ' (Acts 5:42).

Despots and demons have stamped out visible church witness in some countries but they have never stopped its growth. It has simply gone indoors.

A volume of excellent material is available on the conduct of home cell or church growth groups but these are different from the use of private homes for a Gospel reachout to relatives, friends and neighbours. Modern missions often use the church sanctuary for weekend meetings, and private homes for informal women's daytime programs and family evangelism at night. The relaxed and friendly atmosphere helps the missioner establish personal relationships, and invites questions people would never ask in a normal church service.

The hostess plays an important part in evangelistic home meetings by inviting her friends and neighbours and by providing refreshments. This is a test of her Christian witness. She also has to live with the results after the missioner leaves!

If the speaker is not known to the hostess, some inexpensive publicity materials which include a personal profile, details of supporting items and the time and place of meeting will help create interest.

Here are some guidelines regarding format

- As guests arrive, the hostess should introduce them to the speaker and team members. Given names are normally used except with older folk.
- If refreshments are being served first, this will help set an informal atmosphere. When coffee and biscuits are to be served after the message, some hostesses like to provide cold drinks with saviouries or nuts beforehand. There should be no obligation to provide refreshements, to avoid possible financial embarrassment.
Refreshments are not essential to creat informality, as those from the neighbourhood often know one another, and strangers will soon be drawn into conversation while other guests are arriving.
- The program should commence on time or when the majority of the guests have arrived. The speaker or team leader, having been formally introduced by the hostess, should suitably reply, introduce fellow team members and commence with personal warmth, humour and interest. Early features could include guest singers, musical items, country-and-western artists, a good colour-slide presentation, even object lessons with a touch of mystery. This will prevent guests from thinking: 'This is shaping up to be a heavy religious deal, what excuse can I make to escape?' Singing and musical items should be used throughout the program to avoid a 'heavy' atmosphere build-up.
- An ideal method of helping people to relax is to get them to talk about themselves, commencing with their names and places of birth. The period for interaction needs to be watched carefully to leave sufficient time for the Gospel message. Guests should be allowed to say 'pass' if they do not wish to answer any question. Some of the popular questions being used are:
    'Where were you born? How many brothers and sisters did you have? How many in your family now?'
    'What did you like doing most at the age of . . .?'
    'What do you like doing most, now?'
    'What was the centre of human warmth in your home?'
    'What is your aim in life?'
    'What has been the best thing to happen to you this year?'
    'Say one nice thing about yourself.'
    'If there was one thing you would most like to happen to you now, what would it be?'

- The gospel message should be conversational in style, but direct and challenging. A question and answer session may follow, depending upon time and interest. A sketchboard or visual aid approach is ideal.
- A challenge to repentance, faith and discipleship should be made at the end of the message, but avoid a church-type altar call. The friendly home atmosphere calls for a low-key approach, such as materials being offered to people who indicate that they did receive Christ, or wish to. Alternatively, envelopes containing a Gospel tract, letter of explanation and basic follow-up steps may be left in a prominent place to be taken.
- Gospel literature should also be available or given out as the speaker wishes. Tracts should have a clear Gospel message explaining simply what needs to be done to have life in Christ.
- If refreshments are being served, the speaker and team members should mingle with the guests looking for those who have responded to Christ or who may wish to do so taking every opportunity for further sharing or counsel.
- Appreciation should be expressed to the host and/or hostess for the hospitality, and to the guests for coming.

Sometimes coffee meetings are held in the homes of non-Christians. The speaker's conduct should commend the Gospel otherwise what he says may sound a little hollow.

2. Indoor industrial evangelism

Industrial management often resist an evangelistic approach with two excuses. The first is that religion and business should never be mixed. The second is that whoever wants to be religious should go to church on Sunday in his own time. Both are the devil's lies. People are not divided into watertight compartments, and true religion is a life not a visit to church.

The industrial evangelist can expect a very mixed reception in the industrial world. Some industries will not allow speakers of any kind during meal breaks. Others will not have political or religious speakers for fear that prejudice and intolerance may disrupt industrial relationships. Some executives laugh boisterously at a request to preach the gospel, particularly those whose lives are devoted to sex, alcohol and making money. They feel threatened by a preacher of righteousness, and react defensively. But there are many in management who give their fullest cooperation because they believe the gospel will not harm, but may even help, their employees.

The devil has a third lie reserved for Christians. Industrial evangelism can't be done. Don't believe it! It can be done. Certainly, there are obstacles, but they can be overcome, and that makes it all the more of a challenge. The experience of reaching non-church attenders and winning some for Christ is very rewarding. In fact, in industry a worker can reach more unbelievers in one week than would voluntarily go to the average church in one year.

1. Obtaining permission from the management

In order to be able to preach indoors, permission must first be obtained from management. In small businesses this does not present a problem as the manager is usually in a front office, or can easily be found in the factory. Where a foreman is in charge, he can usually be paged. The most difficult places are industrial complexes. Ask to see a senior executive who has the authority to make final decisions; otherwise you may get the run-around with junior staff who will have to go to the top finally. Give a visiting card with some basic details about yourself and your ministry to the receptionist. This will prepare the executive for your approach:

- Introduce yourself (and the name of any group you represent), then ask for permission to speak to the employees during the lunch hour or coffee break, subject to the employees' own approval. You will need the wisdom of the Lord to express your priority (the gospel) in terms which will not turn him off. Over many years in this ministry the writer has found that a card with the word 'Evangelist', 'Industrial Chaplain' or similar wording, and a request to speak 'about the things which matter most in life', convey all that is necessary. Very few ask for more details, but if they do there should be no hesitation about using the word 'gospel'. A copy of the tract you intend using should be left with management as a personal witness, and as a proof that everything is being done openly. The tract, *The Answer in 20 Minutes* was written by the author specifically for industrial evangelism, although it enjoyed a much wider circulation.

- During the interview, make sure it is understood that any permission given will have to be confirmed by the employees, as you realise that what the staff do in their own time is *their* business. The last thing management want is for the employees to feel that they are having 'religion' pushed on them.

- The following questions and answers have been drawn from dialogues with industrial management and may help you to be prepared:

1. **Question** 'Why can't people go to Church if they want religion? Why must they have it stuffed down their necks at work too?'

   Answer 'Because Jesus Christ didn't say that people had to go to church to hear the Gospel. It is the church's responsibility to take it to them. If Jesus were to come back again he would do the same as he did before—go looking for people wherever he could find them. He might find few in church.'

2. **Statement** 'I am sure my employees wouldn't be interested.'

   Answer 'I wrap the message up in an interesting package (with music, object lessons, visual aids) and if they don't like it, they will tell me to go.'

3. **Statement** 'But we have a lot of Catholics (Jews - Moslems - Mormons etc.) here and I wouldn't want them upset.'

   Answer 'No worries, I don't speak about church, I only want to talk about Jesus and they all respect him.'

4. **Statement** 'We don't have a very long lunch (coffee) break.'
   Answer 'That's fine, I can say all I want to say within that time, and have some to spare.'

5. **Question** 'What good will it do them?'
   Answer 'An employee at peace with God will be a more profitable worker, and will relate better to his workmates.'

6. **Statement** 'I'll get the union delegate to ask the men whether they want to listen.'
   Answer 'With due respect, I would prefer to do that myself. The delegate will probably say 'some Bible-basher wants to come and earbash you guys on religion. You don't want that do you?' The answer has got to be 'NO'. But if I go personally and they can see what I'm like and the type of approach I use, the answer will probably be 'YES'.

7. **Question** 'What are you really trying to accomplish?'
   Answer 'First of all, to show people how to trust Jesus Christ as Saviour. Secondly, to break down some of the prejudice against the Gospel and Church. Thirdly, to try and help people at their point of need.'

- When management can't decide whether to say yes or no, throw in one or two of these:

   'We do not take a collection, or ask for money.'
   'We keep rigidly to time. Taking employee's time is the same as stealing money.'
   'If the employees do not give permission, we will leave immediately.'
   'I am here to speak for Jesus Christ, not represent one particular church.'

- Remember that time is valuable to highly salaried executives. Be brief, and leave before you are shown the door.

- When permission is granted, make sure you know where the lunch room is, or if none is provided, where the employees sit during the break. Find out the duration of the break so that you finish before the whistle blows.

2. **The approach to the employees—indoors**

Allow them time to settle before walking into the lunchroom or cafeteria. This will give stragglers time to get their coffee and sit down. The recommended approach is:

- Greet everyone in your friendliest manner. Tell them your name, if necessary whom you represent, and explain that management have allowed you to ask them for permission to speak about the things which count most in life (or your own words) but that they must agree to this. Before asking for that permission, give yourself an advertising boost by explaining anything you do which will be eye- or ear-catching. It stimulates interest.

- To obtain permission, smile, look round the group and say, 'I am sure you won't mind me doing this?' Look for the slightest sign of approval. It may be from only one person—a nod or smile—but in the absence of anyone speaking against it, take it as consent, thank them and commence. In asking for permission don't be negative such as asking 'Do you mind?' Make your question positive, anticipate approval and you will generally get it, even by the consent of silence. A friendly approach will usually bring the fence-sitters onto your side by the time you have finished. Should some object, all is still not lost. Ask them whether they have had some bad religious experience which has turned them off. It may open up a profitable dialogue or a chance to share your testimony. The reasons given are often second-hand, poorly thought-out, or straight out excuses. Keep your cool, and don't argue. If you are unsuccessful, offer literature to those willing to receive it before leaving. Occasionally some who object will not want to spoil it for others, and will go elsewhere so that you can preach to the rest of the group. Don't forget to thank them.

3. The conduct of the Gospel program

- Program contents can be made up from suggestions in Part 1. They should be interesting, positive, communicating, suitable for the group being reached. Conclude by challenging the hearers to repentance, faith and discipleship, explaining the steps clearly. Altar calls are not for industry. Those who respond inwardly may be invited to speak with you as you distribute literature.
- Thank the group for their attention.

Some suggestions from experience

- Make arrangements for indoor programs in advance to avoid delays when management is away, or engaged when you call.
- Always respect private property and avoid trespassing.
- Keep within the available time.
- Keep your word, and don't preach the Gospel unless you get at least token permission. Settle for a personal conversation.
- Avoid controversy, criticising any church or pastor, running down missions, other religions, or those whose views are different to yours. Point to Christ alone.
- Always show your respect to the Gospel you preach by your behaviour and attitude.
- Messages which have the greatest appeal to women employees concern God's love, security, forgiveness, peace and companionship. Men like apologetics, scientific, topical, and hard-hitting messages.
- Wrap your message in an interesting package and people will gladly take it away.
- Wherever you stand to preach, make sure you are not blocking a doorway, an entrance to the cafeteria, or a sports facility such as a dart board.

- Don't turn off a blaring lunch room radio, a polite request will usually have someone do it for you.
- Avoid giving any impression that you are strongly on the side of either management or workers on any subject. It may block a return visit.
- Aim to have a cup of tea or coffee with the workers, even if they won't let you preach. It will build friendships, and may open the way for you to return and speak to them some other time. The writer knows an OAC evangelist whose initial approach to factory workers was to ask for a cup of tea, then introduce the Gospel as they drank and chatted together. If you have been well received, ask if you can return some time.
- A five-minute message in a ten-minute coffee break could mean the difference between life and death for someone.
- Tape-recorded modern music and Gospel songs make a good start to an industrial gospel program, especially by popular born-again singing or musical personalities.
- Be open to the Holy Spirit's guidance with all groups. Forget your planned program if a profitable dialogue session opens up, or if questions are asked which lead directly to sharing the Gospel.
- Some questions can be deferred until after the message knowing that there will be insufficient time to complete the answers. If an invitation to return is not given, one should be requested. The writer has visited the same group of workers day after day for up to a week, using this sanctified tactic!
- Finally, on warm days, many employees sit outside rather than use a lunchroom. If they are on public property, no approach needs to be made to management, but try and get the friendly nod from the group.

3. Prison evangelism

A prison certainly provides a captive audience for evangelism, but there is no guarantee it will be a captivated audience. The lust, greed, hatred, bitterness and violence of the outside world are in a highly concentrated and sometimes very volatile form when men are shut away from society. The gospel which attracts prisoners must assure them that Jesus can free them from the grip of sin and give strength to resist the peer pressures and stand-over tactics so common to prison life. They need to be convinced that Jesus will not only make and keep them clean and decent for the remainder of their term, but will help them in the dangers of readjustment to cilvilian life.

Opportunities for evangelism depend upon the attitudes of prison authorities and chaplains. Most prisons will be open to visits from acceptable groups. Gospel films, music groups, singers, visual aids, sketching and object lessons are ideal for communication provided they do not overshadow the gospel.

Bible discussion groups are ideal for establishing one-to-one contacts, and dealing with issues peculiar to prison life.

1. Negative attitudes to be overcome

- The inevitable 'chip on the shoulder'. Many inmates develop strong resentment towards the society which caused them to be shut away for breaking its rules. It takes time and patience to develop a friendly trustful relationship.
- Some will claim they have been victimised by the Police; their sentence is far greater than they deserved; or they are innocent of the crime for which they were convicted. They look for sympathy, but they need salvation.
- The opinion that Christian workers are 'a soft touch'. The evangelist must show love and concern, and help where he can, but avoid traps set by the insincere.
- Inmates are under intense moral pressures. To break from 'special relationships' for the sake of Jesus Christ could put their lives in real danger.
- Many have a genuine fear of what other prisoners may say or do to them if they show interest in the Gospel. Responses may be kept secret until they complete their sentences.

2. The positive influences which assist the Gospel presentation

- An intense loneliness and desire for friendship because of being shut away from family and friends.
- Genuine repentance and a sincere desire for a new start in life.
- Plenty of time to read Christian literature.

3. Guidelines to preaching and personal work

- Be humble and sincere in presenting Christ, treating prisoners as people for whom Christ died.
- Be strictly impartial and show no favouritism.
- Refrain from enquiring as to a prisoner's crime. It is very difficult to be objective in dealing with a prisoner whose crime would revolt you, if known.
- Choose your preaching and personal work illustrations carefully to avoid offending those who are already very sensitive about having served time.
- Remember there are two sides to every story. Avoid the temptation to believe everything you are told, without checking it out first.
- Do not get emotionally involved in a prisoner's personal or home situation. Let the Lord be the burden-bearer. Let him stand between you and those you help.
- Be candid and to the point, with Christian grace.
- Be prepared for disappointments but not shattered by them. Some may need to be helped time and time again before their faith becomes stable.
- Immediate follow-up after release from prison is essential for continued progress. Those who have grown to feel secure as Christians inside prison sometimes feel very insecure when released.

Prison evangelism is ideal for Bible discussion groups, film ministries, personal evangelism, and Bible study courses. For a selection of program contents, refer to Part One.

4. Hospital visitation

Hospital evangelism can be both rewarding and frustrating for personal workers and patients alike. There was a day when well-meaning people were free to go from bed to bed with a cheery 'Are you saved, brother?', leaving a paper trail of the blessings of heaven and the perils of hell. Changed nursing techniques, hospital regulations, and full-time chaplains have mostly changed this. But people who are sensitive to the situation and who co-operate with nursing staff are still able to visit patients who have no visiting relatives or friends, or who do not belong to a recognised church.

Gospel programs are usually restricted to children's and geriatric wards, or to seasons of special significance such as Christmas and Easter, so personal contact remains the most effective way of reaching patients with the gospel.

The following guidelines may be helpful:

- Be sensitive as to the right time to visit. Screens around a bed – the presence of medical personnel – an oxygen mask – visitors present – are all signs of an inconvenient time.
- Observe hospital visiting rules and do not antagonise nursing staff. Enquire at the ward desk for the most appropriate patients to visit.
- Understand that a patient's mental, emotional and spiritual response will be influenced by pain and medication.
- Show a warm interest in everyone in a ward rather than concentrating on one individual.
- If you wish to share the Gospel, you would be well advised to avoid the natural question 'How are you?' You could be treated to a stitch-by-stitch or pill-by-pill account, and find it's time to leave without having shared the Gospel.
- Be sensitive in speaking about death, particularly with a terminally-ill patient. Patients should be left with the positive assurance of what Christ can do for them rather than fear of death.
- Don't be a health hazard. Talking greatly wearies some patients. Minister Christ to them by your presence, the quality and brevity of what you say, and your smile. Leave them with the warmth of the presence of Jesus.
- Pray for patients discreetly. Never embarrass them by how and what you pray. If they prefer screens, use them.
- Do not force yourself or literature upon anyone. That deep sleep may be put on because they saw you coming!
- Quote a verse of scripture or pray briefly over an unconscious patient. It is never a waste of time. The mind's hearing and memory system never shut down.
- Select and distribute literature appropriate to the need.

5. Camping ground and caravan (trailer) park evangelism

In many Western countries there is almost a mass-migration of city people to country and seaside areas during public holidays and vacation time. Their tents and mobile homes offer excellent opportunities for reaching families with the Gospel. Holiday resorts are generally controlled by local authorities or private enterprise, and permission needs to be received and arrangements made in advance to conduct Gospel programs. Experience has shown that the greatest benefit comes from living among them as well as preaching to them. But effective visitation evangelism is certainly possible, particularly on a regular basis.

Three types of evangelism are possible:

1. **Day-time children's programs**

   Timing depends on local activities particularly if swimming is a major draw-card. An early start after breakfast is an ideal time provided late sleepers are not disturbed. The rest of the day is usually given over to family activities, and it is difficult to gather children together on the beach if they are scattered, or involved with their families.

2. **Evening family programs**

   The best time to reach families is after the evening meal. A children's program should commence about an hour before it gets dark, ending in time for a brief break before the adults' section commences. This gives parents, family members and other campers time to bring their folding chairs and rugs and settle in.

   The second program should be planned for teenagers and adults. Travel films and cartoons make a good introduction, followed by individual or group singing or musical items, personal testimonies, visual aids and a clearly presented sketchboard message. The timing of the Gospel message before the film makes sure that anyone who leaves before the final challenge will have already heard the Gospel. The evening concludes with a Gospel film in which the words 'The End' are not screened. Instead a spotlight is directed on the preacher, or compere, who explains how to receive Christ as Saviour. Those who do so or would like to, should be invited to speak with the preacher or some person afterwards. Voluntary helpers should mix with the people as they disburse, offering prepared materials and doing personal work.

   Materials should also be placed where people can take them without any sense of obligation or embarrassment.

   One word about the compere. He is responsible for introducing items and those taking part, and for the spiritual tone and the general impact of the program. He needs to use humour like salt, comments like seasoning, love and grace like gravy, and know how to present the whole program as a most satisfying spiritual meal.

3. **Visitation of tents and caravans**

   Daytime visits to campers using surveys, opinion polls or tracts will open up many opportunities for conversation and counsel, particularly among those who have attended the night programs. When team members are accommodated in the same area every year warm friendships soon develop.

One advantage of holiday resort evangelism is that people are more relaxed away from home, have time to talk, and don't have to tell you who they are.

Some of these areas have semi-permanent residents for most of the year, and are wide open for local church visitation and Gospel witness.

6. Shipboard evangelism

Shipboard evangelism is really a combination of industrial, home meeting, and personal evangelism. It is not a ministry for the faint of heart, but those who do it count the blessings far above the disappointments.

The Master or Chief Officer must be approached to obtain permission for any activities on board. In some ports chaplains to seamen visit ships to advise of local recreation facilities and distribute publicity materials, but seldom for the purpose of preaching the Gospel.

1. Messroom evangelistic programs

These are held in the same way as industrial programs. The major difficulty is that meal times are usually spread to cover shifts, and a number of programs may need to be held to reach all the crew.

2. Cabin contacts

This is where caution is needed, as certain women from the local red light district may be hawking their wares from cabin to cabin. They certainly regard Gospel preachers as a threat to their livelihood! Sleeping night-shift workers also don't take kindly to being wakened by well-meaning personal workers. Despite this, cabin contacts can be exciting. Souls can be won and lonely Christians greatly encouraged.

3. Evening programs in a lounge

Despite shore attractions, many seamen stay on board, and good numbers will often turn up for a Gospel variety program. Films (dependent upon the language of the sound track), music, singing, visual and sketchboard messages are ideal for these situations.

4. Casual contacts

Seamen are a mixed lot. It is not unusual to find English-speaking officers with foreign-speaking crews. With records, cassettes and literature in a variety of languages, it is possible to share the gospel without being able to hold a personal conversation. Seamen who would not stop to listen to a gospel preacher at home will gladly listen to the gospel in their mother tongue in a foreign country.

Using an outline of Buddha's Turning Of The Wheel Of The Law and the eight steps to Nirvana, the writer once preached to a number of Buddhists on a cargo ship. After the ship had sailed a letter was received from one crew member saying he had received Christ as his Saviour, and that others were interested. On another occasion, while at sea, at the chaplain's request the Gospel was shared with crew members late at night in a messroom close to the engine room. The ships that crowd the sea lanes of our world carry countless thousands of men and women who desperately need the gospel, but seldom hear it.

7. Teenage evangelism

The older the world becomes the younger is the average age of its inhabitants, close to a majority at present being under 25 years of age.

Teenage years are becoming increasingly filled with tensions and fears. More and more young people find themselves either in positions of responsibility once reserved for older people, or lost in the unemployment maze.

Their needs

The restlessness shown by young people needs understanding rather than criticism. Frustrated by the generations they follow, confused by competing philosophies, controlled by drugs, sex, and the occult, they desperately need help more than advice. Their militancy in minority groups is merely an outlet for their pent-up frustration. Jesus Christ alone will satisfy such needs as:

1. the need to belong to something significant.
2. the need to play a significant role within that group.
3. the need for a deep sense of security.

Some suggestions to reach young people

- Show them genuine love. If you are older than they are, do more listening with the mouth closed than talking with the ears closed. Don't allow the so-called generation gap to keep you from learning from one another. The use of a Christian name is friendly, and should not cause lack of respect. Respect comes from how you present yourself rather than a title you use.
- Don't be upset by noise and big talk. It is supposed to impress.
- Keep programs on the move, and use music that appeals.
- Young people like testimonies and good illustrations, but never long or complicated sermons.
- Use humour to bring them on your side but not to be smart and turn them off. Don't take yourself too seriously. Enjoy a laugh with them against yourself.
- Read youth magazines and talk to their social workers if you want to know what makes them tick. Say things in an unusual manner, and talk with them, not at them.
- Don't make them sour by making a fool of them, embarrassing them, or talking them down.
- If they razzle you, give as much as you get, provided it is said with a smile.
- They admire a person who knows what he believes and where he is going, but the know-all will be in for a rough time. Sincerity is flawless.
- Be enthusiastic and show some excitement for the life in Jesus Christ.

- Don't try and bluff them, you could easily get caught out. If you don't know, say so.
- Remember that young people are in transit from fantasy to reality. The process may take a little longer for some than others.
- Don't try pat answers, glib formulae, or worn-out cliches. They won't buy them. They have been trained to question and analyse, but need help in formulating ideas.
- Young people often ask for help very obliquely. It may pay to gently probe behind the question before answering.
- Be natural, and be yourself. There is no argument against your experience of Christ even if they cannot explain it.
- Present gospel truths in a straight line, it suits their logic and way of thinking. Don't confuse them in a maze of doctrines and Biblical references.
- If a young person is right, commend him, and stick up for him if necessary. He won't forget.

Suggestions for programs amongst secondary school young people have been made in the following chapter. More materials may be taken from Part 1.

Suggested reading:

Youth Aflame, Winkey Pratney
Jesus Person Maturity Manual, David Wilkerson
A teenager is many people, Brian Hill
Beginning at Zero, Metcalf Collier
Building small groups in the Christian community, John Mallison
Creative ideas for small groups in the Christian community, John Mallison
    Renewal Publications

Chapter 3

FISHING IN SCHOOLS

Secondary education is to each generation of children what the chrysalis is to the caterpillar—an environment of total change. Under mental, psychological, social and physical pressures, boys and girls who enter the system are expected to emerge as sophisticated young adults ready to play their part in society. For their future's sake they need also to be exposed to the claim of Jesus Christ.

Evangelistic opportunities include:

1. Regular classes of religious instruction

Local pastors and church workers taking regular periods of religious instruction in secondary schools sometimes offer these times of instruction to evangelists and youth workers. Where churches work together, combined classes can sometimes be arranged so that much greater numbers can be reached.

2. Ministers' fraternals sometimes provide special opportunities

Where evangelists are church-sponsored, or work in close co-operation with local pastors, a range of activities is possible:

- With the co-operation of teaching staff, a whole school can be reached by combined classes of junior, intermediate and senior age groups.
- Greater numbers can be reached in less time by a seminar approach. Some clergy in Australia have come up with an answer to student disinterest in religious instruction. The weekly teaching period has been replaced by a quarterly seminar lasting half a day. By the use of films and modern teaching aids interest is held and the teaching

189

more effective. These seminars offer great evangelistic possibilities.

- Where good relations exist between clergy and the principal, school assemblies are sometimes made available to a visiting speaker or team.

3. A series of lunch hour programs

School principals may give permission to hold a five-day lunch hour series of evangelistic programs in the auditorium or other suitable area. If these are not available, the series can be held outdoors. Attendance is voluntary but this usually means the interest level is higher.

There are two necessary conditions:

- **A good quality presentation**

  Teenagers cannot be expected to attend just because someone wants to preach to them. They must be both attracted to the gospel presentation and held sufficiently to be able to make a responsible commitment to Christ. The aim is to encourage daily attendance by building interest until the last day, when a challenge to faith and discipleship can be made. To reach this goal, special thought must be given to a strategy for holding a voluntary audience to convince the principal of the viability of the presentation.

- **The willingness of the school principal to grant permission for use of school facilities**

  Not all schools have regular religious education because of a lack of available clergy or qualified lay teachers. Many principals are genuinely concerned at the lack of religious influence in the light of problems associated with learning attitudes, discipline, morals, rising crime rates, drug addiction, and the increasing prospect of unemployment. While they have authority to grant permission for gospel programs, not all are prepared to do so. Some are against the gospel while others are apathetic and will refer your request to higher authorities knowing there is little chance of approval. Evangelists who want permission should make a personal approach to school principals rather than relying on others to do it for them. There are many questions that can only be answered by the evangelist or team leader himself, and these answers are crucial to a positive response.

  A folder containing sample publicity posters, program information, commendations from other school principals and prominent clergy, question sheets, photographs, and samples of counselling materials makes a very helpful promotional aid.

  When permission is given, it is important to work closely with any Christian teachers and Christian groups working on campus. Staff and students can be most helpful in making public-address announcements, encouraging attendance, and putting posters on noticeboards. Christian teachers who attend lunch-time sessions will be a positive influence on discipline.

190

Suggested preparations for a five-day lunch-hour series

1. Enquire whether more students are likely to be reached indoors than outdoors. Climate, local weather conditions, and school lunch-hour activities will decide this.
2. Suitable advertising materials need to be prepared which stimulate curiosity, are eye-catching, easily read and prominently displayed.
3. Ask for an opportunity to promote the programs at a school assembly.
4. An important preparation is to encourage Christian groups operating in the school to greater spiritual involvement with their fellow students. Study groups and instructional sessions should be offered in counselling, follow-up, and the use of a student questionnaire, during the lunch hours of the week preceding the outreach. This stirs interest and encourages the Christians to witness.

   The following questionnaire has been used by OAC staff in Australia. Each student selected should be asked only 2 or 3 questions so that as many as possible may be reached during the week.

   1. (a) Do you believe there is a God?
      (b) How does this affect the way you live?
   2. (a) If there is a God, do you think he is interested in you personally?
      (b) Why?
   3. Has the Bible anything to do with your belief or disbelief in God?
   4. Has the church anything to do with your belief or disbelief in God?
   5. How often do you go to church?
   6. Do you believe in a personal devil?
   7. Do you believe in life after death?
   8. What do you think is wrong with mankind?
   9. What do you think are the biggest problems facing teenagers today?
   10. Are you completely satisfied with your own life now?
   11. Who do you think Jesus Christ is?
   12. Why did Christ die?
   13. How does a person become a Christian?
   14. Do you think it is possible to know God personally?
   15. Some people express the desire to know God personally. Do you ever feel this?

5. Check indoor facilities for blackout curtains, power outlets, and adequate seating.

Program suggestions for the five-day outreach

1. Day One (Monday)

A good music group is an ideal attraction for the first day. If the program is indoors films will always draw well, such as:
• a sporting film with clear testimonies by well-known personalities.
• a scientific film with a strong Christian emphasis.
• a human interest story with a clear Gospel message.

- a film which deals with psychic phenomena from a Christian viewpoint.

The right type of compere is essential. He should have a good sense of humour, a love for teenagers, and be quick on the uptake. He must be friendly in approach and inoffensive in repartee and reply. The compere must be seen to be a credible, vital Christian, worth hearing again. The Gospel should be clear but not weighty. Positive but not boring. If the students enjoy themselves, they will be keen to return.

2. **Day Two (Tuesday)**

Today's program needs to be different to maintain interest. A question and answer session is ideal for student involvement. Arising from research and surveys in Australian high schools, Mr Robert Coyle assembled a questionnaire, 'Something Inside Is Bugging Me'. Students are given sheets of questions and invited to select those they wish to ask. Answers should be given by the leader or a member he selects from a panel. The session should last no longer than 10 to 15 minutes, being stopped when interest is high. Another session can be promised later in the week. The program should conclude with an interesting gospel message, preferably using the sketchboard. Topical subjects are ideal, such as: 'Is there a hell?', 'The end of the world', or 'Life after death'. The questions used in the 'bug' sheet are given in schedule 'A' at the end of this chapter.

3. **Day Three (Wednesday)**

Another change of format will maintain interest level. Try testimonies selected from well-known sporting personalities, young people known to have had a real change of life, teachers, or students from the school. Musical items, another 'bug' sheet session or a good ventriloquial doll routine will lead to a sketchboard message or some good Gospel visual aid to end the session. Advertise the special feature planned for the next day's program.

4. **Day Four (Thursday)**

A second film will keep the interest of regulars and often bring back those who have drifted away. A brief sketchboard message is ideal for a conclusion. (Some examples of sketchboard messages used in Australian High Schools have been included in Schedule 'B' at the end of the chapter.) Before dismissing the students it should be made clear that the final program will have no entertainment features whatsoever. The time will be given to explaining how to become a Christian. This will limit attendance to those seriously interested.

5. **Day Five (Friday)**

The leader should commence with a clear explanation of the way of salvation. This should be illustrated by sketchboard, chalkboard, enlarged diagrams from wellknown counselling books, or overhead projector transparencies.

Those who wish to receive Christ as Saviour may then be invited to:

- say a prayer of repentance, faith and discipleship of their own choice;
- repeat a written prayer passed around, or given verbally;
- or indicate their response by taking prepared counselling materials. As much personal counselling should be done as possible depending on numbers responding and time available.

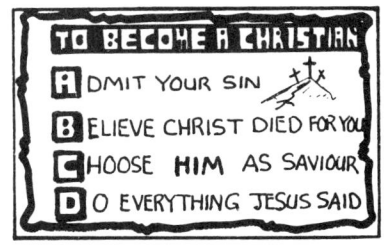

Follow-up should be integrated with Christian student groups and local churches. Where a good number have responded:

1. consider the possibility of commencing a Bible study group in the school if none already exists.
2. ask for permission to visit the converts weekly for several weeks, conducting follow-up classes for Christian growth. Christian study groups in the school may be happy to amend their normal programs for this purpose.
3. consider the long term possibilities of youth rallies, or camps to develop discipleship, but avoid acting independently of local churches.

Suggested rules for the conduct of a five-day evangelistic program

- Do not use high pressure to get responses to Christ. Let the Holy Spirit work, and enquirers will approach you spontaneously.
- Do everything enthusiastically and show the Gospel is exciting news.
- Deal firmly with misbehaviour to keep it from spreading. Do not hesitate to send somebody out of the room if necessary to maintain the right atmosphere.
- Check the exact time of the following day's lunch break. Don't presume it will be the same time each day.
- Make firm arrangements about the key to the auditorium or room you are using, so that you don't find yourself accidentally locked out.
- If you are a confirmed late arriver, give up the idea of High School evangelism. You need to have plenty of time to spare in case of unexpected happenings, and to be ready and waiting to commence as soon as the students arrive.
- Be prepared for your audience to complete their snack lunch while you do your thing.
- There may be a sports day which causes a considerable drop in attendance. Be prepared and plan accordingly.
- Remember to say a personal word of thanks to teachers and students who have helped you. It is a minimum courtesy and may prompt an invitation to return.

Acknowledgments:
R. Coyle—survey questions, bug sheet questions, sketchboard messages.
M. Jensen—program ideas.

SCHEDULE 'A'

The Australian high school bug sheet, which may need cultural adaptation.

A. Bugs about behaviour

1. Is there anything wrong with smoking, drinking and drugs for teens?
2. Do you think that teenagers of today act immaturely because they are not treated like mature adults, but as stupid mixed-up kids?
3. How far should you go with sex?
4. If I swear, does that mean that I'm not a Christian?
5. Why do a lot of parents not understand teens?
6. Do you think that a boy or girl should go out with someone of the opposite sex who is not Presbyterian, Methodist, or Church of England, e.g. Jehovah's Witness, Jewish, Latter Day Saints? Why?
7. Why are 'churchy' people really no different from other people?

B. Bugs about the truth of Christianity

8. Prove to me there is a God.
9. How do you explain the creation story to someone who has studied scientific theories?
10. If God is so great and can do anything, why is there so much trouble in the world today—wars, floods, famines?
11. How do you know Christ ever existed?
12. How do you know Christ is alive?
13. How do we know God is true, and not just made up by these people long ago?
14. Do you think Christians should believe in UFO's and other forms of life?
15. Are there any references to Christ's having a sense of humour in the Bible? Or was he too busy with his serious work and teaching that he never had time to share a joke with his disciples?
16. What's so different about the Bible compared with other books?
17. Why do we have church? Why can't we worship in our homes?
18. Why doesn't the Church get with it?
19. Does the Church agree with modern way-out clothing?
20. Why are there so many denominations if Christianity is meant to unite people?
21. Why is Church so boring?
22. Why doesn't God speak to me?
23. Why doesn't God do a miracle and show himself to me?

C. Bugs about the teachings of Christianity

24. Why does God send people to hell, when he says he loves everyone?
25. What or who is the Holy Ghost?
26. Does God give us a clear conscience and forgive us when we are really sorry?
27. Are Jesus and God two separate people, or are they one person?
28. How do you know there is a devil?
29. Is re-incarnation considered by Christians as a form of eternal life?
30. Will the world ever get better?

31. How can we be sure there is a life after death?
32. What are heaven and hell like?
33. How can Christ mean something to me now, when he lived nearly 2 000 years ago?
34. Why did God create man when he knew he was going to sin?
35. Do good people go to heaven?

D. Bugs about social problems

36. Why does God let children be born handicapped?
37. Do you regard heart transplants as Christians? (Hoping that someone else will die so you can benefit.)
38. What is the Church's view on homosexuality?
39. Do you think the world will ever blow itself to bits?
40. Is there anything wrong with seances, black magic, etc.?
41. Do Christians fight in wars?

E. Bugs about being a Christian

42. How does one become a Christian?
43. 'The results of prayer are not due to divine inspiration, but simply to a positive mental attitude'. What do you think of this?
44. How does a Christian get the best out of life?
45. How do you know you are a real Christian?
46. How can I be sure that God wants me to do something?

SCHEDULE 'B'

Sketchboard messages suitable for High School programs.

1. WHY DID CHRIST DIE?

Christ's death was unique because he as a person was unique. As a lead-in three questions need to be asked and answered.

1. **Who was Jesus Christ?** Speak about his deity as God's Son.
2. **Why did God send his Son?** He alone could deal with man's biggest problem—SIN. Speak about sin and its effects on mankind, and the need for substitution.
3. **Why did he have to die?** Deal with substitution. Christ's death was unique because he is alive today. Explain his claims on our life . . . then make the challenge.

2. THE STORY OF SAMSON

The three things which ruined his life can also ruin the lives of Christians if ignored.

1. **He lost his first love.** Delilah replaced God. Anything that displaces God is an idol. Speak of some.
2. **He lost his strength.** Became weak as water. Speak of habits which beat us. Only Christ gives victory.
3. **He lost his sight.** When idolatry and sin take over we lose our spiritual sight (ability to see God work in our lives).

Conclusion: God met Samson's need when he recognised his need and repented. God will do the same for us if we turn from sin, to him in obedience.

3. JESUS—THE WAY...THE TRUTH...THE LIFE

There are three popular questions asked today. God has the answers.

1. **Where is God?** Jesus ... 'I am the Way'. (a) Who is he? Go through views. He IS God. Take a hard look at Jesus to find answer to this question. (b) Can't see God, because of sin (fill in sketch).
2. **Which one is right?** What Church, philosophy etc. Jesus ... 'I am the Truth'. (Fill in second sketch.) The only way to know ... is to know someone who knows all, and is incapable of lying ... Jesus.
3. **Christianity—so what?** Jesus ... 'I am the Life'. Only Christ can give real life to those who are spiritually dead. The cross means life (fill in sketch). Present the challenge.

4. LOST GENERATION

Introduction: Suicides etc. indicate a world with no purpose in life ... they are lost ... need God, the one who made us, knows how to give purpose.

How do we find God? Bible gives three simple turns.

TURN from SIN. The reason we are lost, lost from God (Is. 53:6) ... sin's effect ... need a Saviour.

TURN to the SAVIOUR. Christ the only one who can save. Why?

TURN straightaway. Necessity to take care NOW.

Picture shadow of cross falls across world, this country, state, room ... claims of Christ now.

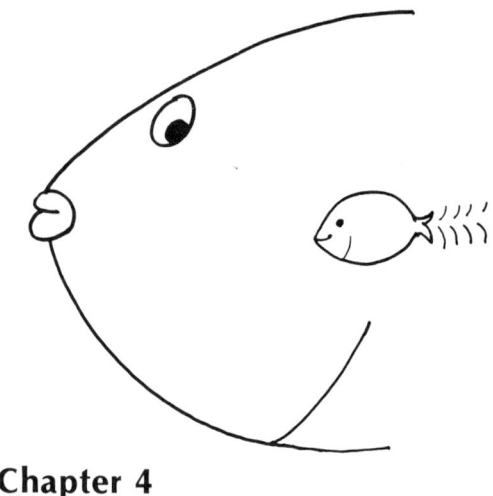

Chapter 4

FISHING THE MINIMUM SIZE
(Children's evangelism indoors)

Children's evangelism indoors certainly has the edge on outdoors:
- cold, rainy, or windy weather doesn't stop children from attending.
- children belong to one district unlike outdoors where many are just visiting.
- contact is made with the same children for a week, most of them attend regularly.
- follow-up is easier, as most of them live close-by.
- parents and family members can be reached at the Family Night program. They will come in the hope of seeing their 'Johnny' get a prize.
- local Sunday schools increase through new contacts.
- larger audiences are usually possible because of advance publicity. Outdoor programs are generally not advertised.

The main openings are:

1. A local Primary School after school hours.

An approach for the use of school facilities should be made to the head teacher. If the applicant is not known personally, some evidence of identity and character needs to be given. Recommendations from other head teachers or the support of a local church or ministers' fraternal will be helpful.

Some governments have established a policy of allowing school facilities to be used by the community out of school hours. This is certainly to the advantage of children's evangelism.

1. Preparations needed
- Obtain the use of a suitably-sized room and washroom facilities

for one hour after dismissal time, Monday to Friday. If possible arrange for a Friday evening family night program.
- Arrange for the children to receive suitable publicity.
  — by public announcement.
  — by speaking to the children at a school assembly.
  — by a leaflet distributed by the teachers during school hours, or by church members after school.
- Head teachers sometimes advise that children should be required to bring their parents' written consent to attend. This will stop parents complaining of their children coming home late without their knowledge, or attending against their wishes.
- Arrangements need to be made for local church helpers to punch attendance cards, help control the children, play the piano, and attend to any personal needs of the children.

2. **Program suggestions**
- The program content is the same as for outdoor programs. One important addition is that each child receives an attendance card to be punched for attendance and various rewards. These include remembering the memory verse, quietness, helpfulness, correct answers, bringing new children, and a host of other activities. Prizes should be given on Family Night to the three highest-scoring boys and girls, both juniors and seniors. Voluntary helpers can punch the cards using inexpensive clippers.
  The attendance card should be prepared with a tear off portion for recording the name, address and Sunday school of each child. A clip should be given to each one completing the slip. The names of those who do not attend Sunday school should be given to a sponsoring or Bible-believing church for contact.
- If the floor is carpeted, no chairs are needed. If chairs are needed they should be put out before each program, making sure that no-one will be facing windows or the sun. All available light should be where the action will be.
- Make sure the program ends on time as parents will be waiting to drive their children home and cleaning staff will be anxious to lock up.
- Family Night invitation cards should be given to the children for their parents at the end of the Wednesday program. To make them more personal, write the names of the parents on each card.
- The invitation to receive Christ as Saviour and the counselling procedures are the same as those covered for outdoor evangelism.

2. A local hall or community centre.

If school facilities are not available, and nearby local churches are not willing to support the programs, local halls can be used. These require more careful preparation:
- Ensure that seating and lighting are adequate, and that the seats are arranged daily by volunteers if there is no janitor.
- See that toilet facilities are open and functioning during the program.
- A suitable advertising banner should be displayed outside the

building, showing the name (such as 'Adventure Time Rallies') and the times of meeting.
- Whenever school principals and staff are unwilling to distribute publicity, a group of enthusiastic local helpers should give the leaflets to the children outside school gates as they leave, the afternoon of the last school day before the mission commences.

3. A church or church hall.

Probably most five-day children's missions and Daily Vacation Bible Schools (holiday missions) are held at the request of local churches or conducted by them in their own facilities. Children of other churches may attend, so programs should always be free of denominational or doctrinal emphases. Parents should be assured that their children can attend without any fear of being influenced away from their own church.

The DVBS holiday program usually has special morning activities added to the regular format. These include sports, handcrafts, film strips, audio visuals, hobby instructions and refreshments. The extra activities are normally conducted by church members. Program details, attendance cards, rewards and seating arrangements are similar to those outlined for local halls.

Finally, the Family Night.

Irrespective of the mission location, a Family Night will draw parents and family members together to hear the Gospel in a way no other program can do. There are some special features to this:
- A review of the choruses, truths and memory texts learned during the week will reinforce the children's memories, and explain the Gospel to the adults.
- A short film or audio visual can be used for entertainment or teaching.
- The distribution of prizes is always a draw card for parents and children alike. The cards are collected and counted during the final afternoon's program, but winners are not announced until the Family Night.
- If a ventriloquial doll has been a daily feature, its appearance will delight all ages.
- A children's message with a clear Gospel challenge aimed at the adults should conclude the evening. Interested parents should be invited to talk afterwards. Gospel literature should be made available.
- If ladies of the church serve light refreshments it will help to build bridges of friendship.

An additional series of puzzle texts and sketchboard messages follows in Schedule 'A'. This means that three five-day evangelistic programs are available. Two may be found in Appendices 'B' and 'C' at the end of Chapter 9, part 2. This will give children's workers a greater selection, or provide materials for three weeks of children's activities.

Appendix 'A'

Puzzle text	**Sketch story**

1st DAY

Text

'All (tall) ... have (shave) ... sinned (tinned) ... against (word from large letters) ... God' (the One Who created the world and caused the Bible to be written) Romans 3:23.

Story: Jonah and the fish lunch

1. Jonah deliberately disobeyed God and paid the fare on a ship for Spain.
2. God caused the storm to have disobedient Jonah thrown into the sea. God knew where he was all the time.
3. Three days and nights in the big fish before being delivered to land.
4. Jonah obeys God—preaches in Nineveh and the people admit their sin and repent.
5. God is willing to save repentant sinners.

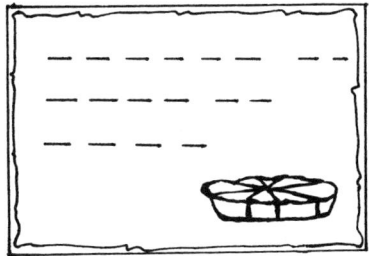

2nd DAY

Text

'Christ is able to save' Hebrews 7:25 (letter guessing versus pie eating).

Story: The only family left alive in Jericho (Joshua chapter 2)

1. Rahab the harlot's reputation ruined by sin.
2. Fearful of victorious army of Israel.
3. Hearkened to the advice of the spies whom she protected.

4. Acted by hanging red cord in window in faith.
5. Was saved by her faith and rewarded by a peaceful place with the people of God.

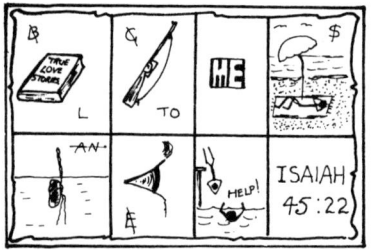

3rd DAY

Text

'Look (book) ... unto (gun-to) ... Me ... and (sand) ... be (bean) ... ye (eye) ... saved' (need of drowning person) (Isaiah 45:22).

Story: Jeremiah and the mud pit (Jeremiah chapter 38).

1. Jeremiah warns the people of judgment (v.1–5). Officials heard and told the king.
2. The officials put him in a dungeon of mud (v.6).
3. Ebed Melech, a palace official, saw them, pleaded with the king.
4. Takes Jeremiah out with ropes. Only Jesus can rescue us from the pit of sin.

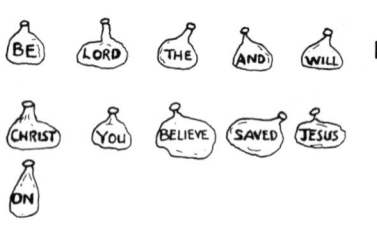

4th DAY

Text

Deflated balloons with the words of Acts 16:31. After the balloons have been blown up and burst arrange the participants into order—'Believe on (or in) the Lord Jesus Christ and you will be saved.'

Story: A sketch story of Matt. 14:23–33. Draw in pictures as story progresses.

1. The disciples in distress.
2. Jesus knew and came down from the mountain—as He came from heaven to save.
3. Disciples frightened (2nd picture). Jesus assures them.

202

4. Peter asked to walk on water—gets eyes off Jesus; sinks; calls out, 'Lord Save Me'. Jesus stretches out his hand and saves Peter, as he will today if we pray same 3 words.

FINAL DAY

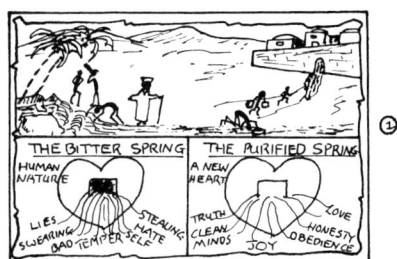

Text

'Create (someone) 'ate' a bite from the sandwich) ... in (pin) ... Me (meat) ... a (first letter of apple) ... clean (use of toothbrush) ... heart.' The words 'O God' may be written in if desired. Psalm 51:10.

Story: Elisha the prophet and the bad water supply. 2 Kings 2:19-22.

1. The bad water made cattle sick and crops wouldn't grow. (v.19) Sin keeps people from being as God intended.
2. The people asked the prophet for help. He threw salt into the spring and said that God himself healed the waters. Jesus himself is the source of the water of eternal life (James chapter 4).
3. A comparison between the sources and results of the springs of the old and new natures.

Family Night: The story Barabbas (Appendix 'C' chapter 2).

Acknowledgments:
1. W. A. Guilford (Winning the Children)
2. N. H. Wyman
3. J. A. Duffecy (Sketchboard Sermons)

Recommended further reading:

Bible Stories, David Kossoff (Fontana Books)
Know how to tell stories, Clifford Warne (Anzea Publishers)
The Jungle Doctor Series, Dr Paul White (Paternoster Press)
The George Goodman Series, Mr George Goodman (Pickering and Inglis)
God's Little Ones, Ivor Powell (Marshall, Morgan and Scott)
Scripture Press Sunday School materials
All books of children's stories written by Lettice Bell

Part 4—INDEX

... OF FISHING TACKLE AND OTHER SPECIALISED GEAR

Chapter 1

THE ADAPTATION OF VEHICLES FOR USE AS PREACHING UNITS

Specially-equipped Gospel vehicles were seen first in 1915 when the Chicago Moody Bible Institute used horse-drawn preaching units. Since then the style has improved and the variety increased. Just to mention a few, Operation Mobilisation use trucks for the sale of literature and open air evangelism in India. The African Inland Mission use enclosed vehicles for outdoor film-screening and preaching over vast areas in Africa. Open Air Campaigners have a variety of well-equiped versatile vehicles and trailers around the world.

No. 1

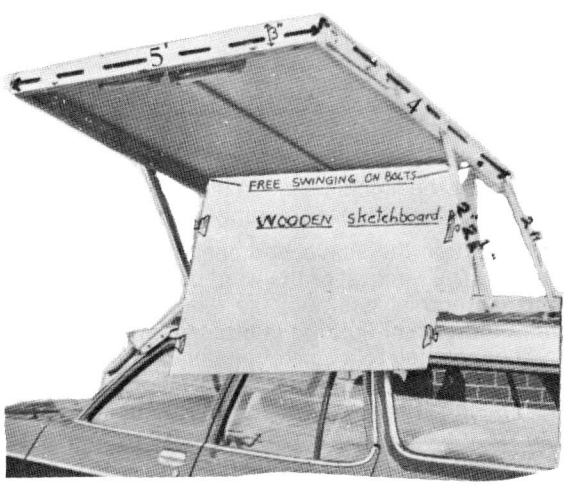

FREE SWINGING ON BOLTS

WOODEN sketchboard

205

1. Portable canopies for sedans or station wagons

Many individuals, Churches, and mission societies want to be involved in outdoor evangelism but cannot afford expensively equipped vehicles. The unit shown fits on to standard roof rods, and may be lifted off for storage by two or four persons, dependent upon the weight of the construction materials.

The size of the unit is shown on the top photo. The base is made from tubular steel. Aluminium would be lighter.

The back view shows the metal supports holding the adjustable canopy to the base section. The pipe fulcrum principle is used to raise and lower the unit.

The canopy is made to swing into position as a screen by undoing wing bolts from the two back supports (labelled 1. in photograph 4.).

A small extension is then added to the arm by use of the same wing bolt, and this in turn is attached to the lower end of the canopy which now doubles as a screen by the use of an extra wing bolt (labelled 2).

No. 2

This extension is only needed on one side of the canopy and will hold the unit in position in the highest wind. A black edging is all that is needed to complete the top for outdoor screening.

During this operation the suspended sketchboard remains out of view behind the screen. The removal of the wing bolts will cause the canopy to swing back to its normal position, the whole operation taking only a minute or two. Fluorescent lighting is attached inside the outer frame of the canopy and connected to a socket installed in the frame itself. A jack with attached cord plugged into the cigarette lighter of the vehicle completes the equipment. It has been found that marine bonded plywood is ideal for the top of the canopy particularly if it is covered by a thin piece of aluminium to protect it from strong sunlight and rain.

Small inverted 'U' brackets need to be welded to the portions of the base of the canopy which rests on the roof rods. The screw-type connectors used for holding garden hoses to taps (the clasp, not screw-on variety) are ideal for holding the inverted 'U' brackets to the roof rods. Rubber gromits between the upper and lower portions of the canopy will prevent rattling on the road. A locking clasp to hold the upper and lower portion tightly together is also advisable. The pipe fulcrum principle for lifting the canopy to the upright position is well known.

No. 3

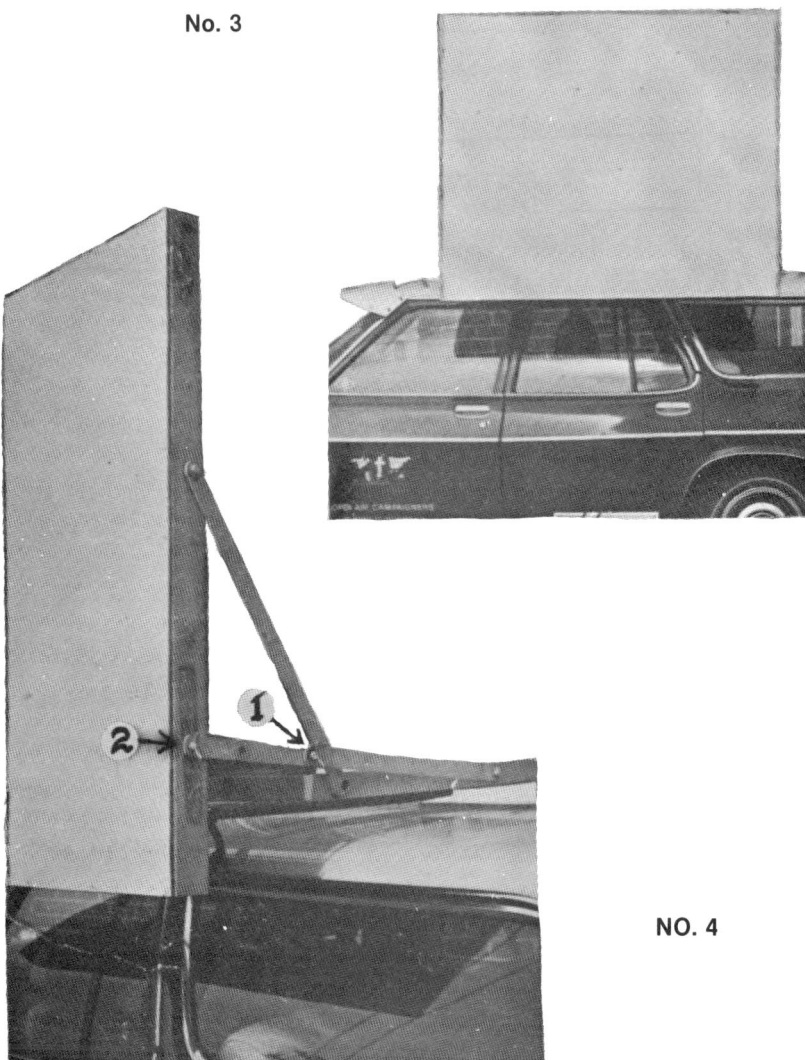

NO. 4

2. Using a car trailer as a preaching unit.

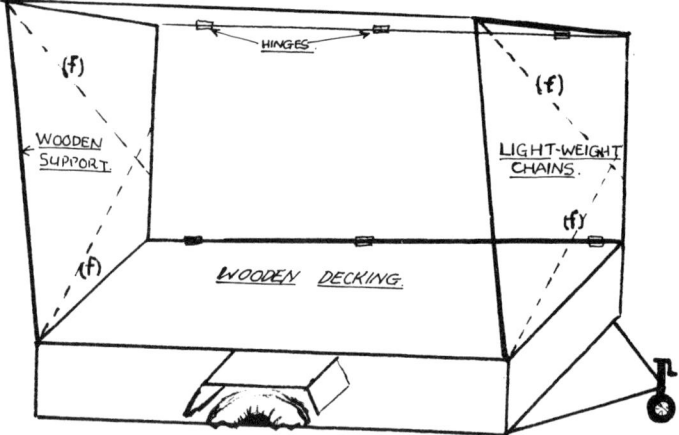

Rough sketch of open unit.

The equipment shown has been designed for the average-sized car trailer so that it may be towed by any type of vehicle. The equipment is compact and easily removed for storage.

The adaptation of ordinary car trailers makes it economically possible for workers to own their own equipment.

Procedure:

1. Build a light wood deck to cover the whole trailer, including the wheel guards. Allow for a trapdoor in the decking (position 'e') for storage of materials underneath the decking.

Completed unit. Note canvas side-flaps can be attached for wet weather.

2. Attach wooden blocks to the underside of the deck in the positions (a) to (d) fitting as closely as possible to the inside of the trailer and tailgate, to prevent the deck from sliding.

3. Secure 'D' type attachments under the edges of the deck protruding over the inside well of the trailer so that the unit may be roped to the trailer itself to prevent any movement caused by travelling, high wind etc.

208

4. Materials for the back and roof need to be lightweight but strong for easy lifting, capable of weathering the sun, rain, and strong wind. Aluminium supports would be ideal. The following construction points need to be noted.

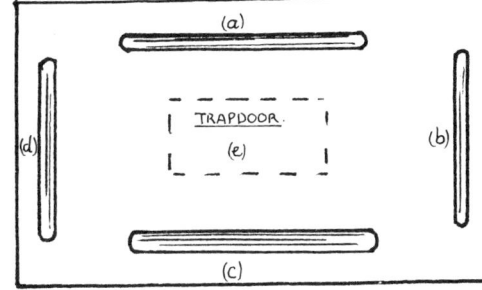

- The size of the folding back and roof sections are determined by the measurements of the base section on which they rest, without overlap.
- The width of each section is the space needed to operate the folding principle. In other words, the roof needs to be hinged to fold on to the face of the back section so that when they both fold down on the deck, the roof rests on top of the deck with back section uppermost. (See illustration.)

5. The roof section and the back portion are supported in two ways:
   - Two wooden supports extend from the front edge of the deck to the outer edges of the extended roof portion, being held in position by anchored bolts and wing nuts. (See sketch of unit opened up.)
   - Light chains (figure 'f' in illustration) keep tension between the rigid back section and the wooden supports.

6. In the event of wet weather, canvas side pieces may be snap-fastened to the edges of the back in the upright position and tied by ropes to the front wooden supports.

7. Suitable lighting and a name plate along the leading edge of the roof section complete the unit.

Illustrations

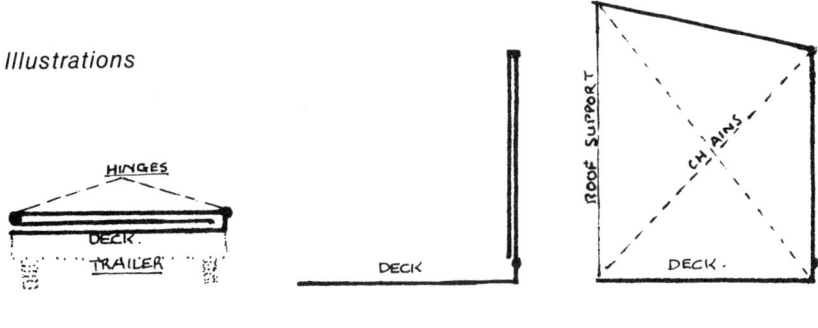

The folded unit   The back in position   The roof angled

Acknowledgment:
G. H. Bradley, OAC, NZ

209

3. Reverse film projection techniques for outdoor audiences.

The following equipment and techniques have been designed for panel vans with side-opening doors, as seen by the photographs taken of a fully-equipped OAC vehicle in the USA. The principle of the reflecting mirror and screen can be used anywhere.

The advantages of projecting a film from inside a vehicle to a screen on top are almost too numerous to mention. The projector is protected from weather and vandals; the audience have a totally unobstructed view; there is no need for projector or screen stands; no speaker or microphone leads are exposed; the projectionist is away from the audience; much less time is needed to set up and put equipment away so more time is available for counselling; and dependence on outside power is eliminated.

Put simply, the film is projected on to a small rear vision mirror mounted directly in front of the lens. This reverses the image and throws it on to a large mirror mounted at such an angle that the image is increased in size and reflected for normal viewing on to a screen mounted on the vehicle roof. The picture loses nothing of its quality in the process of reflection, provided the two reflecting mirrors are good quality. Before dealing with the process, a little needs to be said about equipment.

EQUIPMENT:

While the make and size will be affected by the size of potential audiences and the cost factor, quality must be top priority. The Gospel deserves nothing less. Needed are:

1. A power supply

Either an inverter and heavy-duty battery charged in phase with the vehicle battery, or a small portable generator may be used.

A Trip Lite 1000W model, PV–1000FC (Frequency-controlled) inverter has been most satisfactory. If the battery and inverter are mounted together, they can also be used in beach evangelism. An adequate fuse should be used between the vehicle and portable battery to cope with the surge of power from the generator (alternator) when the vehicle is started after a program, and the projector battery has been depleted.

2. High quality amplification equipment

A Bogen 100Wrms transistorised amplifier is ideal. With this system, a Shure directional (cardaroid pattern) microphone is recommended because of its lack of feedback. (Model 565.D. dual impedence, Unisphere 1. Dynamic.) For crowds of up to 150 people, a 50W. PA can be used— Perma Power Diplomat Model S-210A (40–50W battery-powered), is manufactured by Chamberlain Perma Power Division, Chicago III. 60646 USA.

3. An appropriately-matched speaker system

The Bose 800 series is ideal. Eight small speakers arranged in an inverted 'V' fashion are capable of handling a 350 watt input. A base equaliser gives the whole spectrum of sound and stops feedback. While the capacity of this equipment is far greater than is generally needed, the advantages are high quality at low volume, and great power reserves for those occasions when it could be useful. Bose speaker systems carry a five-year guarantee, and are made at The Mountain, Farmington, Mass. 017701, USA.

4. **A round automobile rear vision mirror.**

5. **A large reflecting glass mirror** approximately four feet by three feet in proportion to the size and shape of the canopy, or screen used.

6. **A good quality projector** with a 250W bulb, transistorised amplifier, and a zoom or wide-angle lens with a focal length of .625″ (⁵/₈″). The lens should be capable of filling the screen in the distance allowed. Bell & Howell is recommended for quality of sound (Filmsound 16 mm model 1574).

7. **Ancillary equipment**
   - A frame for holding the large mirror in position, a wooden base plate for the projector, and a block of wood for mounting the rear vision mirror.
   - A roof mounted speaker system for making public announcements prior to the film screening. This system being weather-protected remains in position at all times. The following photograph shows three outdoor type speakers mounted within a metal frame, and protected by a circular grille. The cover is waterproofed. This system may be bolted to the top of the vehicle, or held in place by springs and clips. Rubber grummets or foam plastic packing between the frame and roof will prevent vibration noise. Hand-held portable speakers are of course suitable alternatives. Each speaker capacity is 30 watts. The 360-degree sound spread is ideal for public announcement prior to film showing.

EQUIPMENT PREPARATION

1. The power and amplification equipment

For portability and saving of space, the battery converter and amplifier should be together. A heavy curtain has been folded back to show the unit mounted between the two front seats, immediately behind the engine. For security, each item should be chained to the floor.

Power and amplification units between front seats.

(a) The base plate mirror and supporting blocks

Prepare a wooden base plate from half-inch plywood, large enough for the projector and block of wood supporting the rear vision mirror. The mirror itself is attached to a rectangular piece of wood by a bolt and thumb screw. The rectangular piece should swivel on the main block fastened securely to the wooden base.

The height of the mirror is determined by the need to have the projector lens lined up with the middle of the mirror.

The position and mounting of base plate mirror.

(b) The mounting of the main mirror

A mirror of this size needs to be wrapped in cardboard, or plastic foam and stored in the vehicle until use.

The pictures show the method of holding and tilting the mirror in OAC vehicles equipped with pull out platforms. The treadplate is hinged at the front, and the angle of the mirror which rests on it may be adjusted with light-weight chains.

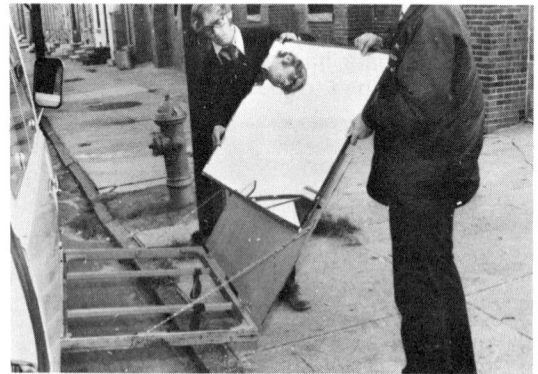

The mounting of the main reflecting mirror.

In place of this equipment, a special frame will need to be constructed to hold the mirror at the correct angle for the screen. A keystone effect of a screen on the roof of the vehicle would be most appropriate. OAC vehicles are equipped with canopies; some can be tipped to any angle.

The principles shown can be used for any size of screen, or for projection onto an opaque sheet of glass in an old TV cabinet.

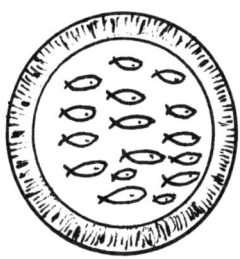

ALIGNMENT

With the projector running, align the image from the small mirror with the centre of the large mirror. (If this is bevelled, tape the edges to prevent wrong reflection.) Using a turn buckle, adjust the supporting chains for the large mirror. Centre the picture on the canopy by shortening or lengthening the chains. If adjusted correctly, there will be a slight keystone effect, with the picture filling the bottom portion of the screen, but overlapping at the top. A little time will need to be taken in making the adjustment in the first place, but it will rarely have to be adjusted again.

When everything is in position, the speakers are placed on the roof. In normal operations, about 50W. capacity is needed.

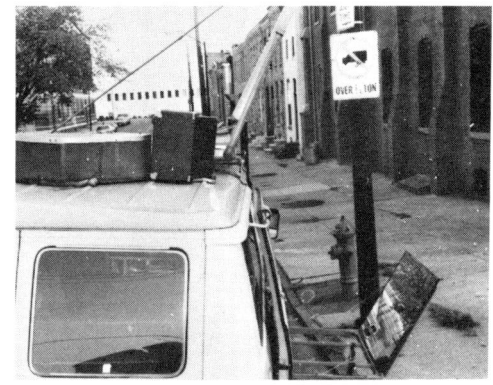

GENERAL HINTS

- If the projector film gate is brushed clean before showing, films will last for over 100 screenings.
- A flat white paint on the plywood will give a good reflection.
- Microphones should be stored away from an inverter. Whether a microphone is alive or not, it will cause hiss if left near an operating inverter.
- Should the amplifier not be of high quality, filters fitted on to the projector amplifier will cut down the hiss.

Note: The equipment outlined will have been updated by the time of printing.

Speakers on the roof.

Chapter 2

FOR THE HANDYMAN
— MAKING YOUR OWN EQUIPMENT

1. A do-it-yourself ventriloquial bird

During an OAC training seminar at Prairie Bible Institute, Canada, a graduate from a previous seminar dropped in to renew friendships. He brought his rather ingenious ventriloquial bird, appropriately named, GREGORY PECK. Gregory had in fact obtained a place of honour during graduation by featuring in the class photo. He had cost his owner-maker only $10.00 to assemble and the writer thought some rough sketches might inspire others to similar creativity.

1. Gregory as he is remembered

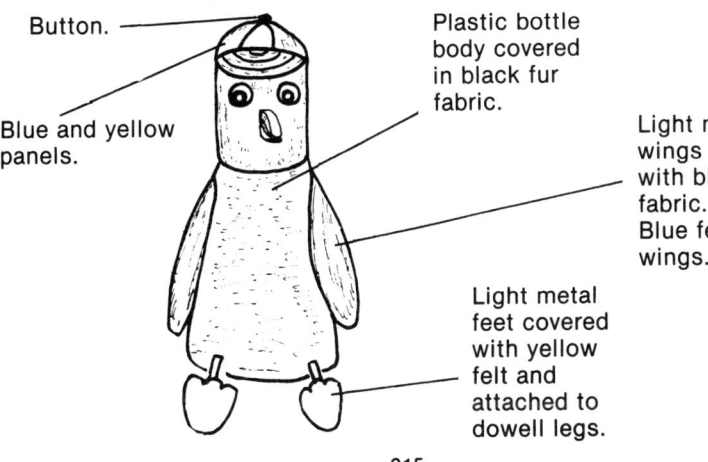

Button. ————

Plastic bottle body covered in black fur fabric.

Blue and yellow panels.

Light metal wings covered with blue fur fabric.
Blue felt under wings.

Light metal feet covered with yellow felt and attached to dowell legs.

2. Gregory's anatomy

Ingenuity plus:
- one empty plastic container suitably shaped with sloping, not vertical sides.
- one empty large jam, or fruit tin.
- one heavy rubber band.
- some scrap metal from which the feet are cut.
- two pieces of dowelling for the legs.
- styrofoam padding for the head.
- black fur fabric for the body and blue fabric for wings.
- blue and yellow felt for the cap.
- pieces of wire, (odds and ends).
- enamel of various colours.
- wood for the two beaks and a piece of 3-ply for gluing the upper beak to the handle.
- a short piece of broom handle.

3. How his head works.

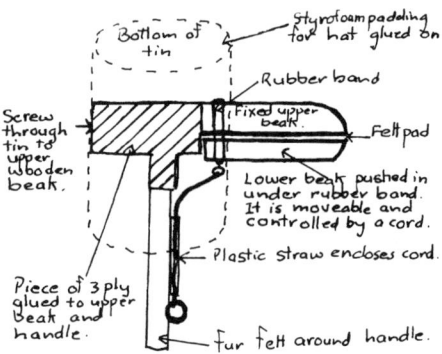

4. He has legs

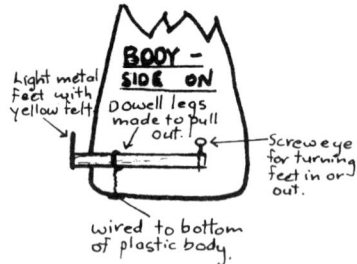

... and flapping wings.

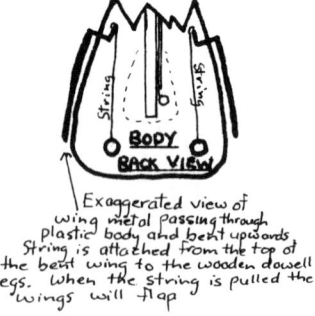

Any voice will do for a bird, or any other animal you may fancy making. There are many books and courses available to teach the art of ventriloquism, and most of them are costly. Apart from special techniques they all say the same thing. Learn to talk with your lips slightly apart. A smile will help you do this, and look quite natural. Use a falsetto voice, or any voice for the dummy that sounds different from your own. Because you do not use your lips to pronounce certain consonants you have to learn to put your tongue behind your teeth to make a similar sound. 'B' becomes 'D'; 'F' becomes 'Eth'; 'M' and 'N' are the same (N); 'P' sounds very like 'T'; 'V' is 'Thee'; 'W' is 'Duggle-you'; 'Y' is made back in the mouth without using the lips. The rest is simple. Practise in front of a mirror, learning to avoid words which begin with the difficult consonants. Coordinate the words you say with movements of your dummy's mouth, keeping its head on the move to add a touch of life. Try yourself out on a small audience of friends first. Keep the practice up and develop a free-and-easy relationship between you both. Mind your dummy's manners and don't let it say anything that may dishonour the Lord or give parents concern.

2. Portable black light equipment.

The use of fluorescent chalks and paints under ultra violet light at night can be quite spectacular. The major problem has been the availability of power. This problem can be overcome by the use of lightweight equipment:

1. **The use of an inverter with flashlight batteries.**
   The equipment needed is:
   a. **The black light unit** (110 volt). This is a long wave unit, non-harming to the eyes. This type has a reflector which makes it as good as two normal type fluorescent tubes (40W). The light has two 15W. tubes. Type BLACK-RAY fixture 18″ x 6″ x 4″ — 2 x 15W tubes 50058, may be obtained from Ultra-Violet Products Inc., 5100 Walnut Grove Ave, San Gabriel, California 91778.

   b. **The Inverter** (110 volt). A 200W inverter is sufficient, a 350W is also available. Size is 3½″ x 6½″ x 5½″ for 200W and 3½″ x 6½″ x 9″ for the 350W. This equipment is available from Tripp-Lite, 133 North Jefferson Street, Chicago, Ill., 60606.

   c. **Ten 'D' size flashlight batteries.**

   d. **Fluorescent paints.** Tempera Fluror paints are recommended rather than chalks. Paint can be applied more quickly and is brighter. Coloured backgrounds may be used with black borders. Green, yellow or orange may be used as a background for jet figures.

The equipment needs to be built into wooden boxes with carrying handles. The inverter needs plenty of air circulating when in use to prevent overheating. The black light unit can be fitted with two arms to clip over the sketchboard.

(**Acknowledgment:** D. Wilson OAC, USA)

2. The use of an electronic ballast.

A lightweight electronic ballast may be used with a 12 volt DC battery or car battery. The Lion Electronic Ballast is recommended for use with a 20 watt fluorescent lamp. It is recommended that the output side is not left without the load of the tube when switched on, as the power transistor may break down.

The fluorescent tube cover may be made from wood. Light guage aluminium or foil, pressed to the shape of the inside of the cover will make an excellent reflector. As in the previous model the light unit needs to be attached to the board with wooden or metal arms.

(Acknowledgment: R. Pocklington OAC—SEND Intl. Philippines)

When using fluorescent chalks at night invisible colours which look white under ordinary light will produce a spectacularly colourful effect when the ultra-violet tube is switched on. By using ordinary coloured fluorescent chalks to provide the major part of the scene or sketch, the real colour is not evident until the chosen point of impact. The chalks are expensive, but worth the cost.

Part 5 — INDEX

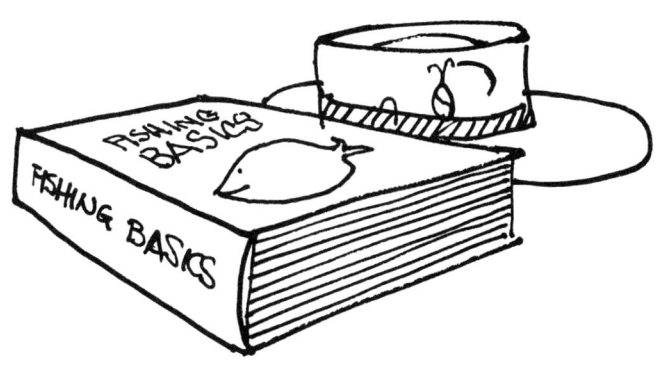

Chapter 1

THE MYSTERY UNDER A MICROSCOPE

The microscope, the telescope and the Word of God have one thing in common. They all highlight the perfection and glory of God in all his ways. The microscope reveals creation invisible to the human eye; the telescope shows us universes in space beyond the sight of the human eye; the Word of God focuses our understanding on the mystery of God's eternal purpose for mankind in redemption. The Apostle Paul explained this greatest revelation in these words:

> 'I have become its [the church's] servant by the commission God gave to me to present to you the word of God in its fulness—**the mystery** that has been kept hidden for ages and generations, but is now disclosed to the saints. To them God has chosen to make known among the Gentiles the glorious riches of this **mystery**, which is Christ in you, the hope of glory'.   (Col. 1:25-27)

An understanding of the basics of this revealed mystery is essential for effective communication of the Gospel of Jesus Christ. Methods of outreach are secondary to this understanding. In the following diagram eight phases of the riches of this mystery are shown.

1. The Gospel Determined

Because the Gospel is revelation, neither its message or objective can be understood without accepting the Biblical teachings concerning its Purpose, Plan and Participants.

2. The Gospel Disclosed

The birth of the Logos (Word) brought truth to incarnational reality. In the fulfilment of his mystical appointments as the Last Adam, the Second

Man and the King-Priest Melchisedek, Jesus Christ provided eternal redemption for fallen man, reconciling us with God.

3. The Gospel Delegated

The resurrection, ascension and glorification of Jesus Christ marked the commencement of a worldwide search for the lost. The terms and conditions of this ministry are as unchangeable as the unvarying nature of God himself.

4. The Gospel Defined

To the general terms of reference in the Great Commission, the Holy Spirit later added the fine print of Gospel detail. From the pen of the Apostle Paul, we have three important Gospel emphases—proclamation, revelation, transformation.

5. The Gospel Depicted

This shows God's progressive dealing with man and his eternal purpose reaching fulfilment in the function of the Body of Christ.

6. The Gospel Deliberated

The conditions upon which sinful man is brought to new life in Jesus Christ need to be carefully examined to avoid reformation without regeneration, penance without repentance, and knowledge without faith. The steps to maturity in Christ need to be practised by soul-winners so that new believers are encouraged by example as well as exhortation.

7. The Gospel Declared

Preachers of the Gospel should study the art of good communication if they wish their message not only to be heard but understood. Effective Gospel preaching and soul winning are the culmination of good communication and the sovereign working of the Holy Spirit.

8. The Gospel Disseminated

The final section is an examination of the various ways of expressing the Gospel message.

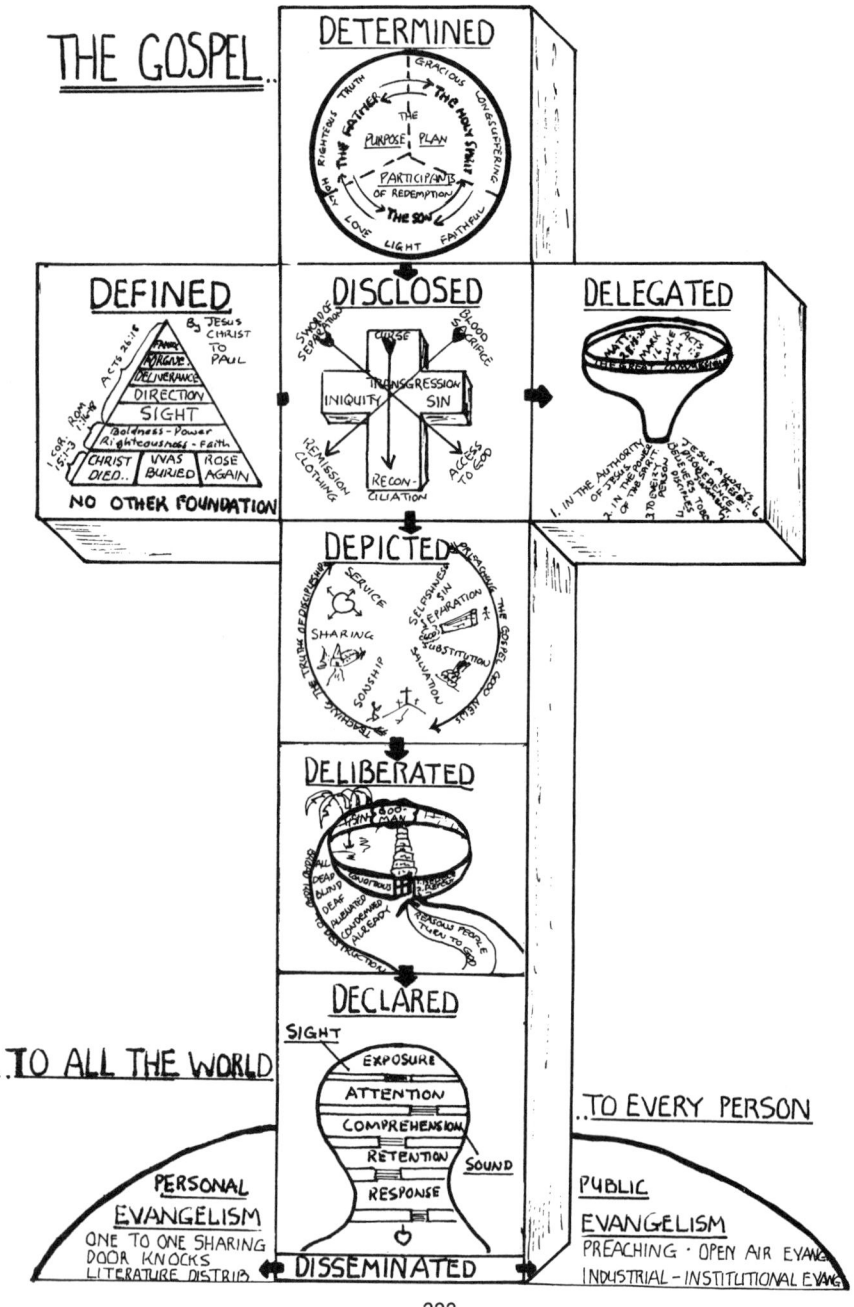

THE GOSPEL..

DETERMINED

DEFINED — NO OTHER FOUNDATION

DISCLOSED

DELEGATED

DEPICTED

DELIBERATED

DECLARED

..TO ALL THE WORLD

..TO EVERY PERSON

PERSONAL EVANGELISM
ONE TO ONE SHARING
DOOR KNOCKS
LITERATURE DISTRIB.

PUBLIC EVANGELISM
PREACHING · OPEN AIR EVANG
INDUSTRIAL – INSTITUTIONAL EVANG

DISSEMINATED

Some of these subjects have been covered in the preceding parts. The contents of this concluding section may have been studied by those who have had the opportunity of taking theological and Bible studies. However, it cannot be assumed that all readers will have this knowledge, and it is for them that these chapters on foundational truths have been prepared.

Chapter 2

CONCERNING GOD ... THE CROSS ... AND THE GOSPEL

These three subjects are an interlocking revelation of the heart of God reaching out to redeem lost humanity.

1. GOD

Without some understanding of God's nature, the Cross of Jesus Christ and the gospel cannot be seen in true perspective. The diagram highlights for personal study, relationships within the Trinity—God's character revealed in his Word—and the heart of God as the first cause of redemption.

This throws light on three aspects of the Gospel's origin.

- **The PURPOSE of the Gospel** (foreordained in eternity) was to make provision for those whom God had created for Himself (Gen. 1:26), to be with him for eternity.

    Matt. 25:34: 'Then the king will say to those on his right hand, Come, you who are blessed by my Father; take your inheritance, the kingdom **prepared for you since the creation of the world.**'

    Eph. 3:10: 'His intent was that now, through the Church, the manifold wisdom of God should be made known to the rulers and authorities in the heavenly realms, **according to his eternal purpose** which he accomplished in Christ Jesus our Lord.'

    In practical terms, this means that the fall of our first parents did not take God by surprise. The Cross of Calvary was no hurriedly-drawn-up contingency plan.

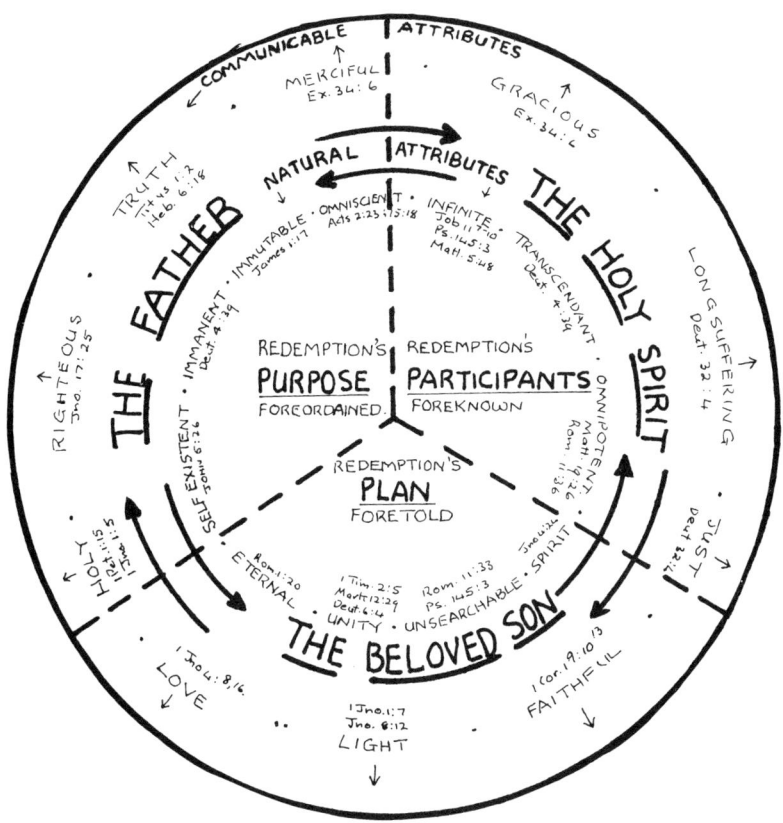

The following text appears within the circular diagram:

COMMUNICABLE | ATTRIBUTES

MERCIFUL
Ex. 34:6

GRACIOUS
Ex. 34:6

TRUTH
Tit. 1:2
Heb. 6:18

NATURAL | ATTRIBUTES

THE FATHER

THE HOLY SPIRIT

IMMUTABLE · OMNISCIENT ·
James 1:17   Acts 2:23; 15:18

INFINITE ·
Job 11:7-10
Ps. 145:3
Matt. 5:48

TRANSCENDANT ·
Deut. 4:34

IMMANENT ·
Deut. 4:39

LONG SUFFERING
Deut. 32:4

RIGHTEOUS
Jno. 17:25

SELF EXISTENT ·
John 6:26

REDEMPTION'S | REDEMPTION'S
PURPOSE | **PARTICIPANTS**
FOREORDAINED | FOREKNOWN

OMNIPOTENT ·
Matt. 11:26
Rom. 1:20

JUST
Deut. 32:4

REDEMPTION'S
PLAN
FORETOLD

HOLY
1 Pet. 1:15, 16
1 Tim. 3:16

ETERNAL ·
Rom. 1:20

1 Tim. 2:5   Rom. 11:33
Matt. 12:29 Ps. 145:3
Deut. 6:4

OMNIPRESENT · SPIRIT
Jno. 4:24

FAITHFUL
1 Cor. 9:10:13

· UNITY · UNSEARCHABLE ·

THE BELOVED SON

LOVE
1 Jno. 8:16

1 Jno. 1:7
Jno. 8:12
LIGHT

- **The PLAN of the Gospel** (foretold from eternity) was that God would himself provide a sacrifice for sin. Long before the institution of the Passover, God had prepared his perfect sin offering whom John the Baptist later called 'the Lamb of God who takes away the sin of the world' (John 1:29).

Acts 2:23: 'This man was handed over to you **by God's set purpose and authority.'**

Acts 4:28: 'They did what your power and will had decided beforehand should happen (against your holy servant Jesus whom you anointed v. 27).

1 Pet. 1:18-20: 'For you know that you were redeemed ... with the precious blood of Christ a lamb without blemish or defect. **He was chosen before the creation** of the world, but was revealed in these last days for you.'

Rev. 13:8: '... the book of life belonging to the Lamb that was slain from the creation of the world.'

- **The PARTICIPANTS of the Gospel provision** (foreknown in eternity)

  1 Pet. 1:2: '... who have been **chosen** according to the **foreknowledge of God** the Father, by the sanctifying work of the Spirit, for obedience to Jesus Christ and sprinkling by his blood.'

  Rom. 8:29: 'For those God **foreknew** he also **predestinated** to be conformed to the likeness of his Son so that he might be the firstborn among many brothers.'

  Eph. 1:4: 'For he **chose us in him before the creation of the world** to be holy and blameless in his sight. **In love he predestinated us** to be adopted as sons through Jesus Christ in accordance with his pleasure and will.' See also 2 Tim. 1:9; 2 Thess. 2:13.

The subject of predestination has been hotly debated for centuries. Regrettably, it has influenced the thinking of some to the exclusion of missionary or evangelistic work. To hold such a view is to disregard both the ministry of Jesus Christ, who stated so clearly that he had come to **seek** and to save the lost (Luke 19:10), and his instructions to the Apostles (and through them to us) to continue the searching ministry. (John 20:21.) It is also clear from Scripture that unless sinful man is prepared to repent and believe savingly, the provision of God in Jesus Christ is of no avail. Saving faith ought never to be regarded as a work for salvation.

Three words used in Scripture need to be understood.

- **'chosen'** W. E. Vine in his Expository Dictionary of New Testament Words states that the use of this word does not necessarily imply that what is not 'chosen' is rejected. God's choosing is always associated with his perfect knowledge as the 'I AM' who presently and continuously fills the eternities with his presence and glory. He simply writes history before it happens and it is no more problem to him to pre-record the names of those he knows will elect to trust Christ as Saviour than to reveal the events of the last days to the prophets and apostles thousands of years before fulfilment.
- **'foreknowledge'**. Again, W. E. Vine stresses that while 'foreknowledge' involves God's electing grace, it does not preclude human will. He foreknows the exercise of faith which brings salvation. The Apostle Paul emphasises the actual purposes of God rather than the grounds of the purpose.
- **'predestination'**. In Rom. 8:29 this word is followed by the calling of God in verse 30. Again, W. E. Vine, states that 'predestination means to call anyone, invite or summons, articulate the Divine call to partake of the blessing of redemption'. A personal response is obviously required before God completes the next step of his intention, namely justification, followed by glorification.

The foreknowledge of God is an aspect of his omniscience, and is in perfect harmony with his great desire that all might respond to the Gospel. When balanced with his love and justice, no living person will ever be able to claim having been disadvantaged. The following verses show that God does not wish a single person to be lost:

Matt. 18:14 '... your Father in heaven is not willing that **any** of these little ones should be lost.'

John 6:40 'For my Father's will is that **everyone** who looks to the Son and believes in him shall have eternal life, and I will raise him up at the last day.'

Romans 5:18 'Consequently, just as the result of one trespass was condemnation for all men so also the result of one act of righteousness was justification that brings life for **all** men.'

1 Tim. 2:4 'God . . . wants **all** men to be saved and to come to a knowledge of the truth.'

2 Peter 3:9 '. . . He is patient with you, **not wanting anyone to perish,** but **everyone** to come to repentance.'

To summarise, predestination to be conformed to the image of Jesus Christ is God's perfect will for his children; the names of whom he has always known through foreknowledge. To proclaim his gospel wherever people may be found, so that they may repent, believe God's gospel and joyfully submit to his will, is our privilege and responsibility.

2. THE CROSS OF JESUS CHRIST

The cry Jesus made just before he died was of the greatest significance. 'IT IS FINISHED' (John 19:30). What did he mean by that statement?

1. The righteous demands of the Law had been fully met.

God's passover lamb had been without flaw or blemish, a totally acceptable sacrifice. 'God made him who had no sin to be sin for us, so that in him we might become the righteousness of God' (2 Cor. 5:21). This was not the first time that Jesus Christ had been found faultless.

At his water baptism (Matt. 3:13-17), Jesus claimed that this public act would be a witness to his perfect fulfilment of the law's demands for holy living. God the Father was satisfied and God the Spirit came upon him in the form of a dove anointing him with power for service. The Father then publicly announced his pleasure in the Son of his love.

From that time onwards, the baptism of blood, of which the water baptism had been but a type, hovered over him. 'I have a baptism to undergo, and how distressed I am until it is accomplished' (Luke 12:50). From the cross the shout of triumph 'It is finished' echoed in both heaven and hell. Unseen hands of Divine appeasement tore the heavy veil of the temple from top to bottom, shook the earth, smashed the rocks, and the Spirit of God quickened some of the righteous dead with resurrection life (Matt. 27:51-53). Father and Spirit together showed that the righteousness of the law had been fully met, and its curse for disobedience paid in full.

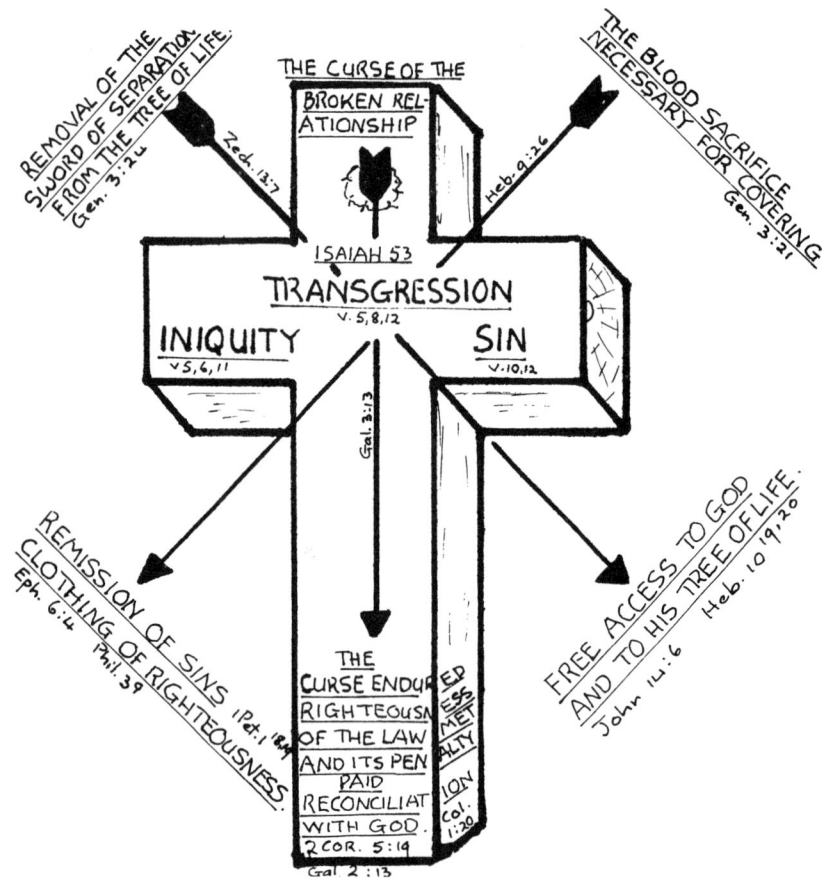

THE CURSE OF THE BROKEN RELATIONSHIP

Zech. 13:7

Heb. 9:26

REMOVAL OF THE SWORD OF SEPARATION FROM THE TREE OF LIFE. Gen. 3:24

THE BLOOD SACRIFICE NECESSARY FOR COVERING Gen. 3:21

ISAIAH 53

TRANSGRESSION
V. 5,8,12

INIQUITY
V 5,6,11

SIN
V.10,12

Gal. 3:13

REMISSION OF SINS 1 Pet. 1
CLOTHING OF RIGHTEOUSNESS
Eph. 6:4 Phil. 3:9

FREE ACCESS TO GOD AND TO HIS TREE OF LIFE. Heb. 10 19:20 John 14:6

THE CURSE ENDURED
RIGHTEOUSNESS MET
OF THE LAW
AND ITS PENALTY
PAID
RECONCILIATION
WITH GOD. Col. 1:20
2 COR. 5:19
Gal 2:13

2. **The vicarious** (in place of the sinner) **and expiatory** (on behalf of the sinner) **sacrifice of Jesus Christ, propitiated** (appeased) **God's holy nature, fully satisfying his righteous demands, so puchasing our pardon and release from the power and penalty of sin, and its attendant guilt.** God could now justify the sinner, making him righteous in his presence after repentance, and faith in Jesus Christ (Rom. 3:22-23; 5:1).

In other words, in love God provided an infinite sacrifice which enabled him to extend mercy to sinners and look upon them as if they had never sinned.

Three words are used in the Old Testament to describe the wickedness of man. They are:

1. 'avon' translated 'perversity' (AV) 'wickedness' (NIV). It occurs 218 times.

2. 'pesha' translated 'rebellion'. It occurs 84 times.
3. 'chattath' translated 'sin'. It occurs 164 times. Another associated word is 'chata' translated 'to sin, err, or miss the mark', occurs 165 times.

At least 15 times these three words are used together, the first time by God himself in Ex. 34:7 where he declared himself to Moses as a God who 'forgives iniquity, transgression and sin' (NIV 'wickedness, rebellion, and sin').

Their association with the death of Jesus Christ is too obvious to be taken lightly.

Psalm 103:10,12: 'He hath not dealt with us after our **sins**; nor rewarded us according to our **iniquities** . . . As far as the east is from the west, so far hath he removed our **transgressions** from us' (AV).

Daniel 9:24:26: 'Seventy weeks are determined upon thy people and upon thy holy city, to **finish the transgression**, and to make **an end of sins**, and to make **reconciliation for iniquity** . . . shall Messiah be cut off, **but not for himself**' (AV).

It is in the 53rd chapter of Isaiah that the full extent of the substitutionary work of Jesus Christ is evident. (Quotations from the AV, Amp.)

The word **'iniquity'** occurs three times, in verses 5,6,11.
The word **'transgression'** occurs four times, in verses 5,8 and 12 (twice).
The word **'sin'** occurs twice in verses 10 and 12.

It is evident that both the root and fruit of the sinner's nature are dealt with in their entirety. Winning people to Christ is not enlisting sympathisers with the 'Jesus-cause', but dealing adequately with the root system rebellion and wickedness in true repentance and total commitment.

3. **The relationship with God lost in the Garden of Eden, can again be enjoyed.**

The only exception is the state of innocence which was forfeited when Adam sold the birthrights of the human race for a piece of fruit. Jesus has restored what Adam lost:

- **Direct access to God** (John 14:6). Through death, Jesus Christ suffered the consequences of the flaming sword (Gen. 3:24), and the sword of separation (Zech. 13:7), so making direct access to God possible through himself (John 14:6).
- **Ability to speak to God, person to person** (John 16:23,24). By suffering the curse and satisfying the righteous demands of the law, fellowship has again been made possible on a personal basis (John 16:23-24).
- **Spiritual life restored after being lost through rebellion** (Gen. 3:17). In total victory over death, the grave and hell, the Lord Jesus purchased freedom and a new relationship with God for those who

believe (John 17:2,5; John 1:12,13).
- **The spiritual light of God's presence** (2 Cor. 4:6). Adam and Eve hid guiltily among the shadows of trees. The Lord Jesus took our guilt to free us from darkness and make us children of light (Eph. 5:8; 1 John 1:6,7; John 8:12).
- **The protection of God** (Heb. 2:18). In Gen. 4:14 Cain showed fear. In conquering sin and death the Lord Jesus not only conquered fear, but promises his protection from it. (John 10:2-10; Paul develops theme in Eph. 6:10-18.)

3. THE GOSPEL OF GOD AND JESUS CHRIST AS REVEALED TO THE APOSTLE PAUL.

Preachers have complete liberty to choose their own methods of Gospel communication, but no liberty to choose the contents of their Gospel. These have been determined by God and are unchangeable. 'I want you to know, brothers, that the Gospel I preached is not something that man made up. I did not receive it from any man, nor was I taught it: rather, I received it by revelation from Jesus Christ' (Gal. 1:11-12).

Paul makes three important statements about the Gospel:

1. **1 Cor. 15:1-3.** 'For what I received I passed on to you as of first impor-tance; that Christ died for our sins according to the Scriptures, that he was buried, that he was raised on the third day according to the Scriptures.' In this verse the Apostle emphasises three essential foundation stones of our faith. (Diagram A.)
   - **'Christ died for our sins'.**
     He fulfilled the predetermined will of the Godhead (Acts 2:23) con-tinuously referred to in prophetical writings (Luke 24:25-27). The Bible provides no basis for preaching a Christ without a cross, or a cross without a Christ. Shed blood was the basis of the Old Testa-ment atonement. Shed blood is the basis of New Testament pro-pitiation without which there could be no reconciliation, new birth, or cleansing for a Christian. God's justice and faithfulness to forgive and cleanse the born-again believer who confesses sin is based upon his covenant in blood (1 John 1:9).
   - **'. . . that he was buried . . .'**
     The burial of Jesus Christ was no routine formality. It was part of fully 'tasting death for every man' (Heb. 2:9). In hell he faced the very powers and principalities he had created for his own glory, and who had been expelled from his presence because of rebellion. He was their conqueror even in the grave. No power could have prevented him from exercising his sovereignty and go-ing down into 'Tartarus', hell's lowest level and proclaiming his blood-bought victory over all Satan's works to the evil spirits chained in darkness since the flood in Noah's day (1 Pet. 3:19; 2 Pet. 2:4). No demonic power, or even Satan himself could have prevented Jesus from leaving Sheol on the third day, taking with him the souls of all the righteous dead from Paradise, leaving behind demons and the souls of the ungodly as hell's only oc-

cupants (1 Pet. 3:19-20; Psalm 68:18). No wonder Paul could say that through the work of the cross, that is by his death, burial and resurrection, Jesus Christ disarmed the powers and authorities (Col. 2:15). Like soldiers of a defeated army they were exposed as shattered and defeated. '. . . he made a public spectacle of them triumphing over them by the cross'. There was victory on the cross. Jesus had laid his life down, no-one took it from him. There was triumph in hell, no-one could bind him. There was triumph in the resurrection. No-one could prevent him from freeing prisoners redeemed by his blood and taking with him all the prison keys (Rev. 1:18).

- '. . . **that he was raised on the third day according to the Scriptures**'.

The Father's greatest sign of approval of His son's perfect work and total victory, was that Jesus was 'declared with power to be the Son of God by his resurrection from the dead' (Rom. 1:4). The resurrection caused great joy in the early church and great apprehension in Jewry. By it prophets were vindicated, the Spirit came, promises of Jesus sprang to life and the ultimate banishment of sin for eternity is assured. The resurrection makes Jesus Christ unique. No founder of any great world religion ever rose

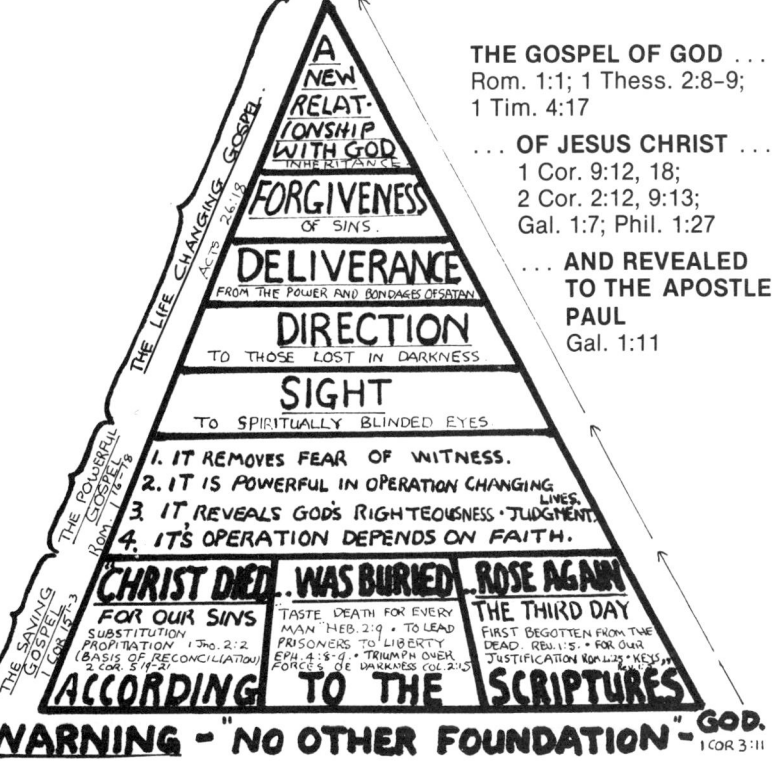

THE GOSPEL OF GOD . . .
Rom. 1:1; 1 Thess. 2:8-9;
1 Tim. 4:17

. . . OF JESUS CHRIST . . .
1 Cor. 9:12, 18;
2 Cor. 2:12, 9:13;
Gal. 1:7; Phil. 1:27

. . . AND REVEALED
TO THE APOSTLE
PAUL
Gal. 1:11

"A" 231

from the dead, and none of their faithful can say as the Christians do—'Our Saviour is alive and well'. The resurrection also affirms the hope of the Second coming. By it the Gospel pulsates with life, eternal and abundant.

It should be noted that social concern is a Christian responsibility arising from the change of life-style and attitude produced through the preaching of the Gospel. It is not part of the historic Gospel, but a very practical partner with the Gospel.

2. **Romans 1:16–18.**

Here Paul emphasises the power of the Gospel. A power to remove fear of witness, and a power to change those who believe. He also stresses faith as the means of justification and the strength for righteous living. God's holy standard in dealing with any form of wickedness and unrighteousness is also strongly stated. If 1 Cor. 15:1–3 emphasises the completed work of Jesus Christ, Rom. 1:16–18 stresses the power now available through the gospel in human lives.

3. **Acts 26:18**

The emphasis is now placed upon the total change in the life of the believer through faith in Jesus Christ. This is not Paul's personal opinion of the Gospel, but exactly what Jesus said to him on the Damascus road before his three-year post-graduate course in Arabia.

The five-fold effect of the Gospel is:

1. **'. . . to open their eyes . . .'**
   The closed or darkened mind cannot respond to Jesus Christ until it sees three things clearly. Firstly, that all are sinners. Secondly, Jesus Christ alone is the Saviour of sinners. Thirdly, God's Word alone can show how Jesus saves sinners and keeps them saved. This 'eye opener' comes when the Spirit of God shines truth into each heart and mind.

2. **'. . . and turn them from darkness to light . . .'**
   With a new understanding and desire to obey truth, there must be a deliberate about-turn to face Jesus Christ, the light of the world. This involves both repentance (having a new attitude of mind and heart), and conversion (the act of turning from the things of darkness), to trust Jesus Christ as Saviour.

3. **'. . . and from the power of Satan to God . . .'**
   The process of being set free from the grip and power of spiritual darkness is very important, particularly for those who have been involved in witchcraft, the occult or Satanism. Personal workers need both the discernment and power of the Holy Spirit to minister deliverance to those in bondage. Without the freedom Christ provides, new believers will never be able to enjoy life in Christ to the full (John 8:31,32,36; Gal. 5:1).

4. **'. . . so that they may receive forgiveness of sins . . .'**
   It is interesting to note the spiritual order. The first three steps are light of understanding, repentance and release from Satan's

power and human responsibility. Now comes faith in Jesus Christ and his blood shed for the remission of sins. On this basis alone God the Son and the Holy Spirit can cleanse, forgive and bring into new life.

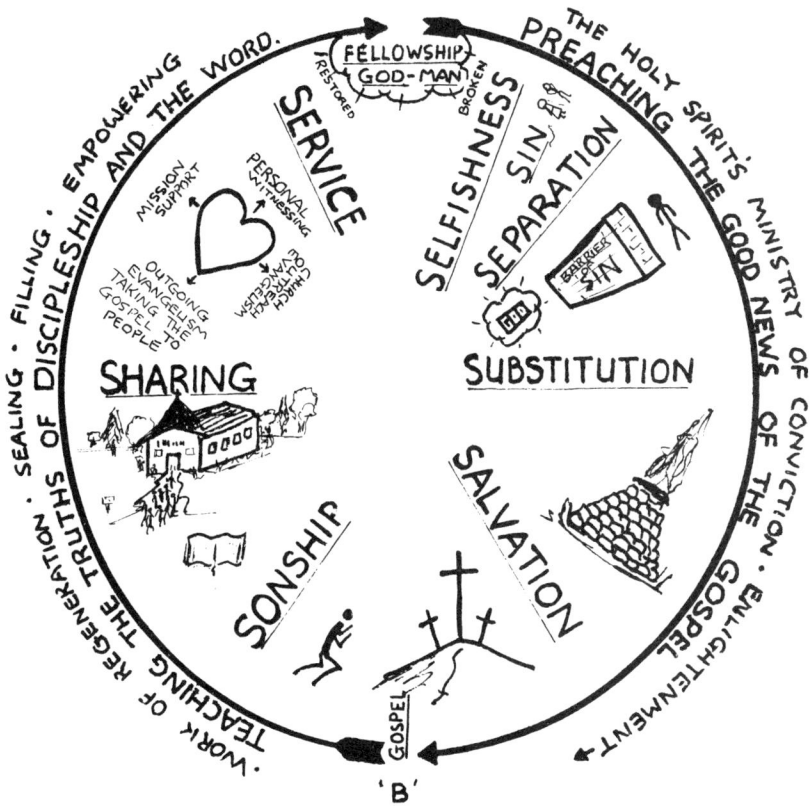

5. '. . . **and a place among those who are sanctified through faith in me.'**

The AV calls this 'an inheritance', the special privilege of a family member. Each new child of God inherits much more than just a small share in the estate of Jesus the elder brother of the family of God. It is the fullness of God himself (Rom. 8:32). In reality, it is not only a living inheritance, but a future destination. From the time of new birth onwards, the believer is a pilgrim on a heavenly journey into all that God has prepared for him. The circle is now complete. From the heart of God came the plan, the provision and the power for man, created in his image to be like him and be with him for ever. (Diagram B.) The Gospel is indeed good news. God has redeemed for himself a family, and we as members of his family have a Father in heaven.

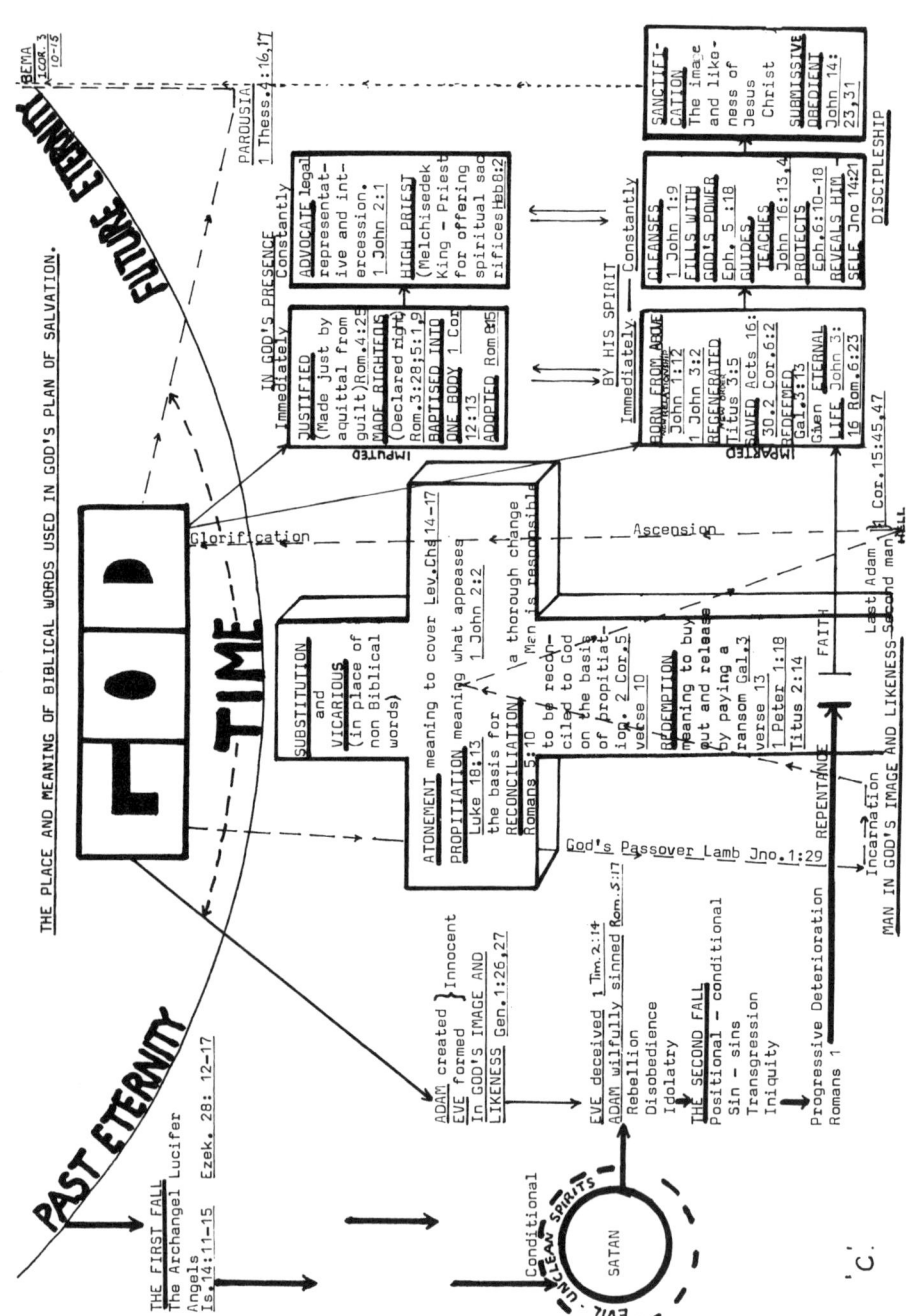

Part 6 — INDEX

Chapter 1

SIMPLE PRINCIPLES OF COMMUNICATING THE GOSPEL

Long before any of us were able to talk, we learned that our voices, faces, expressions, hand movements, and particularly our tempers were effective in getting our message across. In due course, we learned to update our communication. The right words brought us pleasure and the wrong ones sometimes pain. As adults we are not so sure that words alone always convey what we mean, so back we go to square one for some extra help so that people really can understand us. Trying to communicate from a distance sometimes complicates the process. The following (of unknown origin) is an alleged telephone conversation between a caller and the desk clerk of a hotel:

The Caller: 'I would like to reserve a single room for Monday night the 20th of this month please.'

The Desk Clerk: 'Certainly sir, we can accommodate you. Would you care for a room with a tub or a shower?'

The Caller: (who thinks about the difference in cost, and expects any sensible desk clerk would naturally understand this, asks:)
'What's the difference?'

The Desk Clerk: (innocently) 'Well, with a tub you sit down, and with a shower you stand up.'

Maybe the caller dissolved in laughter or got mad, and the desk clerk bristled, but the fact remains that the caller had given no indication of what he meant by his question, and the desk clerk had in fact answered a question the caller had not asked. Good communication depends on both parties knowing exactly what is meant by what is said. Perhaps we need some kind of verbal indication of a change of thought like the turning indicators on a car.

Sometimes well-known and frequently-used words can be interpreted differently. This is particularly so with figurative speech. It is said that a computer which had been programmed to translate English into Russian had these English test words fed in: 'The spirit is willing, but the flesh is weak'. The Russian translation came through as: 'The vodka is good, but the meat's gone bad'. The computer's memory bank obviously had only one meaning for the word 'spirit', and one for 'flesh'. So inadequate terms, unknown words or even words with two meanings lead to misunderstandings.

A motorist was driving his friend through the countryside, when high on a cliff face they saw the words 'JESUS SAVES'. The driver paused, then said, 'You know, that's interesting I've never thought of that before. If Jesus was thrifty, I ought to save too'.

The practical application of all these misread thoughts and misunderstood words is obvious in sharing the Gospel with unbelievers. There is a need for both parties to get on the same word-meaning wavelength.

One of the simplest and most effective experiments in learning how to communicate clearly, is to ask a person to repeat something you say, in his own words. You may be in for a shock or two.

The communication process

Any person who communicates with another is called an encoder. He may use words, signs, pictures, writing or actions to express himself. The person receiving the message is called the receptor. Effective communication is considered to have taken place when the encoder has sent his message so clearly that the receptor's attention has been gained, his understanding reached, and some response given.

Communication cannot be assumed just because a message has been sent. The other person's attention may have been taken up with something else, the message may have been wrongly encoded, misunderstood or inadequately understood, and no clarification requested.

Effective communication then means:

encoding and sending a message clearly,

The message

receiving it clearly, decoding it so that it is understood and acted upon as intended.

The sender
(encoder)

The receiver
(receptor)

Some say words are 'containers of meanings', others 'stimulators to response'. Both meanings should be included in getting the Gospel across. People should understand what God is saying through you, and be moved to respond to him. Good communication will produce:

237

IMPACT, which is more than just making an impression.
UNDERSTANDING, which goes deeper than merely accepting words without knowing what they mean.
RESPONSE, which means reaction, not just passive awareness.

Marshal McLuhan, who taught communication principles in the sixties, said, 'the messenger IS the message'. Jesus Christ certainly was. Those who follow him will need his quality of life to communicate his message effectively. These factors are important:

- **Living an exemplary life.**
  Life and lip should give the same message. Like Jesus, we should be incarnational communicators—God living in us, speaking through us so that no-one ever can say 'I cannot hear what you are saying because of what you are!'

- **Showing personal warmth to others**
  A slot machine communicates well when the right coin is deposited, but it is far from friendly. Chemists dispense doctor's prescriptions for patients they may or may not see, but it is only a business transaction. The Gospel fits neither category. Preachers are living bridges between God and those he longs to save, and should never be aloof. Jesus sat openly with an immoral woman, ate with recognised sinners, touched a leper, healed outcasts and died in the company of criminals. He was never a separatist.

- **Develop cultural sensitivity**
  Jesus was also a healer of breaches, sensitive to cultural and social issues. He was careful to obey local custom, to avoid controversy with the Roman overlords, and to stay with despised Samaritans to win a city to himself. We need that sensitivity to make the Gospel meaningful to people with racial, religious, and social backgrounds different to our own.

- **Share your Christian love, don't hoard or hide it**
  No-one could ever love as much as Jesus did. His disciples and personal friends were continuously surrounded by it. This love has been given to us so that by our unity and concern for one another we will prove to an unbelieving world that Jesus Christ was sent from God, the Saviour of the world. The word 'empathy' appears often in the writings of teachers of communication. Without God's experiential love, they grope for words to define what is normal to a Spirit-filled communicator:
  - 'Empathy is feeling into the experience of another, perceiving what is going on in the feelings of another.'
  - 'It is perceiving the meaning to another of these feelings.'
  - 'It is a sensitive and accurate grasp of and communication with another's inner world.'
  - 'It is being at home in the universe of another.'

God's love flowing in the Holy Spirit needs to be felt, not just defined. Love in action, not words, will reach deep into people's lives, and they will know God lives and loves because you cared.

A French noblewoman who came to Christ looked for an opportunity to share God's love with others. She went into the red-light district of Paris and stumbled upon an underground dungeon-like room where prostitutes slept on straw mattresses. Moving around in semi-darkness she almost tripped over one of them dying of venereal disease. She bent down, put her arm around her shoulders and said 'God loves you, and so do I'. The woman answered through lips covered in sores, 'Then kiss me on the lips'. The noblewoman did so without hesitation. The prostitute wept and trusted Christ as her Saviour. God spared her life a further 12 months, and during that time she led over 50 occupants of that filthy room to Jesus Christ. Love communicates God like nothing else.

- **Be ready to spend time with people to help them understand the Gospel.** Monologue, such as preaching, is undoubtedly the quickest way of reaching large numbers of people, but it is often the least effective method of communication. Interaction is needed if misunderstandings are to be avoided. It may not be practical for preachers to deal with interruptions while speaking, but they should always make themselves available afterwards. Souls may depend upon it.

- **Don't be a talking statue**
  Avoid a droning voice, monotonous hand movements, and cold formality. Put a little personality and variety and a few surprises here and there into your preaching and watch the interest rise! A Spirit-filled communicator should have freedom of expression, liberty of illustration, and an ability to gauge the level of listeners' interest.

- **Answer felt needs where possible**
  Aim to 'scratch where it itches'. People are crying out for a sense of forgiveness, peace, hope, friendship, love, security and self identity, mostly without recognising the spiritual nature of these needs. Initially, they would probably reject a hard-sell Gospel, but they will be open to hear about a Saviour who is willing to meet their felt needs.

Problems may occur anywhere in the communication process. This is technically called static, or channel noise, because it keeps the message from being clearly heard and understood. Static comes from three sources:

1. **Outside sources**
   - heavy rain on a roof, or a thunderstorm.
   - traffic or people noise.
   - environmental noise, factories, household noises, radio, TV.
   - a telephone, baby crying etc.

2. **Problems which cause interference in sending the message**

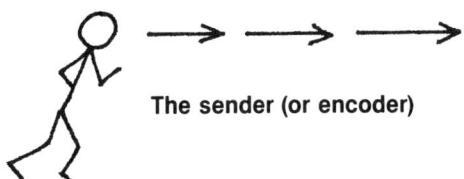

The sender (or encoder)

- Speaking softly so that a person has to strain to hear, or misses some things said.

- Speech problems such as stammering or other speech defects. Indistinct pronunciation.
- Difficulties of expression when using a second language.
- High-handed or proud attitudes which make hearers 'turn off'.
- Prejudices expressed against people, churches, or other faiths.
- Messages which go over people's heads or don't reach them because they are encoded
  — in the wrong type of language.
  — in complicated terms.
  — using unknown theological terms.
  — without logical sequence.

3. **Problems which cause a receiver to be unreceptive to the message.**

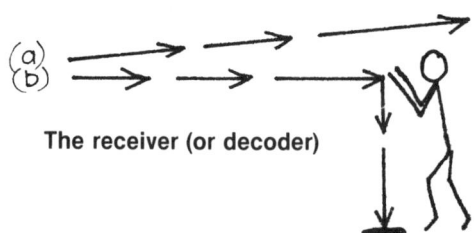

The receiver (or decoder)

- Prejudices against either the sender, or the subject matter.
- Previous unfavourable experiences with preachers or personal workers.
- Messages which are so slow that the mind wanders. Speakers average 125 to 150 words per minute while evidence shows that people think between 600 and 1200 words per minute.
- Messages which are too fast for people to receive and decode in comfort.
- Messages which have too much subject matter.
- Tiredness.
- Insufficient time to give attention to the message and response.
- Messages beyond the receiver's understanding.
- Messages which make the receiver feel threatened.
- Twelve further causes of interference to gospel reception are discussed in the section dealing with personal evangelism.

To communicate the Gospel is to do the will of God. Only by using the principles of good communication can glory be brought to his name.

Recommended reading on communication:
The Mind Changers, Ern Griffin (Tyndale House Publishers)
The Art of Christian Persuasion, Leighton Ford (World Books)
Don't Fake it, Say it with Love, Howard G. Hendricks with Ted Miller (Victor Books)
Evangelism Explosion, D. James Kennedy (Coverdale House Publishers)
The Gagging of God, Gavin Reid (Hodder & Stoughton)
Don't Sleep Through The Revolution, Paul S. Rees (World Books)
Message and Mission (The Communication of the Christian Faith), Eugene A. Nida (Harper and Row)

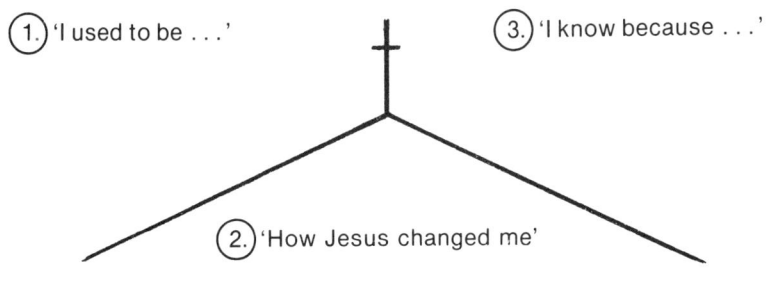

1.) 'I used to be . . .'   3.) 'I know because . . .'

2.) 'How Jesus changed me'

Chapter 2

HOW TO USE YOUR PERSONAL TESTIMONY IN EVANGELISM

God never intends our family relationship with him to be top secret like old family photographs kept hidden away in the old album in the back of the dresser. He wants us to tell the world, our world. One of the best methods is to share our personal testimony.

Manufacturers spend millions of dollars in media advertising in an effort to persuade us to buy their products with the help of well-known personalities. We see their faces smiling at us from billboards, shopfronts, papers, magazines and television screens. Even crammed into our letter boxes. They assure us of profound benefits on becoming the proud owners of their recommended products. The fact that they do influence people's buying habits emphasises the power of personal testimonies.

Andrew, and a friend of his, were disciples of John the Baptist. One day they heard John say that Jesus was the Lamb of God. On the strength of that testimony, they both left John and followed Jesus (John 1:35-37). Jesus so satisfied them that Andrew rushed off, found his brother Peter and told him excitedly that he had met the very Messiah himself (v. 41). Philip convinced Nathaniel the same way (v. 45). In the city of Sychar one woman's testimony was responsible for bringing a city to Jesus Christ (John 4). The young man healed of blindness in John 9 used his personal testimony with the Jewish elders, and the apostle Paul frequently shared his in the book of Acts. Testimonies influence lives.

Every believer has a testimony, but not everyone knows how to give it. The rules of evidence in courts of law are a guide to giving a testimony:

• **Evidence must always be 'the truth—the whole truth—and nothing but the truth'.**

A testimony needs to be open, honest, and to the point, not overdone by the use of words like 'fantastic', 'unbelievable' and 'incredible'. The unconverted want to hear some honest facts about the affect Jesus Christ has on day-to-day living before they will be influenced. And Jesus should never be blamed for things which have not worked out well, particularly when he was not allowed to be in control.

- **Credibility needs to be established**

A witness needs to present himself as a person of character whose word may be accepted without question. The way in which a person gives a testimony should give weight to what is being said.

- **A personal experience is essential**

A witness must either have personally seen or heard the matters in question to be able to give evidence. In the same way, a testimony must come out of one's own experience, never borrowed from someone else, or decorated to make it sound impressive.

- **Keep to the point under examination**

A court witness has to keep to the matter for which he has been called as a witness. Jesus Christ must be kept the centre of the testimony so that he gets the glory. Keep yourself and your church in the background so that the message will not be overshadowed. Be careful to avoid being remembered for your oratory, humour, or long-windedness.

- **People must be able to understand your language**

Before people with language difficulties give evidence in any court of law, an interpreter must be on hand so that questions and answers are clearly understood. Many words used by Christians come directly out of God's Word and although understood in churches are like a foreign language to unbelievers. Imagine their confusion on hearing this—'Beloved, I have been cleansed by the precious blood through the vicarious, expiatory and propitiatory sacrifice of Jesus Christ. I am now justified, clothed in his righteousness, reconciled to God, accepted in the Beloved and baptised into his mystical body as part of the Bride of Christ'. Wow! Speak to be understood, be simple, and explain what you mean.

When professional witnesses use scientific, medical, or highly technical language they are also expected to explain them in laymen's language. Without this, an accurate judgment cannot be given. There was a time when great Bible words were generally understood but those days have gone. Even words like, faith, belief, and sin cannot go unexplained.

- **The witness box is for giving evidence, not a stage for performers**

Courts of law expect clear accurate evidence. A witness trying to make a big impression is bound to end up with a well-deserved rebuke from the bench or counsel. If a personal testimony is to give glory to Jesus Christ, it must be given with humility.

The contents of an evangelistic personal testimony need careful consideration.

Firstly, a testimony is:

- **NOT** preaching the gospel, teaching Bible doctrine, or quoting a string of Bible verses, though it will reflect the influences these have had in your life.

- **NOT** a life history, or a string of boring details, but it should have the authenticity of experience so that it doesn't come across as just theory.
- **NOT** an opportunity to boast of past sins, or confess failures. It must be honest, without offence, and Christ-honouring.

Secondly, a testimony should give people:

- a quick overview of your past life in relation to the things of God, and what caused you to realise you needed Christ as Saviour.
- the circumstances in which you trusted Jesus as Saviour and Lord.
- the ways in which Jesus Christ is still blessing your life.

Each will need to be carefully thought through, and when written should merge together as one overall experience. Now to more detail:

1. **The 'I was' experience** (sometimes called the BC or Before Christ experience).

This is a background to highlight the change of life. Prepare a 'thumbnail' picture of life before your new birth without going into too much detail concerning:

- how you were brought up to think of God, church and the Bible.
- your personal attitude, and how it affected your way of life.
- what caused you to become aware of your need of God or Jesus Christ.

If your experience is unusual, use it for openers to get people's attention as these have done:

- 'Before my air crash I hadn't thought much about God.'
- 'I had too good a time in the Navy to think about Christ.'
- 'When the Doctor told me I had little time to live, I felt desperate, and thought of God seriously for the first time in my life.'
- 'I was on the point of suicide when someone told me Jesus Christ could save me.'

Many people do not have 'spectacular' conversions, but they can still be expressed in interesting ways. A man who came to Christ as a small boy put it this way—'You wouldn't expect a child to understand much about theology, would you?' ... You're right, they don't, but they are often more open to the deep influence of God than grown-ups. I know, I came to Christ at 7 years of age because of a strange heavy feeling inside. I told my father and after a question or two he realised I was grappling with what the Bible called 'sin' and showed me some Bible verses ...'

Unless your whole life is the background to your new birth, condense your past to around one minute. Remember:

DO NOT give intimate details of past sins, particularly those of a sexual nature, and do not hang out your family 'dirty washing'.

DO NOT make yourself out to have been a greater sinner than you were, just to make an impression. You know the style: 'Rescued from a life of crime, a trophy of grace, plucked from the jaws of hell at the age of 12!'

DO NOT create a wrong impression. When ladies say 'I was a great sinner', unconverted people assume they mean sexual indulgence, and may wrongly brand them. Even Christians who don't fully understand God's forgiveness may avoid those whom they think may have been morally indiscreet. After repentance, forgiveness and cleansing, repeated reference to the past may embarrass family members and friends and undermine their own standing in Christ.

DO NOT speak so much about what you used to be that you leave insufficient time to explain the glorious change God has made in your life.

DO NOT forget to say what caused you to think seriously about your need of Christ.

2. **The 'How I became new' experience** (sometimes called RC or Receiving Christ experience).

This is the heart of the testimony, the details of where and how you made Jesus Christ your personal Saviour:

- where you were born again—at home—by your bedside—in a church —at a youth camp—in personal conversation—in prison or hospital, etc. Surveys show that the majority of conversions do not take place in church. This may surprise listeners who think that everything religious must be in a church.
- say exactly what you trusted Jesus to do for you. Don't leave them guessing. Quote any verse which played a real part in your step of faith.
- emphasise the experience you had in Jesus Christ, and not the counsellor who led you to repentance, faith and discipleship.
- leave no doubt that it was not your good works, religious devotion, church membership which saved you, but Jesus Christ alone.

3. **The 'I know because' experience** (sometimes called the LC or Living Christ experience).

This final section should concentrate on the blessings and changes the Lord Jesus has brought about in your life. These include assurance of salvation, pleasure in reading God's Word, consciousness of God's peace with you at all times, answers to prayer, times of special guidance, openings to share Jesus with friends and relatives, strength to overcome temptation, and lots of other significant factors. And **please** . . . see that your illustrations are up-to-date. If something special has not happened to you in the past seven days—are you a backslider? The Christian life is a walk with a living Saviour who wants to do supernatural things for you and through you, to the glory of his Father. Please remember:

- No patting yourself on the back. 'I haven't smoked a cigarette or touched a beer for a long time'. Be positive, and say 'Jesus Christ has liberated me from the grip of my old habits, and I am now able to choose not to do these things.'
- Certainly commend Jesus Christ to others, but remember God didn't give you a new birth to make you happy, but holy! This part of your testimony will show the closeness of your walk with the Lord.

- Make sure your testimony is not confusing. If you have had a number of spiritual experiences, ask the Lord to show you which one was the new birth, and make this clear. There can only be **one** genuine new birth experience so it should not be confused with conviction, assurance of salvation, restoration, rededication or yielding to the filling and control of the Holy Spirit. Be confident of your standing in Christ, because you will never be able to bring anyone to a closer relationship with Christ than you yourself have experienced.

Guidelines for giving testimonies

- Unless your testimony is an unusual one, (and few are), keep to around 2 to 3 minutes. Don't go in for a daschund type testimony—one that droops badly in the middle!

- Avoid cliches such as 'I was brought up in a Christian home'. If you mean your parents were believers, who read the Bible, prayed, and went to church, say so. If they were just nominal Christians or good-living church-goers, say so, but be careful how you use the word 'Christian'. Many people feel that because they have 'Christian' names, live in a Christian country, and do not disbelieve in God, they must be Christians. Your testimony should make it clear that only 'born again' believers are Christians. Another cliche to avoid is 'I was brought up in a church!' If a kennel does not make whatever uses it a dog, neither does the church make whoever goes there a Christian!

- Do not put the Lord Jesus down by saying, 'I have often let the Lord down, but he has never let me down'. What a contradiction and denial of his promise 'I will never leave you, nor forsake you'. If you have been rebellious say so, and explain that when you finally came to your senses and allowed him to help you, he forgave and renewed you.

- Don't paint a picture of the life in Christ as if it were just a 'bed of roses'. And don't make it appear too difficult. Both are wrong. Satan will see to it that there will be trials, temptations, difficulties and problems. God allows these, but his grace and power to cope are always fully and freely available. Some people have more problems after they come to Christ than before. Pressures from friends and workmates, and possible rejection at home are sometimes the earthly reactions to a new-born soul. Paint your picture with contrasting verbal colours, keeping perspective and balance.

- Personal testimonies win when logic won't. Many who argue against the existence of God, become non-plussed when they meet a person who has experienced a complete change of life through trusting the very one they refuse to acknowledge. They may suggest it was psychology, moral reformation, weakness of character or the influence of others, but these are only smoke screens to save face. People know reality when they see it, and you will have set them thinking.

- Avoid giving the impression that the way you came to Christ is the only way. God is sovereign. The disciples were called, but Saul was confronted and commanded. Many come through sorrow, sickness, desperation or a search for truth. Some are loved to Christ, and others want the change they have seen in their friends.

- When speaking publicly, follow the rules of good speaking.
  — look people directly in the eye.
  — stand erect, and avoid leaning or lounging.
  — speak clearly and earnestly.
  — use hand gestures with care.
  — stop when you finish what you need to say—not what you want to say.
  — avoid the resting cow syndrome—chewing the verbal cud, saying the same things over and over. Also the grazing cow syndrome—moving from one memory clover patch to another, not knowing when to stop.

When you have given your testimony publicly, be ready to talk with the interested people. Encourage them to respond as you did.

Chapter 3

A GUIDE TO FORMING AND USING A COUNSELLING PLAN

The focus now falls on the steps personal workers should take to lead a soul into life in Jesus Christ. Four areas are covered in the 4-'S' plan of salvation.

Firstly an overview:

SIN

Many people think that sinners are murderers, rapists, bank robbers and people with a criminal record, certainly not nice people like themselves. Unless the sin question is dealt with, Jesus Christ cannot become Saviour.

SUBSTITUTION

To those who regard Jesus Christ as just a great teacher, philosopher, healer, or guide, his death upon a cross is a mystery and without personal significance. Only those who see him as personally suffering the punishment they deserved will desire blood cleansing.

SALVATION

The death of Jesus Christ makes salvation available to a whole world of sinners. But there are conditions to be fulfilled before the gift of God's grace can be personally received:
- Repentance
- Faith
- Obedience

SONSHIP

The experience of new birth in Jesus Christ means a great deal more than assurance of heaven after death. Full membership rights in God's eternal family backed up with his resources are available to each person trusting Jesus Christ as Saviour and Lord.

Secondly, the details:

1. SIN

1. What is sin?

- 'To cast aside the will of God, and to live according to one's own will, deserting that which is true and lawful in order to satisfy one's own desires.' (Sadhu Sundar Singh).

  The Devil deceived Eve in the Garden of Eden, but he did not deceive Adam. Knowing the consequences, he identified with his wife, turned his back on God and intentionally did what he had been warned not to do. That was:

  Rebellion ... disobedience ... independence ... rejection of God's love ... failure to meet God's standard.

- According to God's Word it is:

  breaking the Law. James 2:10; Gal. 3:10; 1 John 3:4; Matt. 22:37. The two duties of the Law are failing to love God and our neighbours as ourselves.

  failing to be righteous. James 4:17; 1 John 5:17; Rom. 14:23.

  rejecting the person and work of Jesus Christ. John 16:8,9; John 3:18.

- Three common temptations which lead to sin are found in 1 John 2:16. Adam and Eve succumbed to them, Jesus Christ resisted them, and Christians are warned against them. **Appetite** (the cravings of sinful man). **Avarice** (the lust of the eyes). **Ambition** (the aspiration to be or do).

2. Who have sinned?

- **Every person is a sinner by nature.** Eph. 2:3; Ps. 58:3; Gen. 8:21.
- **Every sinner is a sinner by choice.** Eccl. 7:20; Ps. 54:2,3; Is. 53:6.
- **There are no exceptions.** Rom. 3:10; Rom. 3:23; Gal. 3:22; 1 Kings 8:46; Rom. 3:19.

3. God says that every sinner will pay the penalty for his own sin.
Ezek. 18:4,20; Rom. 6:23; Rom. 5:12; James 1:15; Rev. 20:15; Rev. 21:8; Luke 19:10; Rom. 3:19.

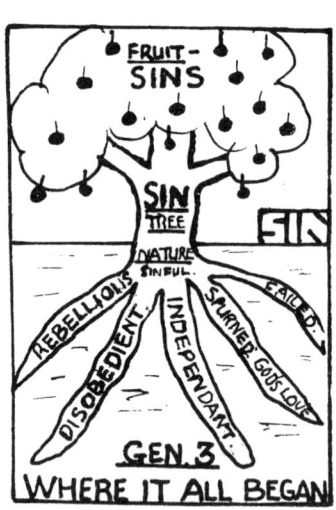

2. SUBSTITUTION

Adam and Eve suffered the full spiritual penalty of death of which God had warned them. They were expelled from the presence of God wearing the skin garments he had made from the animals killed so that blood could atone for (or cover) their sin (Gen. 3:21).

God had kept his word, and the principle of atonement by animal blood was to last a long time, until God provided his own Lamb to take away the sin of the world. John 1:29; Heb. 9:12,14; Is. 53:4-6; 1 Peter 1:9; 1 John 2:2; Ephes. 2:13; 1 Tim. 1:15; 1 Peter 3:18.

The difference between the animals slain first in the Garden of Eden followed by regular sacrifices, and the Lamb from the Garden of Gethsemane is clear:

- The death of animals merely covered sin. The death of Jesus the Lamb removes sin and its guilt for ever.
- Animal sacrifices had to be offered continuously for repeated acts of sin. The death of Jesus Christ was once for all.
- Animal blood was offered for a person, a family or a nation. Jesus Christ offered himself as a sin offering for every person who has lived, or will ever live in the world.
- Animals had no choice as to whether they lived or died. Jesus Christ offered himself willingly.

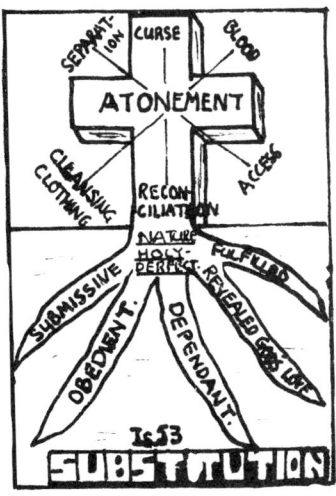

Everything Adam has failed to do Jesus did, breaking the power of Satan once and for all.

Anything man may offer God in exchange for salvation is rejected. Some of these are:

- **wealth.** Ps. 49:6-8; Acts 8:20; 1 Peter 1:18.
- **good living.** Is. 64:6; Prov. 15:8,26..
- **obeying the law, or good works.** Eph. 2:8,9; Titus 3:5; Rom. 4:2; Rom. 3:20.
- **self reformation.** Jer. 2:22.
- **relying on friends or family members.** Acts 4:12; 2 Cor. 8:9.

3. SALVATION

God cannot lightly forgive sins. He has to deal with the root-cause. Our lives are like a tree. What we show on the outside comes from our natures on the inside. To kill a tree, it must first be cut down, then the root system destroyed. Salvation is not just being forgiven like picking off the bad fruit, but demolishing the bad tree to make way for a new one.

1. The necessity of repentance

Repentance involves deep sorrow of heart for thoughts, attitudes, actions and habits contrary to the perfect Law of God, and the forsaking of them all. It must never be confused with feeling sorry for the mess sin has caused in a person's life. That is called attrition. Nor is it contrition or remorse often found in people in prison. Penance and penitence are also confused with repentance. They are often repeated by people who have never let God deal with their sin or found victory through the blood of Jesus Christ. Repentance deals with the root system, making way for a new life style.

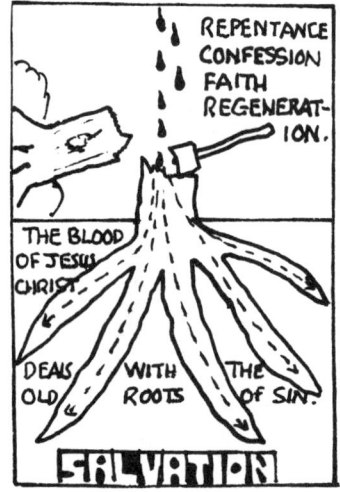

True repentance involves the whole conscious faculty: mind, emotions, desires and will. Repentance has been a key factor in preaching ever since God commissioned men to speak on his behalf. Isa. 55:7: 'Let the wicked *forsake his way* and *the evil man his thoughts*. Let him turn to the Lord, and he will have mercy on him, and to our God, for he will freely pardon'. Prov. 28:13: 'He who conceals his sins does not prosper, but whoever *confesses and renounces* them finds mercy'. See also Job 42:6; Ps. 38:18.

Repentance is mentioned 110 times under both covenants. John the Baptist preached it. The first sermon Jesus preached was simply, 'Repent, for the kingdom of heaven is near' (Matt. 4:17). He also said 'I have not come to call the righteous, but sinners [to repentance]' (Mark 2:17).

Repentance was preached by the apostles and the New Testament Church. Acts 17:30: 'God ... commands all *people* everywhere to repent'. Acts 3:19: 'Repent, then, and turn to God, so that your sins may be wiped out ...'. See also Acts 26:20; 2 Cor. 7:9,10; Ezek. 18:28; Luke 24:47.

A true commitment to Jesus Christ must include repentance. When this is missing, no spiritual progress can be made, and a falling away soon becomes evident. A person may 'convert' himself by turning back to God, but unless he repents, that turning is nothing more than self-reformation. Regeneration has not taken place.

When a sinner genuinely repents and confesses his sin, God forgives, removes the inner stain of guilt and wipes his record clean. Is. 43:25; 44:22; Jer. 33:8; Ex. 34:7; Col. 2:13; Micah 7:19; 2 Cor. 5:19; Ps. 103:11,12; Heb. 10:17.

Genuine repentance is as necessary to salvation as flowers are to fruit. The reality of repentance should be seen in restitution where necessary. Where there has been wrong to another person or property, this needs to be confessed, forgiveness asked, and if necessary restitution made or offered. 'Borrowed' goods also need to be returned. In Luke 19:10 Zacchaeus promised to fulfil the law by offering to make restitution four times any amount wrongly levied. Prov. 14:9 says: 'Fools mock at making amends'.

2. The necessity of faith in the Person and Work of Jesus Christ

Several words are used in the New Testament which produce the same result. They are 'faith', 'believe' and 'receive'. They simply mean the placing of the entire weight of personal trust in the Lord Jesus to implement the blessings of eternal life in the repentant sinner because of his substitutionary death, burial and resurrection on the sinner's behalf. It may be helpful to look at each word in turn.

1. To exercise faith in Christ

To the natural man, seeing is believing. To the man of faith,seeing results from believing. In other words, faith is the bridge between logic and God's fulfilment of his promise. God has paved the path to that bridge with the record of fulfilled promises to nations and individuals who dared to disregard natural instincts and trust his Word. That bridge is the only way to God, for 'without faith it is impossible to please him: for he that cometh to God MUST believe that he is, and that he is a rewarder of them that diligently seek him' (Heb. 11:6 AV).

It is more logical to implicitly trust (or exercise faith in) Jesus Christ for salvation, than to trust a chemist by taking his drugs, or an airline pilot by flying in his plane. The evidence for trustworthiness is infinitely greater. Faith involves three affirmative responses:

- The MIND wants to know why salvation is needed, and who is able to save. The Word of God answers this by bringing awareness of sin, warning of God's judgment of sinners, and presenting Jesus Christ as the only way of salvation.
- The EMOTIONS which dictate so many of our actions must then desire cleansing, forgiveness and life in Christ. It is the Spirit of God who brings conviction and a longing for forgiveness and life. When the mind and the emotions are agreed, this is two-thirds majority, but the most important response remains.
- The WILL can say 'yes' or 'no'. The act of faith in Jesus is based on a positive attitude of mind, the desire of the emotions, and the submission of the will.

It is the activation of the need and desire for salvation that causes a person to place his or her trust solely in Jesus Christ. Tragically many people have had the first two experiences but fear of some kind prevents the vital action of full reliance upon Christ. God will never interfere. He coerces no-one. The whole personality must act willingly.

Acts 20:21 '. . . they must . . . have faith in our Lord Jesus Christ'.

Eph. 2:8,9: 'For by grace are ye saved through faith; and that not of yourselves: it [salvation] is the gift of God' (AV).

Rom. 5:1 (AV): 'Being justified by faith, we have peace with God through our Lord Jesus Christ'.

Gal. 2:16 (AV): 'Knowing that a man is not justified by the works of the law, but by the faith of Jesus Christ'.

See also Gal. 2:15,16; 3:22,26; Phil. 3:9.

2. To believe in Jesus Christ

The word 'belief' means the acceptance of some fact to be true. It may however be just an attitude requiring no positive action. The Greek word belief means much more: 'to trust in, adhere to, or rely upon'. An illustration may throw light on this. A little boy had watched the great tightrope-walker Blondin wheel a barrow over a rope stretched across Niagara Falls. When Blondin asked him whether he believed he could be wheeled across in the barrow, he said he did. When asked to jump in, he quickly backed away, saying that he didn't believe that much. People treat God like that. James said in his epistle: 'Thou believest that there is one God; thou doest well: the devils also believe, and tremble. But wilt thou know, O vain man, that faith without works is dead?' (James 2:19,20 AV).

The important part about believing is doing something about it. To believe is to put all trust and reliance upon Jesus Christ, having confidence in him alone. Active belief is Bible belief.

Acts 16:31: '. . . Believe in the Lord Jesus, and you will be saved'.

John 20:31: 'But these are written, that ye might believe that Jesus is the Christ . . . and that believing ye might have life through his name' (AV).

Acts 13:39: 'And by him all that believe are justified from all things' (AV).

John 11:25,26: 'Jesus said unto her, I am the resurrection, and the life: he that believeth in me, though he were dead, yet shall he live: and whosoever liveth and believeth in me shall never die' (AV).

3. To receive Christ as Saviour

The word 'receive' is also a word of action, explaining in greater detail what is involved by 'faith' and 'belief'. To as many as RECEIVE him, God gives authority to become his children (John 1:12). How does one receive Christ? In the same way as a bride receives a groom to be her husband, by a definite act. The marriage is not legal until both parties have responded with 'I will'. The Saviour says in Rev. 3:20 (AV): 'Behold, I stand at the door, and knock: if any man hear my voice, and open the door, I will come in to him'. Christ has already stated his willingness to enter any door opened to him. All he waits for is a genuine response 'I do receive you Lord Jesus, come into my life as Saviour and Lord'.

This then is the crucial step. The opening of the whole personality to the presence and control of Jesus Christ which he exercises through his Spirit.

The words 'faith' – 'belief' – 'receive' are therefore three interchangeable words giving entrance to life eternal through total submission to the Lordship of Christ at every level of living.

3. The work of regeneration (new birth) is the sovereign responsibility of the Holy Spirit

This is mystical and spiritual, but is the commencement of a new quickening within, a new nature being brought into existence. It began by faith in God's Word, is maintained by faith in his Word, and is NEVER dependent upon feelings. Just as a wedding certificate is the evidence of a ceremony of marriage, so the word of God assures us that:

- we have passed from death to life through hearing and obedience (John 6:24).
- we have received the gift of life everlasting in Jesus Christ (John 3:16; 1 John 5:11,12).
- we have become a child of God through receiving Christ as Saviour (John 1:12).
- we have been born from above (or again) through the Word and the Spirit (John 3:5).
- we have become a new person in Christ (2 Cor. 5:17).
- the new life we have can never end (John 3:36), or be exhausted (John 4:14; 10:10).
- the relationship can never be broken, nor will God forsake us (John 10:27–30).
- the Spirit of God has now taken up permanent residence within us (Rom. 8:15,16).

4. The importance of confession

Confession brings glory to God and confirmation to the heart. The healed maniac at Gadara was not allowed to join the disciples but was sent home to confess (Luke 8:39). The ten Samaritan lepers were sent to confess their healings to the priest (Luke 17:14). All of these people CONFESSED to what they already POSSESSED. The same principle applies in Rom. 10:9–10, where it states a person believes in the heart for justification, and confirms it by open confession.

4. SONSHIP

Just as a newborn baby requires food and care, so the new believer needs to learn:

1. to sustain life and spiritual growth

- **by continuing the closest friendship with the Lord Jesus.**
  He is a constant companion in personal and public living (Heb. 13:5).

- **by confessing recognised sins immediately**
  Sin in a child of God clouds the friendship, but does not break the relationship. 'If we confess our sins, he is faithful and just and will forgive us our sins and purify us from all unrighteousness' (1 John 1:9).

- **by forgiving others who may hurt.**
  'Forgive us our debts, as we also have forgiven our debtors. For if you forgive men when they sin against you, your heavenly Father will also forgive you. But if you do not forgive men their sins, your heavenly Father will not forgive your sins' (Matt. 6:12,14).

- **by keeping an attitude of prayer and communion.** (Talking with God either audibly, or in our hearts.)
  '[Men] should always pray and not give up' (Luke 18:1).
  '. . . in everything, by prayer and petition, with thanksgiving, present your requests to God' (Phil. 4:6).

- **by listening to God's voice through reading his Word daily:**

  —**to always obey him** to be 'approved unto God, a workman that needeth not to be ashamed, rightly dividing the word of truth' (2 Tim. 2:15 AV).

  —**for grace in daily life,** allowing the word of Christ to affect deeply (Col. 3:16). 'Sanctify them by the truth; your word is truth'(John 17:17).

  —**as a guide through life** to make the right choices and avoid pitfalls. 'Order my steps in thy word' (Ps. 119:133 AV).

Diagram: FRUIT OF RIGHTEOUSNESS THROUGH THE HOLY SPIRIT — RIGHTEOUSNESS TREE — A TRUE JESUS / DISCIPLE OF CHRIST — SUBMISSIVE, OBEDIENT, SHARING GOD'S LOVE, DEPENDANT, FULFILLING, NATURE — GOD'S WORD — GOD'S SPIRIT — SONSHIP

2. **What the Spirit of God will do *in* the believer:**
   - Fill him with spiritual ability to produce the character that brings glory to Jesus Christ (Eph. 5:18).
   - Teach the meaning of the Word of God (John 16:13; 1 John 2:27).

3. **What the Spirit will do *for* the believer**
   - Pray for us and give strength in time of weakness (Rom. 8:26).
   - Keep us in close fellowship with God (Jude 24).
   - Answer our prayers (John 14:14).
   - Make us productive Christians (John 15:5).
   - Give strength to resist Satan and his temptations, and live in victory (Heb. 2:18; 1 Cor. 10:13; 1 Pet. 2:9; Col. 1:11,12; 2 Pet. 1:3, 4; Eph. 6:10–18).
   - Teach us how to pray (Jude 20; Eph. 6:18).

4. **What God requires disciples to do**
   - Give themselves unreservedly to him for his unhindered daily use (Rom. 12:1; Prov. 3:6,7).
   - Ask for guidance to fulfil his will in daily living (Rom. 12:2).
   - Obey every instruction in his Word, and every prompting of his Holy Spirit (John 14:21; 16:13–15).
   - Share his love with other believers (John 15:22).
   - Confess Jesus Christ as Lord and Saviour to others. (It is an evidence of salvation: Rom.10:9; 1 John 4:14. It pleases God, and has its own reward: Matt. 10:32,33).
   - Worship with other believers in some Bible-believing, Spirit-filled church (Heb. 10:25). Remember that one coal taken out of a fire soon cools off!
   - Try to win others to Jesus Christ (Matt. 28:19; Prov. 11:30).
   - Trust him to supply needs after sharing in the needs of others (Phil. 4:19).

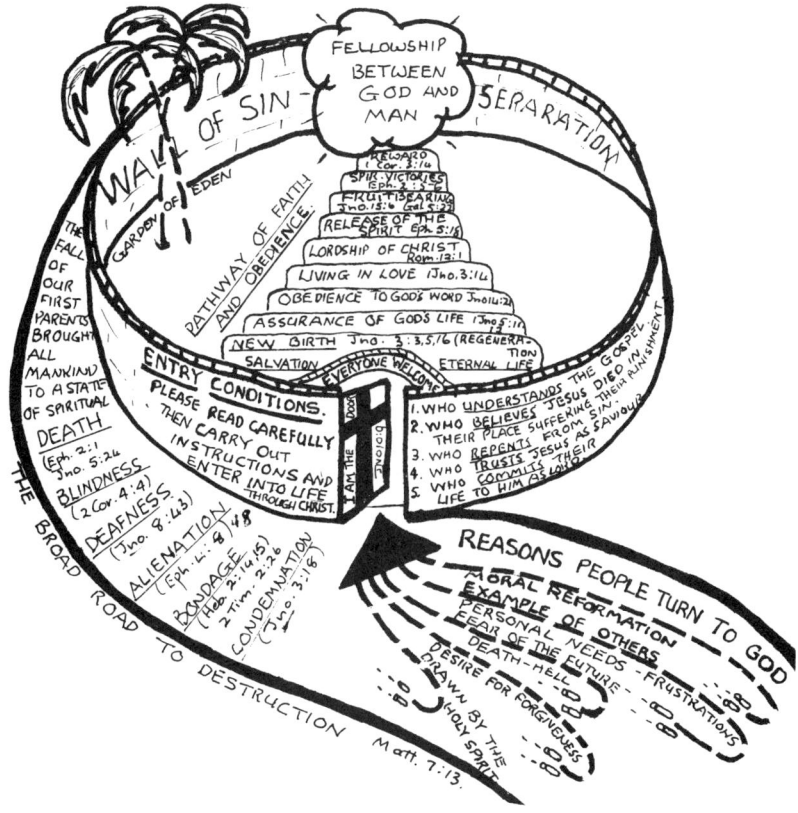

Counselling at a glance

The diagram traces the Fall from the Garden of Eden through the wall of

255

sin and separation from God (spiritual death) to the broad road leading to destruction.

The steps by which man returns to God are most important. Note the process of turning back to God (conversion). Unless repentance is present, they stop short of regeneration. The way by which a person enters into life, grows in maturity in Christ and lives as a disciple, are equally important.

Finally, a delightful comparison between personal work and the threading of a needle. (Author unknown.)

- **Look at the light**
  Because needles have to be threaded against the light make sure you can look to the Lord, without blinking, to see how to centre the thread in the eye.

- **Look the needle straight in the eye to ensure there is no other blockage**
  Make sure the counsellee is receptive and that their mind is not taken up with other things which may hinder understanding or a sincere commitment.

- **Try only one thread at a time**
  Three or four will not fit the eye of the needle at one time. Isolate the interested person, and use other needle threaders if necessary.

- **See that the thread is suitable to the size of the needle**
  A thick thread will not penetrate. Make sure what you say is clear, precise, and easy to understand.

- **Make a point on your thread for easy penetration**
  Never be mechanical. Share the love of Christ and show a personal interest in the counsellee's need of Christ.

- **Don't wave the thread around; bring it into close contact with the needle carefully, and as quickly as possible**
  Use your time wisely, and challenge the counsellee to receive Christ personally as soon as there is understanding and conviction.

- **Push the thread through the eye of the needle—gently**
  Don't stab the thread and split it by being pushy and insensitive.

- **See that the needle is entered fully, and the thread pulled through**
  Don't leave off counselling until the counsellee has assurance of life in Christ.

- **Knot the end**
  Make sure the counsellee is confirmed by the Word of God and has some portion of Scripture to read.

Chapter 4

THE BASICS OF SIMPLE PREACHING

Jeremiah was young and inexperienced when God told him he had chosen him to be his prophet to the nations. It obviously wasn't Jeremiah's choice of a career, so he tried to excuse himself by saying he was too young, therefore unqualified. God took care of that by putting his hand on the young man's lips, saying, 'Now I have put my words in your mouth'. Jeremiah stopped arguing and started preaching.

God still places his hand on mouths and gives the words to say. Sermon construction can be learned by the study of homiletics, but preachers must have the touch of God's hand to speak with his authority. It is no cliché to say that preachers should prepare their sermons as if everything depended upon their preparation, and to wait upon God as if everything depended upon his empowering. This chapter gives some simple basics of preparing evangelistic messages.

Preaching prerequisites

Preserve all scraps of information which you think could be useful in preparing and illustrating Gospel sermons. Get into the habit of carrying a small notebook with you and jot down items of interest you hear, read or see. You will soon accumulate facts, figures, information, quotes, reactions, human interest stories and lots of little details you will find useful. Subject matters, titles for messages and illustrations will often flash into your mind and disappear just as quickly, leaving you frustrated if you have not written them down. Pray over your little 'homiletical seed nursery' and ask the Holy Spirit to germinate those ideas into profitable messages.

But don't stop at the notebook. Develop a filing system most suited to your needs. Start with a large folder with alphabetic divisions, or large labelled envelopes into which you can drop cuttings or notes under different headings. A card-index system within a large cardboard box is another inexpensive system. As materials increase, a commercial filing system may be needed, but whatever you do, resist the temptation to be mesmerised by size and complexity. Be concise and simple. Cull materials frequently. Do your writing or printing in small letters, and if you are liable to be on the move, keep everything portable.

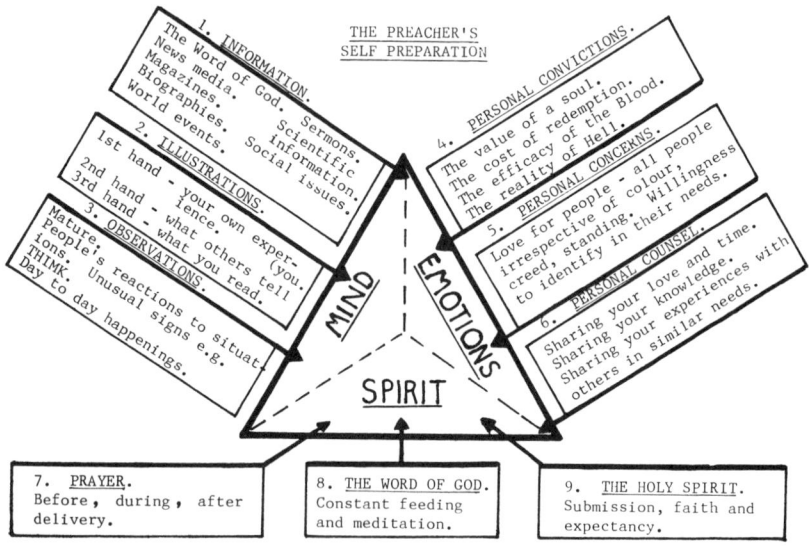

THE PREACHER'S SELF PREPARATION

1. INFORMATION.
The Word of God. Sermons.
News media. Scientific
Magazines. information.
Biographies. Social issues.
World events.

2. ILLUSTRATIONS.
1st hand - your own exper-
2nd hand - ience. what others tell
3rd hand - what you read. (you.

3. OBSERVATIONS.
Mature. reactions to situat-
People's Unusual signs e.g.
ions. to day happenings.
THINK.
Day

4. PERSONAL CONVICTIONS.
The value of a soul.
The cost of redemption.
The efficacy of the Blood.
The reality of Hell.

5. PERSONAL CONCERNS.
Love for people - all people
irrespective of colour,
creed, standing. Willingness
to identify in their needs.

6. PERSONAL COUNSEL.
Sharing your love and time.
Sharing your knowledge.
Sharing your experiences with
others in similar needs.

MIND EMOTIONS

SPIRIT

7. PRAYER.
Before, during, after delivery.

8. THE WORD OF GOD.
Constant feeding and meditation.

9. THE HOLY SPIRIT.
Submission, faith and expectancy.

Preaching preparation

Types of evangelistic messages are varied.

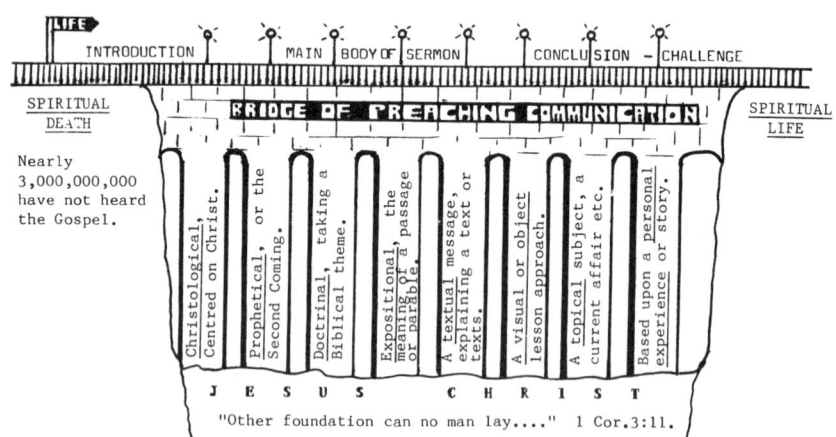

LIFE

INTRODUCTION   MAIN BODY OF SERMON   CONCLUSION - CHALLENGE

SPIRITUAL DEATH   BRIDGE OF PREACHING COMMUNICATION   SPIRITUAL LIFE

Nearly 3,000,000,000 have not heard the Gospel.

Christological, Centred on Christ.

Prophetical, or the Second Coming.

Doctrinal, taking a Biblical theme.

Expositional, the meaning of a passage or parable.

A textual message, explaining a text or texts.

A visual or object lesson approach.

A topical subject, a current affair etc.

Based upon a personal experience or story.

J E S U S   C H R I S T

"Other foundation can no man lay...." 1 Cor.3:11.

258

A few bridge-building rules:

- Unless there is a Rock foundation, the finest bridge will not be safe.
- The type of sermon chosen must adequately explain the way from death to life.
- To get strength in sermon construction, preach and explain the Word of God faithfully, and let your illustrations and supporting material be used wisely.
- Never finish a bridge in mid-air, connect with reality both sides.
- Make sure the bridge is sufficiently well-lit by the lights of simple language, adequate explanation and good illustrations for people to make their way across.

Some background information

Before you begin to prepare your Gospel sermon, ask five simple one-word questions each commencing with the letter 'W'.

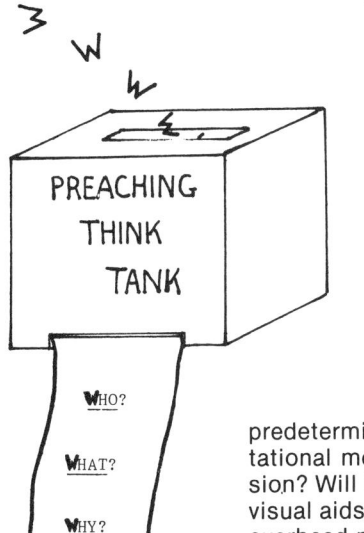

WHO?

Who will make up your audience? Is it a particular age or interest group? Your approach and subject matter will obviously vary between children, teenagers, youth groups, adults, families, senior citizens, university students, professional people or service clubs. Use your imagination and ask yourself, 'What approach would appeal to me if I were in that group?

WHAT?

What is the aim of the gathering? Is it to win people to Jesus Christ? A regular or special church service with a predetermined subject? A missionary or deputational meeting, a devotional, or a teaching session? Will there be a question time? Will you need visual aids, a sketchboard, a slide projector? Is an overhead projector available?

WHY?

Why have I been asked to preach? Am I expected to do something of a special nature? It may cause you embarrassment if people have been told to expect something about which you have not been briefed.

WHEN?

When does the service commence? When do I begin preaching and how much time do I have? These are important details. Don't assume you will have all the time you want to preach. Find out, and prepare accordingly. The less time you have to preach, the more exact your preparation will need to be. The timing will also regulate audiences. For example, children and senior citizens attend morning rather than evening services, and public holidays often reduce the size of the congregation.

WHERE?

Where exactly is the venue? Don't arrive red-faced, out of breath, and full of apologies thirty minutes after the service began because you thought you knew where to go.

Sermon preparation

Never ask God to bless what he has neither given nor approved. Preachers are constantly faced with the temptation to reach for their well-used sermon notes and select a favourite, or hunt through books for ideas, rather than wait upon God for what he wants to say. What God gives will carry his authority. Ask him to originate, not patronise your sermons.

It is not the delivery which makes a sermon powerful, but the contents. Never substitute perspiration for inspiration, or rhetoric for an anointing of the Holy Spirit. Another significant omission from modern sermon preparation is—tears. They have a vast effect on the preacher's attitude to the lost, his relationship with God, and how he preaches. Dr Stephen Olford, one of this generation's powerful preachers, recommends that preachers pray their sermons over before God first, and that unless they hear a concluding 'Amen' from heaven, they should be abandoned. The sermons which God delights to bless are those which make much of the person and work of Jesus Christ. God-fearing preachers say what God wants people to know, not what people want to hear. Make this your number one aim and see what God will do for you.

Time with God should always have top priority in preparation. It is better to have a sketchy outline because you have spent time with God, than a powerless sermon with elaborate notes. The warmth of heaven in the heart, and its glow on the face, will lift messages far beyond human ability. Unction always rates before oratory in preaching (1 Cor. 2:3-5; 1 Thess. 1:5, 2:4; Eph. 6:19).

Set aside sufficient time for adequate preparation

Words need to be accurate, meaningful, informative, easy to understand and relevant to the hearers. Use variety. The approach and means used need to be adapted for your audience.

Another reason for good preparation is that research may turn up further information, or it may prevent you from saying something which could be contradicted.

When you have the basic details of subject matter, title and research materials, let the Lord shape your message into three inter-related parts. Whether you write your sermon in full then reduce to working notes, or simply preach from an outline is a matter of personal choice.

1. The introduction

Your introduction should be friendly, maybe with a touch of humour, short, simple and alive. Don't let your introduction encourage your hearers to fluff up their mental pillows in anticipation of forty winks!

If you haven't already announced your subject, the introduction should let people know where you are heading. One hazard is the danger of taking so much time over the introduction that more important materials have to be omitted, in order to keep reasonably to time. The only known remedy is self-discipline.

Preachers who follow other speakers may have to forego their planned introduction, and key into the previous message for a smooth flow-on. Basically, the introduction is the launching pad for the theme of the sermon. You need wisdom to make the right start.

Some suggestions are:
- the use of a human interest story.
- the asking of a challenging or metaphorical question.
- a summary of information which throws light on the subject matter, perhaps historic, geographic, analytical or scientific.
- the use of quotations made by significant people—'As Abraham Lincoln once said . . .' etc.
- the use of a humorous story which opens up the subject. Moving from the opening into the sermon itself should be natural and smooth.

2. The main body of the sermon

The subject matter is developed stage by stage in preparation for the final application, or challenge. If its aim is to win people to Jesus Christ, it must be full of teaching about him, well illustrated, heart warming, conscience awakening, and challenging to the will.

The Rev. Dr John Stott claims 'Evangelism is offering Christ to the people. Take Christ from the Gospel and you disembowel it'. The Rev. John Wesley once summed up his own preaching in four words: 'I offered them Christ'. Evangelistic sermons should offer Christ:

- **as the Divine Lord**, the Eternal Word made flesh, forever identified with man whom he created, and for whom he died.
- **as the historic Christ**, confirmed by history, but not confined to it.
- **as the crucified Saviour and risen Lord of Glory**. The resurrection was the key factor of New Testament preaching. Without it the Gospel is meaningless, no promise may be claimed and no power is available.
- **as the reigning Christ**. King of his eternal kingdom who regards nations as a drop in a bucket. The determiner of all future events.
- **as the Saving Christ**. People must be told that he is always ready to save. Again quoting Dr Stott, 'The most pregnant phrase in the New Testament is: "HE BORE OUR SINS".'
  James Denney once said that the cross is like the barb on a fisherman's hook. He told of a friend who had lost his bait while out fishing and caught nothing. When he pulled his line in, he found that the barb had broken off, the fish had taken the bait and escaped. 'So', said Denney, 'the condemnation of our sins in Christ upon his cross is the

barb on the hook. If you leave that out of your Gospel, I do not deny that your bait will be taken, but you will not catch men'.

- **As the expected Christ**, the Messiah of Whom both Old and New Testaments constantly speak concerning his return to earth.
- **as the judging Christ**. Appointed by God his father to judge the living and the dead in his eternal kingdom.

1. **Three main points are ideal.**

   Firstly, complicated sermons cause mental fatigue, and if the seats happen to be uncomfortable, boredom and restlessness will soon be evident. Secondly, people can only absorb a certain amount at one sitting; the rest is forgotten. Three good points are as much as people can remember with ease, and people will bless you for them. Maybe the negro preacher asked about his preaching habits knew this when he said, 'Fust of all ah tells em what ah is goin to tell 'em. Then ah tells 'em. Finally ah tells 'em what ah has just told em'.

   Open air sermons should be committed to memory as notes are not practicable outdoors. In the case of interruption, a preacher will be able to recall his message much more easily if the main points have been clearly impressed on his mind.

2. **The theme should be progressively developed**

   An experienced preacher was giving advice to a younger man on this point. He picked up a piece of paper and sketched a large iron spike—the type used to secure a plate to a railroad wooden sleeper. Then he drew a sledge hammer driving in the spike, and made the point that only direct hits on the head of the spike will drive it into place. Then he looked up and said, 'Make every part of your sermon a telling blow to drive the point of the message further into place. Don't waste blows'. That young man never forgot the message. He was the writer.

3. **Arrange your materials in logical sequence**

   We live in an ordered world and do things in an orderly manner. For example, who ever dresses with underwear on top of street clothes, or serves a meal which commences with sweets and concludes with the soup? Preaching is no different. Be logical, and people will follow your line of reasoning.

4. **Be simple in the way you speak, even if the subject matter is profound**

   Theological wording is essential for study and academic dialogue, but the average church attender is not impressed. If he is looking for forgiveness, strength, or help in a special time of loneliness, grief or temptation, he needs words he can understand and rely upon. The words Jesus used were simple, and well illustrated by parables and real life stories. No wonder people flocked to hear him.

5. **Using suitable illustrations**

   Illustrations should be used like windows in a building. Enough to throw light into dark areas without weakening the structure. They ought:

- not to overshadow the deeper teachings of the sermon.
- never be so graphic or emotional that people respond under the pressure of emotionalism.
- not be so complicated that the hearers leave off listening to puzzle over their meaning. The best illustrations are from daily life.
- never to be out of taste, or offensive. When preaching in other cultures, enquire if there is anything which should be avoided to protect your credibility.
- not too boring in detail, but accurate, with touches of authenticity such as the spelling of an unusual name, or the giving of an important date.
- to be suitable to the age group and level of understanding.
- never be used to fill in time, or make up for lack of substance in the message.

3. The conclusion and climax

The Apostle Paul had one objective in preaching to the Corinthians. It was that their faith would not depend on men's wisdom but on God's power (1 Cor. 2:4-5). He looked to the Spirit of God to make such an impact that people would believe, not on the basis of his reasoning, but because God had given them understanding. As a result their faith rested on revelation received from God, not on argument or rationalistic reasoning.

Because public responses to Gospel preaching are sometimes not permissible or advisable, preachers should aim to climax their Gospel messages with a personal challenge to respond to Jesus Christ in repentance, faith and discipleship. Hearers should be left in no doubt as to how to exercise faith in Christ. The timing of the response is then their personal responsibility.

Where public responses are expected, or customary, an invitation should not be made automatically, but only as the Holy Spirit directs. With indoor congregations, people may be asked to indicate their willingness to respond to Jesus Christ as Saviour and Lord by a variety of ways:

- by the raising of hands during a time of prayer, then coming forward for counselling during the last hymn.
- by coming to the front while everyone is standing, during the singing of a hymn.
- by remaining in their seats afterwards, to indicate they wish to speak to a counsellor.
- by going to a counselling room at the conclusion of the service.
- by asking someone nearby to go with them to be counselled.

Personal embarrassment needs to be avoided at all costs such as asking Christians to sit down, leaving only unbelievers standing. Another wrong method is to tell people their response is between themselves and God alone, then invite them to come forward publicly for counsel. The writer has seen some very angry responses to preachers using these tactics.

If it is impracticable or impossible for people to come to the front of an auditorium, the following steps are suggested:

1. Explain step-by-step the meaning of turning from sin (repentance); the asking for forgiveness (confession); the manner in which a person enters into life in Christ (receiving Christ by faith); the open acknowledgment of Christ as Lord (confession); and obedience (discipleship).

2. Invite those willing to enter into such a commitment to Jesus Christ to repeat the following prayer, said slowly:

'Dear God,

I realise I have sinned against you by going my own way, doing my own thing, and failing to honour you. I am truly sorry for this and now by your strength turn my back on these things. Thank you for punishing your Son Jesus on my behalf. Please forgive all my sin and wrongdoing. (Quietly name them.)

Lord Jesus, I trust you as my Saviour, and invite you to take over my whole personality by your Spirit. Please live your life in me, and make me the kind of person you want me to be.

Amen.'

Whether people responding are dealt with by personal workers or repeat the preacher's prayer, workers should distribute literature, and obtain names and addresses for follow-up purposes.

Types of Preaching

Preachers inevitably express their personalities in their delivery styles, and hearers often react by turning 'on' or 'off'. Those who like forceful preachers will quickly lose concentration with a slow or quiet speaker, and the quiet type freezes when he hears someone become demonstrative or enthusiastically raise their voice level. Preachers need to be sensitive to the Holy Spirit, and flexible in delivery so that the message will not be hindered. Warmth, sincerity, conviction and spiritual authority can be expressed in any type of delivery without offence. Delivery styles include:

1. **The fire-cracker or bouncing-ball type** who is perpetual in sound and motion. His words are forceful, even verbal explosions, and they swamp the audience at tidal-rate volume. Every part of this preacher works at one time, and at speed. The audience grows tired as they watch him throw himself into it. He makes an ideal outdoor speaker, or revivalist, but is a disaster where peace and quietness are needed. Powerful speakers are needed, provided God supplies the power. Remember that:
   - forcefulness, word volume and restless movement may be the flesh making up for the lack of Holy Spirit anointing.
   - if the message is accompanied by distracting mannerisms, the impact is drastically reduced.
   - too many words at high speed will reduce effectiveness. Stop occasionally to let your hearers get their 'mental breath' again.

2. **The efficient, steady-pace, unexcitable teacher type.** Wind him up and he won't vary his speed or run out of words until he presses the stop

button. He makes an ideal pastor-teacher rather than evangelist. He is easy to follow, methodical, and a delight to the note taker. He seldom makes his hearers uncomfortable, and those who like an undisturbed church atmosphere love him. He would probably not volunteer to preach outdoors, and will certainly satisfy those who are allergic to fireball preaching. But he too should remember:

- that his message must contain sufficient quality and interest to keep chins from sinking to chest level.
- to vary the rate and tone of his delivery.

3. **The easy-going, conversational type** creates his own drawing room atmosphere. He looks and sounds relaxed and proceeds to treat his audience as one big happy family. He may call for answers to questions, carry on an imaginary dialogue, or have a brief conversation with someone in his audience, but he gets through. He holds interest, uses everyday language, and thoroughly enjoys himself. The people like his humour, stories and actions, because he is alive and one of them. But remember:

- if the message has not penetrated, a warm personality does not save people.
- the free and easy style could become a lazy way of avoiding time for prayer, study and preparation.
- there is a danger of allowing an easy-going atmosphere to compromise the seriousness and challenge of the Gospel.

Preachers must develop their own distinctive preaching style, but not wear it as a straight jacket. Solomon was right; there is a time to be dynamic and a time to be quiet, a time for confrontation, and time for friendliness. There are times for questions and times for authoritative teaching. The timekeeper is the Holy Spirit, but 'Woe to me if I do not preach the Gospel' (1 Cor. 9:16b).

Finally, some reminders.

Just as students have last minute cramming before exams, and players last minute coaching before games, so preachers need last minute reminders.

- Stand tall when you preach, don't slouch or spread yourself over the pulpit.
- Don't let people see you are nervous. Tell-tale signs are fiddling with your tie or the microphone stand, jingling coins in your pocket, or continuously raising and lowering your spectacles.
- Treat your hearers like friends, be your nicest, relaxed self.
- Remember humour is like fire, good to warm the atmosphere but dangerous when nothing is serious.
- Avoid letting your sermon wander wherever a nice thought leads it.
- Remember to stop when you have finished—the first time.
- Aim to express everything positively; outlaw the negative.
- Be enthusiastic, but don't overact, use your spiritual authority, but don't be an authoritarian.
- Never preach down to people. Speak as one of them.
- Don't prepare too much material. Convince, not confuse your hearers.

- Apply your message as you go, so that anyone who leaves before you finish will take something of substance with them.
- Let your conclusion call for action, not just the forming of an opinion.
- Use hand gestures to emphasise important points.
- Never say what you don't believe, God is listening.
- If you hold strong opinions, avoid being dogmatic.
- Be faithful in preaching God's word, don't select what suits you or worse still, what the audience wants to hear (Rom. 15:19).
- Don't point your finger at your audience and say 'you'. Spread your hands and say 'we'.
- Always look your audience in the eye as you speak. Shifty-eyed wall and ceiling inspectors don't communicate.
- If the unexpected happens while you are preaching, handle it in a dignified and God-honouring manner (Phil. 1:27).
- Preach in a firm, even strong voice, but don't shout. That means you are out of control.
- Pronounce your words clearly and distinctly.
- Vary your style from time to time by a tone change, a pause, or a question such as 'I am sure you agree, don't you?'
- Practise your sermon over and over again if you are an inexperienced preacher. Get used to the sound of your own voice, and correct any wrong facial expressions in front of a mirror. Ask your wife or a friend to evaluate your sermon (that is if the relationship is strong enough to stand for frankness!)
- Keep your message for future use in your filing system.
- Sermon outlines should be merely referred to during delivery, rather than read. A preacher who relies on the Holy Spirit will communicate much better than a person reading a sermon word for word.
- For outdoor preaching there are some additional 'don't forgets':
  — a good outdoor message will be well-received indoors, but a good indoor message may be a disaster outdoors.
  — please don't try raising your voice tone at the end of a sentence, or placing the tips of the fingers together while preaching.
  — maintain the interest level otherwise you can say 'goodbye' to your audience.

Don't be discouraged by your mistakes as you gain experience. Persevere, pray more, learn from your mistakes and those of others. Books provide knowledge, but wisdom comes from the Lord. Apply the principles of sowing given in Psalm 126, and gather your harvest in eternity.

Chapter 5

FINALLY — A SPIRITUAL FITNESS TEST

A famous Italian mountain climber by the name of Walter Bonatti once placed his life on the line. He set out to climb the Matterhorn by the seemingly impossible vertical ice-covered north wall. A Swiss guide when he heard of it, shuddered, and said it was a route 'that a drop of water would follow'. Together with two friends, Gigi Panei aged 50, and Alberto Tassotti aged 47, Bonatti took two days to reach the shelter of the Hornli Ridge at the 10 500 feet level. They paused only briefly to rest before attacking the 3550 foot cliff of the North wall. Going up hand over hand on nylon ropes they climbed 420 feet the first day and 550 on the second. Both nights they slept in mid-air on ropes anchored to pitons with sleeping bags pulled up to their shoulders and nylon tents over their heads to protect them from the bitter cold. On the third day at 3 a.m. it began snowing and 60 mph gusts lashed them. One gust ripped the tent off Bonatti's head, and with his face rimmed with ice, he felt excruciating pain. None of them could move, the slightest movement would have been fatal. At 10.30 a.m. the next morning the ascent was abandoned, and it took until 6 p.m. to descend the freshly ice covered wall to a narrow ledge, the first horizontal surface they had seen for five days.

What incredible dedication to training, fitness, discipline, mental concentration, and endurance must have been needed to even attempt such a feat! And for what purpose? Probably just for the personal satisfaction of achieving the seemingly impossible, or for a place in the record book. Bonatti and his two friends missed their goal, but saved their lives.

Jesus Christ reached his goal at the cost of his life, and left his disciples no option about the dedication he expected from them, and those who followed them.

'If anyone would come after me (desires to be my disciple, Amp.) he must **deny himself** and **take up his cross** and **follow me**. For whoever wants to save his life will lose it, but whoever loses his life for me will find it' (Matt. 16:24,25).

In other words, those who make disciples, must first learn themselves to be disciples. There are three distinctive specifications.

1. Discipline of self. ('If anyone would come after me, he must deny himself . . .')

If the Christian life were an obstacle course, this would surely be the first tough hurdle. The self life acts so often like a pet dog, always barking and jumping all over you, wanting attention. Just feed it, stroke it, or play with it, and you will be smothered with licks of approval. If you give that dog the chance, it will lead you around and you will become its servant. It takes rigid discipline to allow Jesus to be Lord over the thousand and one things that claim first place. The best type of discipline is the self-administered kind. It hurts initially, but by perseverance, it becomes a habit. Then there is submission to the discipline of others. That hurts a lot more because it whittles down pride. God also disciplines us because he loves us so much. He believes in house-cleaning before house-furnishing. Solomon talked a lot about discipline but finished badly because he didn't take his own advice. What can we learn from him?

1. **Discipline leads to truth, wisdom and understanding**

    'Buy the truth and do not sell it; get wisdom, discipline, and understanding' (Prov. 23:23).
    'Whoever loves discipline loves knowledge, but he who hates correction is stupid' (Prov. 12:1).
    'The fear of the Lord is the beginning of knowledge, but fools despise wisdom and discipline' (Prov. 1:7).

    Dr Watts had a fruit tree in his garden which was his pride and joy. Every summer it fruited prolifically. One year when it was laden he was horrified to see his gardener cut down a lot of suckers which had grown up around the trunk. In his opinion the extra growth made the tree even more attractive. Where the good Doctor saw beauty, the gardener saw danger. For the sake of the size and quality of the coming crop, he used the pruning knife. It is most unwise to allow matters of secondary importance to sap what God sees as best.

2. **Discipline keeps a person from sexual sin and its ruin**

    'At the end of your life you will groan, when your flesh and body are spent. You will say "How I hated discipline! How my heart spurned correction" ' (Prov. 5:12,13).

    A young man in prison asked to see the writer. He was a university student and a professing Christian when moral temptation hit him. He couldn't resist, and lost his professional career, his family respect, and his life's ambitions. At the end of the conversation he said with moving sincerity 'Would you please warn Christian young people wherever you see them, that I came into this prison for one reason only. I did not keep up my Bible reading and prayer'. A fence at the top of a cliff is better than an ambulance at the bottom.

One frightening trend among God's people today is an acceptance of sexual situation ethics. God's 'thou shalt not' becomes 'under normal circumstances thou shalt not. However, should an unexpected situation arise where it is difficult to do anything else, or where no harm is done by it, or where it is the nicest way of two people expressing their love, then it's permissible.' Like the trapdoor spider, Satan cleverly camouflages the doors to his death-dealing traps.

He has special lures for pastors, evangelists and full-time Christian workers. They include laziness, money, overwork, pride, and sex sometimes the most subtle of all. Jesus Christ was tempted that way, and because he did not yield, he has promised victory, even in the hottest temptations (Heb. 2:18).

3. **Discipline preserves from poverty and disgrace**

'He who ignores discipline comes to poverty and shame' (Prov. 13:18).

It wasn't Solomon who said 'the way to hell is paved with good intentions' but his proverbs pointed to that conclusion.

Disciples need deliverance from the tyranny of time consuming nonessentials. Paul set his goal, and refused to settle for anything less. 'I want to know Christ and the power of his resurrection and the fellowship of sharing in his sufferings.'

Each one of us has 24 hours per day at our disposal. Each hour has 60 minutes containing 60 seconds each available for some chosen activity. Think of it, 84 600 seconds in one day. What a huge investment potential for Bible study, prayer, personal preparation, and service for Jesus Christ. If a dedicated communist devotes eight hours to work, eight hours to sleep and relaxation, and eight hours to the party, surely a disciple of Jesus can better that? Wasting time while the devil works turns the call of God into a mere hobby.

4. **Self discipline shows a person has a healthy self-respect**

'He who ignores discipline despises himself' (Prov. 15:32).

One of the most common causes of spiritual weakness is a low self-image. It is understandable when unbelievers sometimes suffer from lack of identity, but should a child of the King immortal, invisible? How dare we? Are we not heirs of God and joint heirs with Jesus Christ? Then let us live like princes and princesses, it costs no more than living like a pauper.

If you happen to be flat on the floor of self-pity and low self-image, welcome discipline as a friend and let it help you stand tall in Jesus Christ. Realise your potential in God, and possess your possessions as a true disciple of Jesus Christ. (For further references on the need for daily self discipline, see Rom. 6:16–23; 8:1–13; Gal. 5:19–24; Col. 3:1–10).

2. Distinctiveness of standard ('... and take up his cross ...')

Nobody ever sets out with the intention of becoming second-rate. They just perform at a level that is less than their capability, like the business firm with the sign: 'This is a non-profit company, but it was not intended to be that way'.

Most preachers start off by wanting to be another Spurgeon, Moody, or Billy Graham, but few make it. Little thought, if any, goes into the cost price of carrying the cross day and night which is the ceaseless vigil of thinking and doing everything as Jesus would.

It is not the size of the emblem of the cross we wear that counts, but the inner standard of character and life which shows the Lordship of the Christ of the cross. Many a hairy arm used in violence has a cross tattoo on it, and many an ear of a prostitute has a good luck symbol of a cross dangling from it. Meaningless symbolism is not the believer's cross. To him, or her, the cross means being nailed to the holy ethical standards of the living Christ in mind, emotions, will and body.

The standards of the cross feature largely in evangelism. Paul reminded the Church at Corinth of his objectives in visiting them (1 Cor. 2:2). It was not to flaunt his degree from Gamaliel College (where he only averaged a 'C' for sermon delivery), or to show off his impressive intellectual approach. He even said he had really only one sermon title: 'Jesus Christ and the matter of his crucifixion'. The fact that he had already earned the antagonism and scorn of the cultured Greeks and the legalistic Jews didn't embarrass him in the slightest. He lived the cross and preached the cross, so God gave him the power of the cross.

Taking up the cross of Jesus Christ may mean going without some of the goodies of life. Jesus did not say take up your four wheel drive vehicle and fully equipped trailer home and follow me.

The writer had a doctor friend who lived with his wife and family above the 12 000 foot level in the Andes of South America. Asked what his standard of living was, he said it was better than most of the people. Pressed further, he admitted he had packing case furniture self-made, with one luxury, a canvas deck-chair. There was not a word about missing the family monogrammed china-ware, or an extensively equipped surgery. He bore his cross without flinching, even when trying to change a punctured tyre in freezing temperatures at high altitude!

Little pieces of gold jewellery were not what Jesus had in mind. The cross Jesus bore was so heavy, he fell. So rough, he bled. To carry a disciple's cross calls for spiritual fitness as three young men found out to their surprise in Luke 9:57–62.

1. The first wasn't prepared to forego his personal rights.

When he heard that Jesus had no accommodation booked for the night, he backed out. No soft pillow, feather bed, and eight hours sleep? The cross wasn't padded enough to suit him. If you are set on a 'career' in evangelism without financial insecurity, late hours, poor accommodation, little or no food, and a lot of hard work for the sake of the Kingdom, you too had better turn back.

2. **The second wasn't prepared to forego his personal possessions.**

Of the three, he was the only one Jesus invited personally. He may have been on the point of accepting when he suddenly thought of the large slice of his father's estate which would be his when the old gentleman died. He wondered whether he could trust the rest of the family to treat him fairly, so he asked for a later call-up date. It never came. The cross was too inconvenient for him.

3. **The third wasn't prepared to forego personal relationships.**

At the very least, he felt he should go home and say goodbye to Mum and Dad, throw a farewell party for his friends, get some clean clothes and catch up with the rest of the gang later in the week. He didn't make it either, the cross was bad timing for him.

The longer the time gap between God's call and obedience, the less chance that it will be honoured. God is the God of the NOW. 'Follow me', means right away. Discipleship offers neither excuses, nor reasons for delay, only 'Yes, Sir, certainly Sir!' (Further references concerning taking up the cross daily—Luke 9:23; Rom. 6:11–13; 8:12–13; Col. 1:23, 2:6–7, 3:5–10).

3. Diligence of submission ('. . . and follow me')

This final discipleship specification means 'Quick march, left–right-left–right . . .' Spiritual soldiers obey orders, no answering back, no privileges, no meddling in other's affairs, no disobedience, no strikes, and no idleness. These daily parade ground activities are basics of everyday Christian living.

1. **Following obediently honours God, and glorifies Jesus**

Disobedience in a soldier, or disciple, means mutiny. The writer has printed two important verses in his prayer folder as a daily warning against spiritual revolt.

'For you must worship no other gods but only Jehovah, for he is a God who claims absolute loyalty and exclusive devotion' (Ex. 34:14, Living Bible).

'You have laid down precepts that are to be fully obeyed' (Ps. 119:4).

There is one important difference between the soldier and the disciple. The soldier may hate the person giving orders and obey only because he is forced to. The disciple loves the one he obeys, and his greatest reward comes from joyful obedience. Very few of us take to obedience without some protest. The writer still remembers his father's leather strap. It was a well used deterrent to disobedience when he was young. First the feel, then the sight, and finally just the promise of its use was sufficient to produce obedience.

Adam learned that disobedience brought instant punishment. Abraham learned that obedience delighted God, and was rewarded. Pharaoh always disobeyed, and never learned. When the children of Israel were called to stand between the Mountains Gerazim and Ebal they heard the blessings of obedience and cursings of disobedience. Jesus said the same things because God's requirements are unchangeable.

- 'If you love me **you will obey** what I command' (John 14:15)
- 'Whoever has my commands **and obeys them,** he is the one who loves me. He who loves me will be loved of my Father, and I too will love him and show myself to him' (John 14:21).
- **'If anyone loves me he will obey my teaching** (John 14:23a) '. . . he who does not love me will not obey my teaching; (John 14:24).
- 'If you obey my commands you will remain in my love' (John 15:10).

Discipleship means following close enough to hear every word of command, and obeying it.

2. **Following attentively means nothing is missed.**

Jesus said 'Follow me and I will make you fishers of men'. The process took more than 3 years to complete and the finishing touches were supplied by the Holy Spirit. The Book of Acts is in fact a textbook on discipleship. Comparing the 20th Century with the 1st Century we cannot but ask a leading question.

Why are there so many professing Christians today and so few practising disciples? Many answers rush defensively to mind. The Gospel is not being preached with its old-fashioned clarity. There is lack of depth in follow-up, and church failure in Christian education. But let us be wary of quick answers and give the subject more thought.

The parable of the sower and the seed sounds a loud warning to all would-be scatterers of the Gospel seed.

- **The seed which became bird feed.** (Matt. 13:1–9, 18–23; Mark 4:1–20; Luke 8:5–15).
  The devil doesn't want anyone to believe the gospel so he shuts minds and confuses thinking. Unless the light of God penetrates the darkness the Gospel doesn't mean a thing. He then removes all memory of it like a bird picking up seed.
- **The seed which had no chance to germinate.**
  No plant can survive without a reasonable amount of soil, and a Gospel response coming from emotional feelings and good intentions will never produce a sound Christian. A little opposition from friends, family or workmates and the effervescence of emotion and good intentions dry up. There is no nourishment in rock.
- **The seed which grew into healthy plants and died.**
  Some people would be Christians if they could hang out a sign 'Business and parties as usual!' Some seed fell among the thorn bushes, but germinated. The people were sincere, the soil produced healthy looking plants. But before long the thorns grew all over them. The leaves got no sun, turned yellow and finally the plants died. What looked so promising was lifeless.

The test of a good plant is not who sowed the seed, and when, but does it bear fruit? The Bible says we are not to judge other people, but if a piece of fruit happens to fall into your hand, an inspection will soon show the type of tree it came from. 'By their fruit you will know them.' The writer once owned a house with a large peach tree in full view of the road, and sometimes people stopped to photograph the tree smothered in pink flowers. In due course the peaches arrived, grew to a certain size, and fell off. That tree produced cases and cases of rotten fruit. Not one piece was ever eaten because the tree suffered from a fruit-fly disease. The show was terrific, the results were terrible.

- **The reproducing seed.**
  Finally, Jesus showed in the parable that good seed always produces good fruit when people understand the Gospel and obey it fully. Faith and obedience commence together at salvation and go hand-in-hand as a process to the fruit-bearing stage. No wonder it was said of the heroes of faith in Hebrews 11: 'All these people were still living by faith when they died (v. 13). Obedience is the self-discipline of discipleship. The problem of non-practising professions is not the clarity of Gospel preaching, but the completeness of it. The necessity of continuing obedience in discipleship is not being preached. The emphasis is on short-term response, rather than long term results. Preacher and hearer alike need to note the warnings of Scripture:

'... and we are his house **IF** we hold on to our courage and the hope of which we boast' (Heb. 3:6).
'But now he has reconciled you by Christ's physical body through death to present you holy in his sight, without blemish and free from accusation—**IF** you continue in your faith, established and firm, not moved away from the hope held out in the Gospel' (Col. 1:22,23).
'By this Gospel you are saved **IF** you hold firmly to the word I preached to you. Otherwise, you have believed in vain' (1 Cor. 15:2).
'We have come to share in Christ, **IF** we hold firmly till the end the confidence we had at first' (Heb. 3:14).
'We want each of you to show this same diligence to the very end **IN ORDER** to make your hope sure' (Heb. 6:11).
'Let us not become weary in doing good for at the proper time we will reap a harvest **IF** we do not give up' (Gal. 6:9).
'**IF** anyone does not remain in me, he is like a branch that is thrown away and withers' (John 15:6).

The Lord Jesus clearly showed what type of fruit he had in mind for mature plants of discipleship (John 15:5,8).
- Greater love for him, than anyone or anything else (Luke 14:26–27:33).
- Greater love for one another (John 13:34–35).
- Greater obedience to his word
  'To the Jews who had believed him Jesus said, "If you hold to my teaching, you are really my disciples. Then you will know the truth,

and **the truth will set you free**" ' (John 8:32). (See also Heb. 5:9; Rom. 1:5; 1 Peter 1:2.)

The deeper truths of the Word of God are never reached by the casual reader. It is to disciples who faithfully obey all the Word says, that the power of its liberating truth is revealed. Disciple-makers must themselves be such close disciples that their hearers will see as well as hear Jesus in them.

Finally, following Jesus means going anywhere, anytime, regardless of cost. All the information in this book, and all the time taken to read it will mean nothing if it ends only in armchair dialogue. Walter Bonatti and his two friends mortgaged their lives for one thing, reaching a goal by a route no-one had ever conquered. When Jesus says 'Follow me' he has already been the route he leads his disciples.

The writer once attended a Congress on Evangelism in Devlali, India attended by selected nationals from Asian countries. During this time, the following story was told about how the Gospel entered Korea during the 19th Century.

Two Korean brothers were studying medicine under a famous doctor in China. He was a fine Christian, and in the process of their studies both brothers trusted Christ as Saviour. This immediately presented them with a problem. They both felt they should return home with the Gospel, but knew the Korean authorities would never tolerate the Christian 'religion' in their country. The younger man wanted to go first because he was unmarried, and if he lost his life, he would not leave a wife and family like his older brother. Finally, it was the elder brother who went, carrying on his shoulders a large copy of the Bible. When he arrived, the Bible was found, confiscated, and the guards angrily cut off the doctor's head. News of this reached the younger brother in China. Saddened, but determined to take the Gospel back to his people, he prayed for guidance. Then he dismantled the parchment leaves of his Bible, soaked them in water, and rolled them tightly into ropes which he used to tie up his luggage. When he reached Korea, he was searched carefully, but no evidence of the hated foreigner's religion was found. He reached home and was given a joyful yet tearful reunion. Then he carefully unrolled the ropes, re-soaked and flattened them. When dry he sowed them back together assembling the first copy of God's Word in Korea. Many years later when Presbyterian missionaries arrived in the country they found a church flourishing on Biblical lines, literally nourished by the blood of a martyr.

If you are fit and ready, shall we go? He is still calling—**'Follow ME and I WILL MAKE YOU FISHERS OF MEN'.**

And . . .

. . . good fishing.

Part 7—INDEX

THE RESOURCE LOCKER

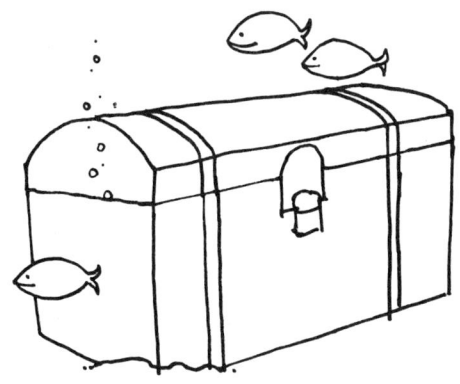

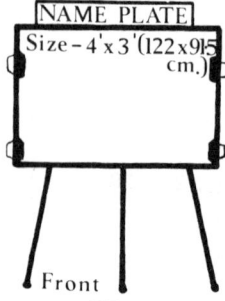

Front

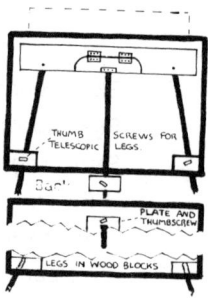

The solid-as-a-rock model. Dimensions are 4′ × 3′ or 3′ × 3′. The main difference to previous models is the way in which the back support is attached, and the type of legs used. Steel or aluminium pipes (one sliding inside the other) which may be held by a thumbscrew, or by a screw-together mechanism are ideal. As an alternative, pipe or wooden legs may be pushed into holes drilled into the blocks of wood holding the thumbscrews. Boards of this nature can be carried underarm, and strapped to a car's roof, or rods.

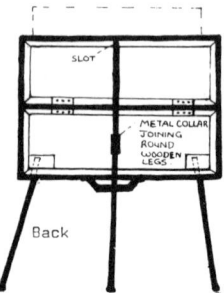

Back

The suit-case model, is inexpensive and easy to carry and store. Made from wooden 1″ × 1″ frames, covered with 4′ × 3′ plywood, the two halves are hinged to fold together. A small holding clip and a carrying handle completes the unit. The legs may be metal or wood, and fit inside the board when it is closed. Because the back support is too long for the frame it must be made in two pieces with a metal collar to hold them together while in use. The outside cover of the board may be painted in attractive colours, or with a gospel text. A canvas bag will keep the board from damage in vehicles.

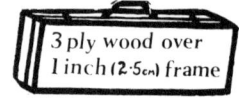

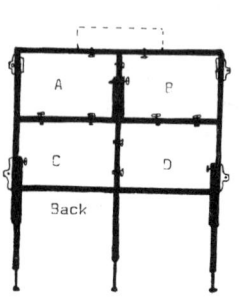

Back

The deluxe model is more expensive, not as stable, but light and very portable. Make four trays of light gauge aluminium (aluminum) so that tray A fits inside C, and tray B fits inside tray D. The two sets of trays fit together with the other materials into a canvas bag for carrying. To assemble, place the trays in alphabetical order face down, and secure tightly together with brass bolts and wing-nuts. Use telescope legs from camera tripods and fasten to the sides of trays C and D with large bolts and wing-nuts. Fit the third leg to the upper join of trays A and B with a large bolt and wing-nut. For more length use a piece of wooden dowel. Cover the front with canvas for a smooth surface for the paper.

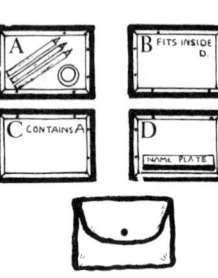

Ack. P. Edwards

ack. C. Vines

Ack. D. Fanstone

ack. R. Coyle

Ack. S. Sexton

Ack. K. Thompson

SINGLE FRAME PICTURE.

SINGLE FRAME PICTURE WORDS.
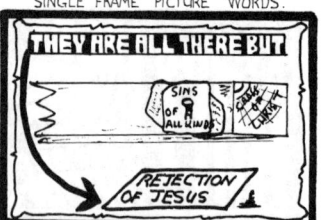

DOUBLE FRAME MESSAGE.

DOUBLE FRAME PICTURE BIBLE STORY.

TRIPLE WORD MESSAGE.

TRIPLE FRAME MESSAGE.
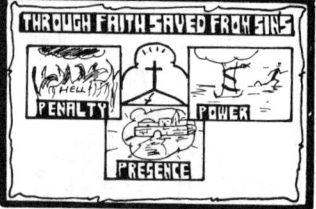

QUARTER DIVISION - WORDS · PICTURES
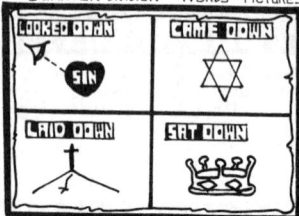

QUARTER DIVISION - STORY.

278

Ack. R. COYLE

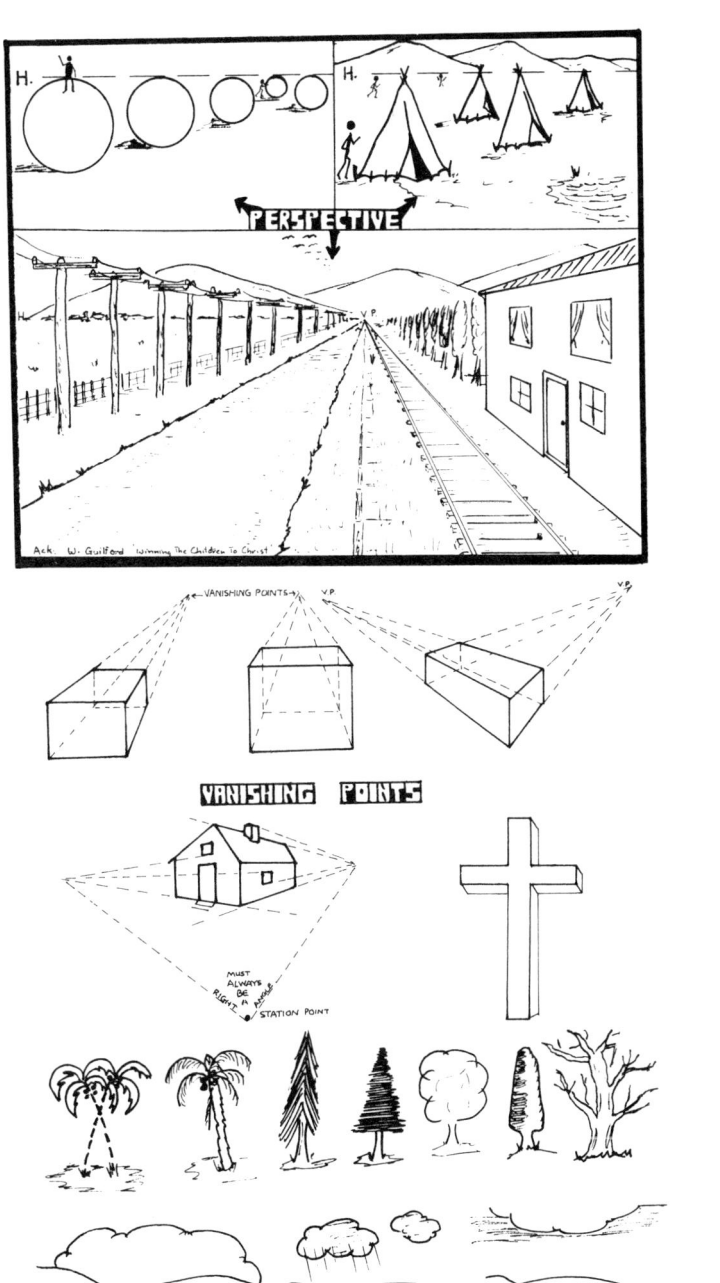

PERSPECTIVE

Ack: W. Guilford "Winning The Children To Christ"

VANISHING POINTS

VANISHING POINTS

MUST ALWAYS BE RIGHT ANGLE

STATION POINT